Marxism and the good society

Marxism and the good society

Colloquium in Social Theory.
University of Washington

EDITED BY

JOHN P. BURKE
Professor of Philosophy
University of Washington

LAWRENCE CROCKER
Professor of Philosophy
University of Washington

LYMAN H. LEGTERS
Professor of Russian and East European Studies
University of Washington

CAMBRIDGE UNIVERSITY PRESS

Cambridge
London   New York   New Rochelle
Melbourne   Sydney

Published by the Press Syndicate of the University of Cambridge
The Pitt Building, Trumpington Street, Cambridge CB2 1RP
32 East 57th Street, New York, NY 10022, USA
296 Beaconsfield Parade, Middle Park, Melbourne 3206, Australia

First published 1981

Printed in the United States of America
Typeset by Huron Valley Graphics, Ann Arbor, Michigan
Printed and bound by BookCrafters, Chelsea, Michigan

Library of Congress Cataloging in Publication Data

Colloquium in Social Theory, University of Washington,
1973–1974.

Marxism and the good society.

Papers originally presented at the 1973 and 1974
conferences.

1. Communism and society – Addresses, essays,
lectures. I. Burke, John P. II. Crocker, Lawrence.
III. Legters, Lyman Howard, 1928–   IV. Title.
HX542.C623   1974   335.43   80–24020
ISBN 0 521 23392 5

Arthur DiQuattro's chapter entitled "Alienation and justice in the
market" appeared in revised form in *The American Political Science
Review,* vol. 72, no. 3 (September 1978), and is reprinted substantially as in that version by permission of the American Political
Science Association.

Lyman Legters's chapter entitled "Marxism and dissent in the
Soviet Union" appeared in a shorter form in *Forschungen zur
osteuropäischen Geschichte,* vol. 25 (Berlin, 1978) and is reprinted here
with permission.

Paul M. Sweezy's chapter entitled "Theory and practice in the
Mao period" appeared in *Monthly Review* 28, no. 9 (February 1977)
and is reprinted substantially as in that version by permission of
Monthly Review Press. Copyright © 1977 Monthly Review, Inc.

Contents

v

Contents

Contributors

JOHN P. BURKE
Department of Philosophy
University of Washington
Seattle, Wash. 98195, U.S.A.

DAVID A. CROCKER
Department of Philosophy
Colorado State University
Fort Collins, Colo. 80521, U.S.A.

LAWRENCE CROCKER
Department of Philosophy
University of Washington
Seattle, Wash. 98195, U.S.A.

RICHARD T. DE GEORGE
Department of Philosophy
University of Kansas
Lawrence, Kans. 66044, U.S.A.

ARTHUR DIQUATTRO
Department of Political Science
Indiana University
Bloomington, Ind. 47405, U.S.A.

NORMAN FISCHER
Department of Philosophy
Kent State University
Kent, Ohio 44240, U.S.A.

Contributors

LOREN R. GRAHAM
Program in Science, Technology, and Society
Massachusetts Institute of Technology
Cambridge, Mass. 02139, U.S.A.

LYMAN H. LEGTERS
School of International Studies
University of Washington
Seattle, Wash. 98195, U.S.A.

DAVID MCLELLAN
Eliot College
University of Canterbury at Kent
Kent CT2 7NS, England

PAUL M. SWEEZY
Monthly Review
New York, N.Y. 10003, U.S.A.

Preface

The essays that form this volume were all offered originally as papers in the Colloquium in Social Theory at the University of Washington. The series on Marxism and the Good Society began in 1973 when, through the generosity of the Institute for Comparative and Foreign Area Studies (now School of International Studies), the Colloquium was able to invite participation by scholars from outside the University of Washington. They, like the local members who contributed, were asked to treat some aspect of the general theme. In balancing outside and local contributions, we sought also to balance the subject matter between more purely theoretical studies and examinations of actual postrevolutionary situations. Although some of the local contributors now find themselves elsewhere, this book reflects both kinds of balance embodied in our original plan.

LYMAN H. LEGTERS, *Chairman*
Colloquium in Social Theory

Introduction

JOHN P. BURKE, LAWRENCE CROCKER, *and* LYMAN H. LEGTERS

Visions of a good society emerge, at least by implication, from concrete social criticism. It is a truism that one can criticize a given society without offering a blueprint for its replacement. But it is also clear that any but the most superficial criticism of existing society delimits the range of alternative societies that the critic would find more congenial. These could only be societies lacking the feature that is the immediate target of criticism in the present society. Vague as it may be, a vision of a good society is, if nothing else, at least the hidden agenda of all social criticism.

It was once common for many Marxists to claim that Marxism, properly understood, was an evaluatively neutral science whose products were explanations and predictions, not criticisms and recommendations. That Marx and Engels were not engaged in, among other things, social criticism is, however, difficult to reconcile with the texts. It is now nearly universally granted that their social theory is a critical one. That theory must therefore tell us something about its authors' views of what a better society would be like.

Marx had early perceived the prevailing social system as being so deeply flawed, from the standpoint of realizing human freedom, dignity, and community, as to be irreparable. And, being as impatient with utopian fantasies as he was with mere tinkering, he was driven to develop not only the intellectual forecast of bourgeois capitalism's necessary demise, but also the plan of human action that would at once hasten that demise and school the revolutionary actors for the postrevolutionary task of constructing a good society.

Although we can only conjecture about the way in which we would remember Marx if the social movement launched in his name had met with conclusive defeat, it is probably safe to suppose that he would, in any event, belong to the most exclusive pantheon of profound nineteenth-century European social thinkers, albeit with a difference. That difference lies in the exceptional quality of Marx's construction, whether expressed as the unity of theory and practice, as the dictum of the eleventh thesis on Feuerbach, or as the history of a theoretically informed social movement. In short, Marx's system was provided with intrinsic armament against the prospect of becoming a mere intellectual artifact.

In fact, of course, we are spared the conjecture, and for precisely the same reasons: Virtually alone among historic plans for social reordering, Marxism provided for the continual process of adjustment to changing social reality, thus becoming, as Lenin correctly understood, a guide to action even under drastically changed conditions. Hence the uninterrupted invocation of Marx's name and theory by a succession of social movements right down to our own era, when Bentham and Mill, Rousseau and Proudhon, Hegel and Herzen have ceased, regardless of their permanent intellectual significance, to offer a practicable course of action in the contemporary world.

This singularity is, to be sure, not without its problems, even on a purely intellectual plane. The wide range of variation among contemporary Marxisms poses special difficulties for those who like their intellectual history to be tidy or neatly compartmentalized. Unchanging texts are much more convenient, in this sense, than a body of teaching that is undergoing constant evolution in a deliberate interaction with social experience. Just as the history of Christianity is not only a study of doctrine but also a study of the evolution of the church, so the history of Marxism embraces a plethora of movements and parties, as well as a body of theory. And as the range of derivative versions fans out to include an ever-widening assortment of circumstances, coherence and intelligibility has to give way to perplexity.

The bickering of the various Marxist parties and tendencies cannot be entirely dismissed as sibling rivalry. The differences among Marxists run deep on such central matters as material equality, democracy, liberty, and individuality. Consider a Marxist whose vision of a good society is equality of consumption (adjusted for need) and a close agreement within the society on all questions of substance – all presided over by a single benevolent party. Such a Marxist will undoubtedly exhibit uncompromising antagonism toward a Marxist who emphasizes liberty, individuality, and a multiparty democracy. Each would be a revolutionary within the good society of the other.

Such disparities among branches of the Marxist tradition may be either intensified or overshadowed by the landmark occurrence of accession to power. If there is a natural history of social movements, wherein political or strategic considerations assume a growing importance in comparison to purely theoretical considerations, then a revolutionary seizure of power by a theoretically informed movement or party is surely *the* crucial sea change. No longer is it a question of the adequacy of the plan for a future good society, or of the practicality of the means for attaining it: The central issue becomes, immediately or as soon as tolerance of post-revolutionary difficulties wears thin, a testing of the degree to which the new regime measures up to its professed norms. Up to that point, the movement for change and its informing theory have posed a critical or normative challenge to the established order; then, abruptly, the normative questions turn back upon the movement-come-to-power and it is asked to show at least that it is on the way toward realization of those qualities – freedom, equality, justice, and the like – the absence of which it has criticized in the past and the realization of which it has promised for the future.

That this represents a special problem for regimes that proclaim their dedication to Marxist teaching is repeatedly demonstrated by the elaborate exercises in self-justification in which they engage. A different sort of problem arises, however, for those equally devoted to Marx's message who happen to live outside the jurisdiction of governments that authorize themselves to define the content of Marxian orthodoxy. Their dilemma, shared by growing numbers of independent-minded observers from within the post-revolutionary social orders, consists of a belief that the essential features of a good social order are unobtainable within a bourgeois capitalist system along with the growing conviction that the known substitutes are equally unpromising. Occupants of this uncomfortable position thus feel compelled to defend the original Marxist theory against those who, while claiming to implement it, seem instead to have corrupted it and, simultaneously, against those who believe, or profess to believe, that Marxism is to be judged according to what a particular revolutionary experience has made of it. And, as if this were not a sufficient hardship, however much they argue in good faith, the activist imperative of Marxism is likely to force them into a condition of bad conscience. The position might seem to be altogether unattractive, then, except for the fact that it also entails grappling with the most acute and consequential intellectual problems of "the good society" that are posed to us in this era.

Since the time of Marx's writing, reflection on the good society is constituted by concern, first of all, with that problem and its attendant issues in his own writings, together with later resonances of that theme within the tangle of Marxian interpretation and criticism. Second, it focuses attention on problems that have arisen from the various attempts to implement Marx's theory in practice. The centrality of the good society – as a conception, as a historically plausible aim, and as a program of human action – is hardly to be doubted in the context of Marx's theory. And as long as socialist regimes continue to invoke Marx's name, they necessarily render themselves subject to the norms contained within or implied by Marx's understanding and endorsement of freedom, equality, justice, and human self-realization in a community. This volume deliberately attempts to address the general theme in both contexts.

More specifically, twentieth-century reflections on the good society invite, perhaps necessitate, considerations that explore a cluster of related issues, only some of which are represented by the contributions to this volume. Such an ambitious project thus commits us to conceptual clarification and perhaps legitimation of the good society. And in the absence of a definitive image of a good society drawn from texts of Marx and Engels, it may be necessary to reconstruct a coherent image by identifying and arguing for particular properties of such a society in a "Marxian spirit." The problem of the existence of theoretical differences between Marx and Engels on a future society, and how such differences are to be determined, is another issue that may have to be addressed.

Because Marx and Engels both believed that bourgeois society was irreparable and that socialism would constitute a decisive transformation and repudiation of capitalism, it is important that we examine their views on the need for and the nature of revolution. Might there be room in their theory for nonrevolutionary advance to socialism? What was their perception of the relationship between democracy and socialism?

Considerations of the Marxian understanding of human nature, freedom, equality, and economic and political justice are relevant as well. What is the place of science and technology in the Marxian conception? Given Marx's indictment of the capitalist market, is it nonetheless conceivable and defensible that market processes could function in socialism without violating justice? That is, is market socialism a viable concept?

Diverging from these issues, which are largely theoretical, we are led to consider problems linked to the contemporary existence of societies that profess to be socialist societies and that implement Marx's theory in diverse, although not wholly singular, ways. Our reflections must be augmented by considerations about the Soviet Union and China, as well as smaller existing models such as Yugoslavia. What is the role of dissent in societies that are avowedly socialist? How is one to contend with the problems associated with bureaucracy? Does examination of such existing models of functioning socialist societies suggest that they serve to advance or repress those aspects of a good society that were of concern to Marx and subsequent Marxists? It is not at all implausible to expect that inquiry into the nature and problems of existing socialist societies will provide reflected illumination back upon the theoretical corpus of Marx, suggesting fresh directions for thought and study, assessment and criticism.

Although this hardly exhausts the spectrum of issues that can be evoked by reflections on Marxism and the good society, those that have been briefly identified may be found to constitute a coherent focus, a fitting texture of thought directed upon an intellectually defensible and timely topic in social theory. If such reflections are pursued by a number of individuals working in different disciplines, the ambitiousness of attempting to present together their various understandings of the general theme will become only too apparent. Yet, this is precisely what the editors and contributors to the present volume have sought to do.

The first two chapters are both introductory, although in different ways. Professor De George, aware of the plan of work that his paper was inaugurating, offers some fundamental intellectual discriminations against the background of Marxism as a historical movement. Professor Crocker, eschewing the historical dimension, prepares the way for subsequent offerings by proposing a set of conceptual norms as belonging properly to any Marxian undertaking.

The next two contributions, by Professors Fischer and Burke, continue the theoretical orientation by examining two of the most salient features of Marxism – the linkage between socialism and democracy and the manner in which human actors function both as subjects and objects of the revolutionary process.

Chapters 5 and 6 form an intermediate segment, incorporating both theoretical concerns and examples of the working out of the Marxian ideal in practice. Professor McLellan scrutinizes certain differences between Marx and Engels in their vision of a communist future; Dr. DiQuattro uses the model of market socialism to illuminate the problem of justice in Marxism.

The next two offerings address different manifestations of resurgent Marxist thought in the socialist world. Professor Crocker singles out Marković as representative of the Praxis group in Yugoslavia and Professor Legters focuses on Medvedev as a Marxist critic of the Soviet order.

Finally, Professor Graham examines the crucial role assigned to and assumed by science in a socialist society as beset by problems of modernization as by the norms of Marxian thought. Dr. Sweezy concludes the volume by weighing the Maoist variant of revolutionary experience as, potentially, a way out of the impasse in which the socialist world finds itself.

It would, of course, be absurd to pretend that this assortment of essays can be any more than a sampling of the salient issues. By stressing the issue of realizing the good society, and by comparing original theory and current practice, we hope at least to have achieved a measure of coherence in this varied set of illuminations of the Marxist tradition.

I

Marxism and the good society

RICHARD T. DE GEORGE

A good society and the good society

The difference between speaking of *a* good society and speaking of *the* good society is considerable. The designation of "a good society" could be applied to an indefinite number of different kinds of societies organized in various ways. A society might be called good if it had a large preponderance of goodness over evil in it; or if it had a smaller amount of goodness but almost no evil. The nature of the goodness or evil might vary from society to society. A society with no poverty, in which all the members enjoyed social justice, might be called a good society despite the fact that the arts failed to rise above a mediocre level. Another society in which the large majority of people enjoyed a high standard of living, comfort, and creativity, but in which some crime – maintained within tolerable limits – remained present, might also be considered a good society. A society might be considered a good society by its members but not by those outside of it; or there might be general agreement among most individuals about whether a certain society was a good one. There might be a number of good, although different, societies existing simultaneously. To call a society a good one, moreover, is not to say that it is perfect or that it could not be improved.

To speak of *the* good society, however, is a different matter. The use of the definite article implies that there is only one good society – whether this means one given society or one type of society. It is not one among many, but one that is unique and good for everyone. The use of the definite suggests as well that if societies can be graded, then not only is the good society *a* good society, but it is in some ways the best – perhaps the best possible, or if this is too strong, then at least it is basically the best, although there may be room for some improvement here or there.

7

The notion of a best society, however, is an abstraction and not the description of an achievable society. For if we imagine any supposedly best society it will be possible to think of ways to make it better, if only by increasing the amount of happiness it contains. The ultimate perfect society in which everyone is perfectly happy, in which there is perfect harmony among all the inhabitants, in which there is no pain or sadness, in which death, if it occurs, is gentle, timely, accepted, and appreciated, in which no parting causes sorrow and no presence impatience, in which there is no want or desire that is not satisfied at the optimal time and in the optimal way, in which there are no accidents, and so on, is a description possibly of heaven, but of no earthly society. Nor is it entirely clear that such a society would be better than one in which there is some pain to make the experience of pleasure more sweet by anticipation and longing, in which there is some separation to make someone's presence more appreciated, in which there is some unfulfilled desire to make the attaining of other desires more precious, in which there is some labor and sweat to make the achievement of one's endeavors more satisfying. To speak of one ideal good society, *the* good society, is to limit the imagination of man too radically, to assume a homogeneity of human tastes and desires, some of which may not in fact be completely harmonious with others, or to prescribe for mankind with an unfounded arrogance.

The same difficulties exist if we interpret the good society to mean the best *kind* of society, of which many, differing in detail, are possible.

The notion of *a* good society, although not open to the same objections, suffers primarily from vagueness. I suggested that any good society would have an overwhelming preponderance of goodness in it, possibly together with a tolerable amount of evil. The number of ways to mix the good with the bad, however, are limitless. As I have suggested, the presence of some evil might enhance, and so increase, the good present in a society. Some evil might also be tolerated if any attempt to eradicate it would produce more evil of a different kind, or inhibit more good than its toleration would. Suppose, for example, that in a good society drunkenness, although not a problem, was considered (and actually was) an evil. The complete eradication of drunkenness might

8

necessitate prohibition of the sale of alcoholic beverages, or a close scrutiny of citizens' private lives – measures that would produce more harm than the toleration of the evil of occasional alcohol abuse. Whether the evil tolerated affects small segments of the population, or whether it affects all of the population in some small way are again differences that might exist in different societies. Suppose that a wealthy society of free, enterprising citizens contains a small population that has some strange ideas. These people are recalcitrant and dangerous to others. As a result they are placed in penal or mental or other institutions. The society would be better off without them; however, the society that cares for them is better than one that simply eliminates them. Another society enjoys comfort and justice for all its citizens, and cultivates the arts. But in order to achieve this it creates some tolerable, but nonetheless annoying, amount of pollution. It would be a better society if it created less pollution, if the air everyone breathed and the large bodies of water that all could enjoy were purer, but it cannot eliminate the amount of pollution it does have without lowering its standard of living.

We might argue that any good society cannot contain overwhelming misery, poverty, disease, repression, exploitation; that its members must have some rather high level of comfort, culture, freedom, security, and peace. But once we reduce the "overwhelming" to "some," the questions of exactly what mix is preferable to which, and exactly when a society becomes a good society are moot. If, during the Middle Ages, someone had foreseen and described American society today, would it have been called a good society? Would Soviet society have been called a good society? Some American and some Soviet citizens feel their respective societies are already good societies, despite the presence of certain evils. Would a society with more social justice and less personal freedom or vice-versa be a better society? Some would argue one way and some the other way. Can a society be a good society if it exists in a world in which there are other societies that can in almost no way be considered good societies; that is, societies in which misery, poverty, disease, oppression, and exploitation are rampant? Again there is room for disagreement. Our language assigns no clearcut meaning to the phrase "good society," and the questions already raised preclude any possibility of general agreement.

I have claimed that one of the characteristics of a good society is a large preponderance of good over evil. Insofar as the notion of a good society is a moral notion, however, it seems reasonable to maintain that the goodness of a society must include not only material goods and the satisfaction of needs, but moral goodness as well. And there is a tradition in political and social thought that maintains that preeminent among the social virtues is justice. Hence a *necessary* condition for any good society is that it embody justice to a preeminent degree. If it does not enjoy justice in this way, despite the other goods it might contain, it cannot be considered a good society. Yet justice is not a sufficient condition for a good society. A society in which all men were treated equally and fairly and in which justice reigned, but in which all lived at a subsistence level might be called a morally good society; but most people would agree that more of the goods of life should be present for a genuinely good society.

If justice is not only a necessary, but the most important condition for a good society, it might seem plausible to argue that the notions of *a* good society and of *the* good society become so close as to coincide for all practical purposes. *The* good society is one in which justice is widespread and preeminent, the other conditions – as long as basic needs are satisfied – being of lesser importance. The uniqueness of the concept of *the* good society would then stem from its being the just society. But despite its plausibility, this notion will not do, for several reasons. The first is that we can imagine very disparate societies, each of which enjoys justice, but that are so different in other ways that to speak of *the* just or *the* good society, as if there could be only one or only one type, would be to combine what it would be more fruitful to keep separated. The second is that the meaning of justice and the specifics of its implementation are sufficiently ambiguous in some respects so as to produce drastically different societies. Consider the difference, for instance, between a society in which justice is embodied in the maxim "From each according to his ability, to each according to his need," and one in which, following Aristotle, distributive justice consists in proportioning what is received not by the recipient's need but by his merit.[1] A third difficulty comes in considering the possible mix of justice and other values. If, for example, in order to achieve perfect justice the freedom of the members of a society must be extremely limited, a society that achieves less than perfect justice but maximizes the mix of justice and freedom might well be preferable.

The point of this line of argument is once again that there is no one best society, but a great many different possible good societies. The various utopias that we find in the history of human thought describe good societies, none of which has been without its critics. Each is *a* good society, but none, despite the intent of their creators, is *the* good society, where this carries with it a connotation of being the only good society or the best possible society.

A reply to this line of reasoning, however, could be offered by someone who maintained that, although we can imagine different societies, given existing societies and the dynamics of their development, there is actually only one good society that can develop; and although from the point of view of other conceptual models it might be called *a* good society, it is *the* good society, because it is the one and the only one that mankind can attain. Hence there is only one actually possible good society, the others being merely conceptually possible. The ground for the claim of uniqueness, in turn, might either be that there is only one way for any society to become a good society – for which there seems to be no sufficient a priori argument; or more plausibly, it might be that mankind is moving toward some sort of single society and that as a whole its development is leading to a certain social condition that will in fact constitute a good society and so it will be the good society. This is the contention of classical Marxism, and so from this point of view it deserves closer scrutiny.

Marx's notion of communism

The term "communism" is used by Marx (and Engels) in three different, although related ways. The term signifies a doctrine (communism$_d$), a movement (communism$_m$), and a stage of historical development (communism$_s$). Both the doctrine and the movement have a history that preceded Marx, although Marx put a special stamp on the meaning of the term, and influenced the doctrine and the movement so profoundly that it is difficult to separate them from him. Communism as a stage of historical development is yet to be achieved.

Marx and Engels also used the term "communist" in several ways, relating it either to communism$_d$ or to communism$_m$; they did not use it to refer to a member of communism$_s$. The adjective "communist" is used sometimes to refer to some aspect of communism (in any of its three meanings) and sometimes to refer to some aspect of the noun "communist": The *Communist Manifesto* is a manifesto of the communists; a communist society is one in which communism is the form of social organization.

Communism$_s$ constitutes the good society and it *is* the good society insofar as it *will be* the good society. Communism$_m$ comprises the organizations and the activities of those organizations and of their members that help bring about communism$_s$. These activities are guided by communism$_d$. Communism$_d$ consists of a description of communism$_s$ and a theory of how communism$_s$ is to be achieved.

Communism as a stage of historical development

Marx's explicit references to communism$_s$ cover a comparatively few pages of his voluminous works. The description of communism$_s$ used by later Marxists is, in fact, usually a composite of these references. By sorting these references, we can distinguish what can be considered either four types of description, or, if they form a whole, four components of communism$_s$. First, communism$_s$ for Marx is the next stage of social development; that is, the stage that will succeed the capitalist stage.[2] This is a definite description, and the one by which Marx most frequently refers to communism$_s$. One of the primary aims of his study of capitalism is to discover where the laws of its development will lead it and the society to which it will give birth. Secondly, the basic characteristic of communism$_s$ is that it involves the abolition of private ownership of the means of production.[3] For Marx, periods or stages of social development are defined by the kinds of ownership and the relations of production found in society.[4] Communism$_s$ is thus *defined* as the stage of social development in which both production and ownership are communal and social.[5] This basic definition thus constitutes another definite, identifying description. The third set of features in Marx's description of communism$_s$ comes from his critique of capitalism. They are negative features, namely, those negative aspects of capitalist society that will not exist in communism$_s$. These for Marx are the evils that private ownership has brought in its wake: the alienation, exploitation, and the oppression of the worker,[6] the division of labor,[7] the division of society into classes,[8] the domination of workers by the ruling class,[9] and the existence of the instruments of oppression – the state, religion, bourgeois family relations, education, law, and oppressive ideologies.[10] None of these will be present, at least with their oppressive capitalist features, in the new stage of social development. They thus form a negative description of communism$_s$. The fourth set of ingredients are the positive characteristics that communism$_s$ will have. Under communism$_s$, man will be emancipated and rehabilitated,[11] labor will not be "only a means of life but life's prime want,"[12] the productive forces will increase,[13] the all-round development of the individual will be possible,[14] each will contribute according to his ability and receive according to his needs.[15] Some of these positive features are for Marx a positive extrapolation from the negative qualities (for example, when the division of labor is eliminated, then men will be free to develop themselves in a well-rounded way); but as positive qualities they form another definite description of communism$_s$.

The first two of the four components are basic (first-order components) for Marx and are the chief means by which he identifies communism$_s$; they constitute Marx's basic addition to the description of communism, and help distinguish it from what Marx and Engels call the utopian descriptions of communism that were developed by such writers as Saint-Simon, Fourier, Owen, Dezamy, and Gay.[16] Because these are the descriptive means by which Marx distinguishes his theory from utopian theories, they can be called the scientific elements of his description. Yet it is the third and fourth (second-order) components that actually make communism worthwhile, and although the choice of descriptions is in part deduced from the essential attribute of the abolition of the private ownership of the means of production, they constitute Marx's and communism$_s$'s humanism.[17] These humanistic elements include values that formed parts of most earlier utopias and that were and are championed by many people other than communists.

For Marx communism as the stage of social development that

follows the capitalist stage and as the stage of social development in which private ownership of the means of production has been abolished were inseparable. The one would be the other. Yet the two are conceptually distinguishable. If we were to ask whether the term communism should be applied to the stage following the capitalist stage even if it did not involve the abolition of private ownership of the means of production, the answer would have to be no. For the term does not apply to the next stage no matter what that stage might be like; it applies only if there is communal ownership. Similarly, if we inquire whether the next stage is preferable to the present stage and valued simply because it is the next stage, the answer – though this time less clearly – would also be no. It is less clear because, in Marx's view, each stage thus far in the history of social development has been progressive. Capitalism, despite its evils, marked progress over feudalism. But it is unlikely that if Marx had lived and written at the end of the feudal period he would have been an active advocate of capitalism in the same way that he was of communism. For it is not only because communism is the next stage of social development but primarily because it is a desirable stage that Marx champions it. Although both of these basic characteristics are descriptive, not evaluative, the more important element of the two is the abolition of private ownership of the means of production, because the higher-order components follow upon it.

The abolition of private ownership thus becomes *the* distinguishing characteristic of communism. Because Marx spoke about crude communism[18] and the higher stages of communism,[19] it has become customary to refer to the first stage of communism$_s$ as socialism – in which the private ownership of the means of production have been abolished, but in which the other conditions that Marx indicated would be present have not yet been achieved.[20] Although these other conditions should, in Marx's view, follow the elimination of private ownership, he realized that they would not follow immediately.[21] Moreover, he certainly realized that he was not giving an exhaustive description of what that society would be like.

The higher stage of communism$_s$ was for Marx preferable to the lower stage and it is only in the higher stage that man achieves freedom and that communism is humanism.

The good society

If we think of that higher stage of social development and start listing the negative and positive second-order components, such as absence of alienation, absence of oppression, presence of wealth, freedom for all-round development, and so forth, we can call these characteristics $a, b, c, \ldots$ and we can consider the set of these characteristics. The set is indefinite.[22] All of the characteristics should follow from overcoming the capitalist stage if Marx's analysis is correct. The second-order characteristics in the set are values that most men would acknowledge as worth having and pursuing. They are the stuff out of which utopias were constructed, the qualities that make communism$_s$ attractive, and the ingredients of a good society. For Marx they will follow upon the overthrow of capitalism – which is the aim of communism as a movement.

The achieving of communism

The second part of communism$_d$ constitutes the Marxist doctrine on how the abolition of private ownership is to proceed and how it will lead to communism$_s$. It is this portion of Marxist theory that, according to Marx and Engels, raises communism$_d$ as a theory from the status of a utopian ideal to the status of science. This distinguishes scientific socialism from utopian socialism. Moreover, if the theory is correct, it entails the fact that communism$_s$ will not only be a good society, but it will be the first good society humanity will have achieved. Communism$_s$ will be the fulfillment of the centuries-old dream of mankind, it will be worldwide and so embrace all of human society, and, consequently, although it may improve with time, it will in fact be *the* good society.[23]

The transition from communism$_d$ to communism$_m$ is a short one. The two were closely intertwined for Marx. Communism as a movement preceded Marx, but not by so long as did some components of communism as a theory. Communism$_m$ had as its object the abolition of private property and the overturning of "the basis of all earlier relations of production and intercourse."[24] But Marx did not always clearly distinguish his statements about communism as a movement from his statements about communism as the stage of future society. Thus in *The German Ideology* he says, "Communism is for us not a *state of affairs* which is to be established, an *ideal* to which reality [will] have to adjust itself. We call communism the *real* movement which abolishes the present state of things."[25] Later in the same work he lists three presumptions of the movement, which are also three preconditions for the establishment of the movement's end, namely, communism$_s$. These are (1) that the great mass of humanity be propertyless – "cut off from capital" (2) that wealth and culture be present and that a high degree of the development of productive forces be reached; and (3) that the development of productive forces and the communist movement be universal or world historical.[26] The communist movement for Marx was clearly an international one.[27] The movement has a history,[28] is real,[29] and will overturn the basis of all previous relations of production[30] by a total revolution that will abolish the present state of affairs.[31] The movement, however, can achieve the end of total revolution and so introduce the first stage of communism$_s$ only when the material conditions are ripe.[32]

This emphasis on the necessary material conditions is another trait distinguishing Marx's version of the theory of communism from earlier versions. Earlier versions did embody the idea of total revolution and ideals of what a good society would be like. Communism as "the doctrine of the prerequisites for the emancipation of the proletariat"[33] according to Marx and Engels did not leave its utopian status and become placed on a sound footing until the proper conditions arrived for such emancipation.[34]

The important point to note is that communism as a movement focuses on the first-order, not the second-order components of communism$_s$. Although the ideals make communism$_s$ worthwhile, Marx was so convinced that they follow upon the elimination of private property that the basic concern of the movement is a revolution in the sphere of production. Whereas communism$_s$ is humanistic and embodies a set of characteristics expressive of man's hopes and desires, these do not form part of the *movement*.

Marx never considered the possibility that his analysis was not correct. If, for instance, the second-order components of Marx's description could be achieved without abolishing all private property, it can be argued that such a society is preferable to one in which all private property is abolished but the higher-level components are not achieved. Or if private property is abolished, is it more important that wealth flow abundantly or that the members of society have the ability to achieve their all-round development? Are all the characteristics in the set compatible and equally important? Can, for example, the division of labor be abolished and productive wealth still flow abundantly? If not, which is to be preferred?

Marx did not consider these questions because he was not describing *a* good society but *the* good society. He claimed that such a society cannot be achieved without the abolition of private ownership; and once this occurs, the rest will ultimately follow.

The gap between the humanistic components of the higher stage of communism and the aim of the movement to abolish private property is significant in evaluating the results of the movement and the present state of Marxist theory. Because Marxism postulates an interaction of theory and practice, instead of simply looking at and attempting an evaluation of what Marx and Engels said in the nineteenth century, it is enlightening to consider the status of communism in the new Marxisms of the contemporary period. How is Marx's theory of communism faring today, and is his view of the good society still viable?

The new Marxists

Contemporary Marxists are of many stripes and sometimes it seems that there are almost as many Marxist positions as there are Marxists. The Marxism of Jean-Paul Sartre, of Roger Garaudy, of Ernst Bloch, and even of Louis Althusser are, despite their few followers, idiosyncratic. The list could be augmented considerably. Maoism, Castroism, Debrayism, Trotskyism, and Eurocommunism, among others, represent identifiable political and tactical positions. Each is instructive in its use and interpretation of Marx's writings. I shall concentrate, however, upon three important contemporary groups of Marxists, each of which represents a different view of communism$_s$ and the means of achieving it. I shall call the three groups the scientific Marxists, the humanist Marxists, and the critical Marxists.[35]

The first group consists of Marxist-Leninists. It includes the large majority of Marxists in the Soviet Union and a great many others who follow the Engels-Lenin line of Marxism. The second group consists of those Marxists in non-Soviet Eastern Europe who were and some of whom still are concerned with developing a humane socialism. They have to some extent been silenced. But preeminent in this group are the so-called creative Marxists of Yugoslavia, among whom Gajo Petrović, Mihailo Marković,[36] and Svetozar Stojanović are best known.[37] The early writings of Leszek Kolakowski[38] of Poland, the pre-1968 writings of Ivan Svitak,[39] the works of Karel Kosík of Czechoslovakia, and those of the followers of Georg Lukács in Hungary can all be grouped together here. The critical Marxists are found in Western Europe and the United States. They have focused on and developed Marx's criticism of capitalism and have attempted to bring him up to date. This group includes most of the members of the Frankfurt School – for example, Theodor Adorno, Max Horkheimer, and Jürgen Habermas – Herbert Marcuse,[40] and many of the New Left who go to Marx for inspiration, method, or vocabulary. They criticize Western society and its institutions, class division, racism, militarism, and so on. For the most part, they are not overly taken with the Soviet Union as a model for social development. They share this trait with the humanist Marxists.

The fact that the three groups are divided geographically reflects their different socioeconomic and historical conditions, and helps explain their concentration on differing elements of Marx's theory of communism. Each of the three groups goes to Marx with equal legitimacy and finds texts in support of its position. The scientific Marxists go primarily to the writings of the mature Marx, such as *Capital,* with its emphasis on the laws of social development, and to dialectical materialism as developed by Engels and Lenin. The humanist Marxists focus on the early works of Marx, which deal with man, alienation, and human values. They interpret Marx's later works in the light of his early ones, finding in them the same basic values. The critical Marxists make equally good use of both the young and the old Marx. Whereas the humanist Marxists are primarily interested in the positive aspects of Marx, the critical Marxists are primarily interested in his negative critique and his attacks on the status quo.

The nonscientific Marxists join non-Marxist philosophers in rejecting the claims of Marxists to be scientific. They read such claims as ideological or mythical and interpret them sociologically or psychologically or in some other similar manner. This is true of Herbert Marcuse's and Jean-Paul Sartre's critiques of Marxist-Leninist ideology.[41] In a similar vein Mihailo Marković says, "It was typical of Stalinist dogmatism to misuse science and to look for a quasi-scientific form for its doctrines. The party line had to be presented as the result of the 'scientific' examination of existing reality and an exact expression of social necessity."[42]

What is the status of communism and of the good society according to these three groups?

The doctrine of communism has been transformed into an ideology in Soviet hands. Although the first stage of communism is said to have arrived in Eastern Europe, the humanistic Marxists no longer anticipate the development of the second stage in the same way as it was anticipated by Marx. Communism as a movement is of little concern to the critical Marxists, and has been identified by them with political parties in Eastern Europe.

The view of the scientific Marxists is the most dogmatic and stereotyped. Their doctrine of communism can be characterized in three ways. First, the notion of scientific socialism has been extended to scientific communism.[43] Those who pursue this doctrine have attempted to formulate the laws of the transition from socialism to communism in a way analogous to the way in which Marx attempted to uncover the laws of the development of capitalism.[44] Second, they accept the October Revolution as a communist revolution, the development of socialism in the USSR as a model for such development as described by Marx, and developing Soviet society as on the road to the achievement of communism.[45] The willingness to subject each development to critical testing has been replaced by a drive for the scientific development of what has already begun and is in progress. Third, communism is considered not only the stage of social development following capitalism, but it is raised to the level of the moral ideal of mankind.[46]

Lenin continued the communist movement and following Marx's lead concentrated on the revolution that would expropriate the expropriators. The essential goal was to eliminate private ownership of the means of production. Lenin, as Marx, understood that the humanistic aspects of communist society would not be achieved immediately, and that was not his immediate aim.

19

After Lenin, the doctrine of the possibility of socialism – and eventually of communism – in one country was accepted by the Marxist-Leninists.[47]

The scientific Marxists continue to emphasize the importance of the laws of social development. The scientific aspects of their doctrine lead to an insistence on the knowledge and leadership of the CPSU and on the importance of developing the economic base of the USSR. The scientific Marxist line continues to maintain that the positive, humanistic aspects of communist society will follow upon economic development. The scientific Marxists are still looking for laws governing this development; but they have been unable to find them.[48] Scientific communism is the name of a doctrine looking for its Marx. For Marx's laws – to the extent they are laws at all – were the laws of the development of capitalism and of its inevitable tendencies. These were to lead to the demise of capitalism and the end of private ownership of the means of production. He did not claim that the humanistic aspects of communism would follow according to laws he uncovered. He could not, because the next stage of development had not yet arrived to be investigated.

The scientific Marxists continue the dichotomy introduced by Marx between the humanistic components of communism$_s$ and the means of attaining such a society. In their ideological development they have explicitly elevated the former to a moral ideal in a way Marx did not. In practice their emphasis remains on production, on economic goods, and not on the all-round development of the individual. Faced with choices Marx ignored, such as whether the elimination of the division of labor is compatible with the increased productivity they desire, they have opted for productivity and all but ignore the alternatives that might favor the humanistic aspects of Marxism at the expense of productivity.

At the same time, however, the Soviet scientific Marxists are willing to claim that communism$_s$ in its second stage can be achieved in one country with the state apparatus, army, and police not withered away but maintained to protect their good society from capitalist encirclement.[49]

What Soviet history has shown is that the elimination of the private ownership of the means of production does not necessarily lead to the abolition of oppression, alienation (whether or not it is of the same type as Marx describes is not important here), the division of labor, and negative features of the superstructure. State ownership can carry with it as much oppression and repression as private ownership did in Marx's eyes. This is scarcely admitted by Soviet scientific Marxists but it is a commonplace observation among the other two Marxist groups.[50]

In the USSR the break between the scientific and humanistic aspects of communism$_d$ and communism$_m$ has so far led to a society that is not notably humanistic. There is little reason to believe that the existing repression, lack of personal freedom, and alienation will be abolished by the continued economic development that Soviet Marxists advocate in accordance with their scientific communism.

The scientific Marxists maintain that despite changes that render the standard of living of the workers in nonsocialist societies higher and higher, these societies, essentially infected by the exploitation and injustice that characterize societies built on the private ownership of the means of production, can never be good societies; thus there can never be other good societies coexisting with a good communist society. The possibility of nuclear warfare, however, makes these other societies tolerated in an uneasy peaceful coexistence. If worldwide communism remains a dream of some of these Marxists, most now maintain that communist society will be *the* only existing good society, although in the foreseeable future it will not be *the* good, worldwide society.

The humanist Marxists go not to the scientific socialism of Engels or to the doctrine of dialectical materialism as it developed after Engels in the Leninist and Soviet tradition. They go more to the early works of Marx where they find his humanism most clearly expressed. They use these early works to interpret the later works, and so emphasize the humanistic aspects of *Capital,* and not its scientific aspects. Communism is seen not only or not primarily as the next stage following capitalism, but it is seen as the stage in which justice will be achieved, in which man's essence and existence will be rejoined, in which the state will wither away and man will enjoy freedom.[51] Their view of Soviet communism or socialism is that it has not achieved the humanism of which it is capable;[52] that it has substituted one type of alienation for another;[53] that it has restricted freedom and is antihumanistic, despite the fact that it has developed sufficient wealth to have become a truly humanistic socialist state.[54] The primary focus of these Marxists, however, is not criticism of either capitalism – which their countries have left behind – or of Soviet state socialism – which they wish to escape – but of humanistic socialism and communism, which they are trying to build. The attempts in Yugoslavia at socialist self-management in society and self-management socialism in industry are examples.[55]

What emerges in the writings of these Marxists is an attempt to develop the social structures necessary to establish the humanistic communism$_s$ that is contained in what I have called the third and fourth components of Marx's description. One of the essential differences between the humanist Marxists and the scientific Marxists is that the former, unlike the latter, do not believe that the humanistic superstructures follow in some quasiautomatic, scientific, regular, lawlike fashion upon changes in the economic base.

Gajo Petrović in a manner characteristic of the humanist Marxists asks, "But is it not of vital importance for mankind today to distinguish between the social condition in which private property is abolished (communism), and the humane community of men in which a man is a *socius* to another man (socialism, or, more adequately, humanism)?"[56] He similarly claims, "The texts of Marx speak in favor of regarding socialism as a higher phase compared with communism. The etymology of the words also supports such a terminology. 'Communism' (compared with *communis* – common) suggests a society in which means of production are common, and 'socialism' (corresponding to *socius* – comrade) points to a society in which a man is comrade to another man. And the second is certainly higher and more difficult to achieve than the first."[57]

A second difference between the humanist and the scientific Marxists is that whereas the latter emphasize the means necessary in order to achieve an ultimate humanistic end (communism$_s$), the humanist Marxists argue that the means taken must be humanistic as well as the end itself. Leszek Kolakowski was the most outspoken champion of this position. In objection to the view that certain otherwise immoral actions are historically necessary and so morally justifiable, he said: "A soldier is morally responsible for a

22

crime committed on the orders of his superior; an individual is all the more responsible for acts performed – supposedly or in fact – on the orders of an anonymous history."[58] And, "Thus we profess the doctrine of total responsibility of the individual for his deeds and of the amorality of the historical process."[59]

The concern of the humanist Marxists is with building *a* good society that is characterized by the third and fourth levels of Marx's description. The emphasis in their writing is not against capitalism (not that they favor it) but against the developing forms of social relations in the socialist countries. Although critical of Stalinism and of the Stalinistic repression, they are constructive in their attempt to find alternate ways to achieve a good society in their own countries. The concrete attempts in this direction – whether of self-management or of communal living or of other forms of social organization – have thus far not yielded very positive or impressive results. For even when workers can manage to run their factory cooperatively and efficiently, cooperation among factories, industries, suppliers, and users on any large scale is extremely difficult to achieve. Yet the thrust of these experiments seems to be definitely in the right direction. The aim, however, is to achieve *a* good society, not *the* good society.

The third group, the critical Marxists, are critical of capitalism. For the most part they are critical as well of Soviet socialism. They do not accept the scientific side of scientific socialism, which enunciates laws of social development. They have been disenchanted with the accuracy of these laws because the working class in the United States and Western Europe has prospered, despite their claimed exploitation. Most are not naïve enough to expect a proletarian revolution in these countries. But for the most part they accept Marx's analysis and criticism of the evils of capitalism and attempt to extend that criticism, update it, and apply it. Their view of communism – or in general of a good society – is not a view of Soviet society; and their emphasis is not on a utopia that they attempt to describe. With some justification, their position can be called Marxism without communism. Thus Max Horkheimer says, "One cannot determine what a free society will do or permit . . . There is no patent system to work out . . . The modalities of the new society will be discovered only in the course of the transformation."[60] For although their emphasis is on the next stage of social development after capitalism they are by no means unanimous in believing that that stage will be communism. Exactly what that stage will be is not clear. But if they are against private ownership of the means of production, they are equally opposed to state ownership.[61] Government is to be taken out of the hands of the ruling class and given to the people.[62]

For some critical Marxists the stage following the present stage will be one of anarchy.[63] For others, such as Marcuse, a new elite will help the masses achieve their liberation.[64] Still others admit they have no programs for reform or for rebuilding society; but what is clear to them is the injustice and immorality of the present system, which they would like to topple. They are willing to face the problem of what to do with the rubble that results only when necessary, armed with a faith that things cannot be any worse.

Unlike Marx, however, they have given up hope in the workingman as the instrument whereby the social revolution will come about. The average worker in industrially developed countries is no longer impoverished. If he is exploited he is generally not aware of it, and he thinks his position in society is fairly good and looks forward to its getting better. He is less interested in social justice than in bettering his standard of living, which is already higher than ever before in history. Many critical Marxists thus either become champions of such minorities as the blacks, Chicanos, or migrant farm workers, or they become independent critics of governmental and social policy – antiwar, antipollution, antimilitary-industrial complex, antibourgeois values, and antiauthority in general.[65]

Some of their criticism has been salutary and has served to focus attention on social ills and injustices with respect to minorities, civil rights, and the Vietnam War. The revolution they so ardently desire is unlikely to occur. But their aim is clearly not to produce *the* good society but to help bring about *a* good society.

Thus, original Marxism with its critique of capitalism, its theory of social change, and its view of communism$_s$ has survived in fragmented fashion in the doctrines of the new Marxists. The scientific Marxists pursue the elusive laws of social development that they hope will lead to the good – though restricted – society, the humanistic Marxists attempt to find an alternative to the capitalist and Soviet paths to a humanistic society, and the critical

Marxists continue a Marxist-type critique in an effort to attain neither a communist nor necessarily a socialist society, but a better, more moral, more just society than the one in which they live.

The goal of achieving the one good society, although it was once a Marxist goal, is no longer clearly a goal of most new Marxists, the majority of whom are willing to settle realistically for more limited good societies.

The new Marxists go to Marx for doctrine, method, vocabulary, or conceptual framework and all legitimately continue a tradition he started. If Marx had been born in 1918 instead of 1818 would he be writing what any of the three groups of Marxists are writing, and would his view of communism as the good society be the same as it was? Although the question is unanswerable, we know that there are presently threats to social development that Marx did not and could not anticipate. In their quest for a good society neither socialist nor nonsocialist nations can ignore the implications of population growth, air and water pollution, limited natural resources, or the reality of nuclear warheads. No nation can build a good society without paying attention to these dangers; and these dangers, more likely than any common ideal of a good society, will force cooperation and planning on a global level. The countries of the earth have become too interdependent to behave as if they were independent, self-contained units. This interdependency, moreover, has come about not because anyone wished or willed it, but as a natural result of the development of industry and technology. The progress of communications, the need for raw materials from various parts of the globe, the international distribution of manufactured goods, the dangers of nuclear contamination, the pollution of air and water, population pressures, and the limits on food production in some parts of the world while surpluses exist elsewhere, all serve to bind the world closer together. In such a world, it becomes more and more difficult to build a good society in any one country. The ancient Greeks could rest satisfied with justice in their city states because they considered the non-Greeks to be barbarians. To those who believe that all human beings have the right to life, liberty, and the pursuit of happiness, a society that closes its eyes to poverty and suffering throughout so many countries and that rests contentedly as long as it achieves wealth, comfort, and justice for its own members can be called a good society only from its own short-sighted perspective.

But this does not mean that there must be one homogeneous society on a world scale in order to achieve a good society. Communisms in the Soviet Union, China, Yugoslavia, and some of the other Eastern-European countries may all develop differently. Provided they have the humanistic third- and fourth-order characteristics described by Marx, they will certainly have many of the ingredients necessary for a good society. American and Western-European societies may also develop differently, each approaching some ideal of a good society, whether or not private property is abolished, as long as its evils are mitigated. We have already seen that the abolition of private property is not sufficient to create a good society. It is not yet clear that its abolition is a necessary condition for a good society, for, as we have seen, even if its preservation involves some injustice, this may be compensated for in various ways.

I have already argued that conceptually the claim for the uniqueness of the notion of *the* good society is excessive, and that it is possible conceptually to consider a great many different types of social organization that can be termed good. The additional claim that there is only one real possible good society – the original Marxist claim – was too narrowly drawn without sufficient justification, and it has been given up by all except the most dogmatic scientific Marxists. Capitalism, or what now passes under that name, may not last forever, and something better may come after it, if we work for it. But that something better, if it is ever achieved, in all likelihood will not be a monolithic system that can be described in economic terms, but a plurality of good societies, organized in different ways and peacefully and cooperatively co-existing together.

To the extent that Marxism proposed the good society, it is no longer – if it ever was – viable. To the extent that the new Marxists enunciate and carry on the work toward a good society, or toward good societies, they are positive forces that share much of the best to be valued in Western democracy. Their efforts thus constitute positive social experiments and possible social programs from which we may learn how to cope with our own social problems in our attempt to achieve a better society. We can ignore them only at the expense of our own impoverishment.

Notes

1 Ernest Barker, trans., *The Politics of Aristotle* (Oxford: Clarendon Press, 1946), pp. 116–21.
2 Karl Marx, *Economic and Philosophic Manuscripts of 1844* (Moscow: Foreign Languages Publishing House, 1961), p. 114.
3 Ibid., pp. 99, 103.
4 Marx, "Preface to *A Contribution to the Critique of Political Economy*" in Marx and Engels, *Selected Works in Two Volumes,* vol. 1 (Moscow: Foreign Languages Publishing House, 1958), pp. 362–4; Engels, "Socialism: Utopian and Scientific" in Marx and Engels, *Selected Works,* 2:136–8; Marx and Engels, *The German Ideology* (Moscow: Progress Publishers, 1964), pp. 32–3.
5 Marx, *Economic and Philosophic Manuscripts,* pp. 98–104; Engels "Socialism: Utopian and Scientific," in Marx and Engels, *Selected Works,* 2:145–55.
6 Marx, *Economic and Philosophic Manuscripts,* pp. 67–83.
7 Marx and Engels, *The German Ideology,* pp. 43–58.
8 Ibid., pp. 60–2; Marx and Engels, "Manifesto of the Communist Party" in Marx and Engels, *Selected Works,* 1: 34–45.
9 Marx and Engels, "Manifesto," pp. 34–45.
10 Marx, "Preface to *A Contribution to the Critique of Political Economy,*" pp. 362–3; Marx and Engels, "Manifesto," pp. 46–54; Marx, *Economic and Philosphic Manuscripts,* p. 114.
11 Marx, *Economic and Philosophic Manuscripts,* p. 114.
12 Marx, "Critique of the Gotha Programme" in Marx and Engels, *Selected Works,* 2:24.
13 Ibid.
14 Ibid.
15 Ibid.
16 Marx and Engels, *The Holy Family* (Moscow: Foreign Languages Publishing House, 1956), pp. 176–7; Engels, "Socialism: Utopian and Scientific," in Marx and Engels, *Selected Works,* 2:120–8.
17 Marx, *Economic and Philosophic Manuscripts,* pp. 98–103; *The Holy Family,* pp. 168–9, 177.
18 Marx, *Economic and Philosophic Manuscripts,* p. 101.
19 Ibid., p. 102; Marx, "Critique of the Gotha Programme," p. 24.
20 Gajo Petrović, *Marx in Mid-twentieth Century* (Garden City, N.Y.: Anchor Books, 1967) disagrees with this interpretation, arguing (pp. 155–62) that socialism is the higher stage.
21 Marx, *Economic and Philosophic Manuscripts,* pp. 98–103; Marx, "Critique of the Gotha Programme," pp. 22–5, 31–4. In the latter Marx speaks of the period of transition from capitalist to communist society as the "period in

27

which the state can be nothing but *the revolutionary dictatorship of the proletariat.*" See also Marx's letter to J. Weydemeyer of March 5, 1852, Marx and Engels, *Selected Works*, 2: 452.

22 For a more detailed analysis of this type see Richard T. De George, *Soviet Ethics and Morality* (Ann Arbor: University of Michigan Press, 1969), pp. 41 ff.

23 This is the case despite Marx's statement that "*Communism* is the necessary pattern and the dynamic principle of the immediate future, but communism as such is not the goal of human development – the structure of human society" [*Economic and Philosophic Manuscripts*, p. 114], which seems to identify communism$_s$ only with the first of his four types of definition, and Engels's claim that "communism no longer signified an attempt to use your phantasy in order to concoct an ideal society as nearly perfect as possible. Communism meant henceforward understanding the nature, the condition and the resulting general aims of the struggle conducted by the proletariat" ["History of the Communist League" in *Birth of the Communist Manifesto*, Dirk J. Struik, ed. (New York: International Publishers, 1971), p. 156] which seems to identify the term communism not with communism$_s$ but with communism$_d$ and possibly with communism$_m$.

24 Marx and Engels, *The German Ideology*, p. 86.

25 Ibid., p. 47.

26 Ibid.

27 Ibid., pp. 47–8; Marx and Engels, "Manifesto," p. 46.

28 Marx, *Economic and Philosophic Manuscripts*, p. 102.

29 Marx and Engels, *The German Ideology*, p. 47.

30 Ibid., p. 86.

31 Ibid., p. 47.

32 Ibid., p. 50. In his "Preface to *A Contribution to the Critique of Political Economy*," p. 363, Marx says, "No social order ever perishes before all the productive forces for which there is room in it have developed . . . " Obviously there was much more room for the development of those forces in capitalism than Marx realized, and this led him to anticipate that the new stage would follow much sooner than it has.

33 Engels, "Principles of Communism," in Struik, *Birth of the Communist Manifesto*, p. 169.

34 Ibid., p. 167; Marx, *The Poverty of Philosophy* (Moscow: Foreign Language Publishing House, n.d.), p. 125; Marx and Engels, *The German Ideology*, pp. 50–1.

35 Of the other groups I mentioned, the Maoists and the Eurocommunists deserve at least a brief mention. The Maoists, at least during Mao's lifetime, emphasized egalitarianism in a poor society, an approach that found fertile soil in China, parts of Southeast Asia, and portions of Africa. The Eurocommunist views are perhaps best expressed in Santiago Carrillo's *Eurocommunism and the State* (London: Lawrence and Wishart, 1977). For our purposes, however, neither group has developed a clear, distinct theoretical position on communism$_s$.

36 In January 1975, Marković and seven other faculty members were removed from their positions at the University of Belgrade. They continue to write (although not to publish in Yugoslavia). Members of the humanist group teaching at the University of Zagreb, including G. Petrović, have been allowed to retain their official positions.

37 For a survey of the Yugoslav group, see Gerson S. Sher, *Praxis: Marxist Criticism and Dissent in Socialist Yugoslavia* (Bloomington: Indiana University Press, 1977).

38 Kolakowski was one of the most outspoken Marxists in post-1956 Poland. The essays collected in his *Toward a Marxist Humanism* (New York: Grove Press, 1968), are some of his most influential. He was dismissed from his professorship at Warsaw University in 1968. He is presently at Oxford and claims no longer to be a Marxist (a claim once made by Marx himself).

39 See his *Man and World: A Marxian View* (New York: Delta Books, 1970). Svitak left Czechoslovakia in 1968 and presently teaches at California State University, Chico. Like Kolakowski, he claims to have given up Marxism. Karel Kosík is still in Czechoslovakia but has been removed from his teaching position and is no longer allowed to publish.

40 Marcuse was an early member of the Frankfurt School, but left it and developed independently. He became an important figure for many in the new left movement.

41 Herbert Marcuse, *Soviet Marxism: A Critical Analysis* (New York: Columbia University Press, 1958); Jean-Paul Sartre, "Materialism and Revolution," in *Literary and Philosophical Essays* (New York: Criterion Books, Inc., 1955), pp. 191–208.

42 Mihailo Marković, "Humanism and Dialectic," in *Socialist Humanism*, Erich Fromm, ed. (London: Allan Lane, 1967), p. 83.

43 See for example, V. Afanasyev, *Scientific Communism* (Moscow: Progress Publishers, 1967).

44 A. Verbin and A. Furman, *Mesto istoricheskogo materializma v sisteme nauk* (Moscow: Moscow U.P., 1965), pp. 146, 155; D. I. Chesnokov, "Predmet i zadachi istoricheskogo materializma," *Filosofskie nauki* 8, no. 1 (1965): 50; *Filosofskaia entsiklopediia* (Moskva: Izd. "Sovetskaia entsiklopediia," 1962, 2:58.

45 See the "Programme of the Communist Party of the Soviet Union" in *The Road to Communism: Documents of the 22nd Congress of the Communist Party of the Soviet Union* (Moscow: Foreign Languages Publishing House, 1961), pp. 445–589. The document claims (p. 512) that by the end of the decade 1971–80 "*a communist society will in the main be built in the U.S.S.R.*" The reference is obviously to the higher stage of communism; but the distinguishing notes are not freedom or humanism but public ownership and distribution of goods according to need.

46 *Filosofskaia entsiklopediia*, 3:18–20. For an analysis of communism as a moral ideal see Chap. III, "Good and the Moral Ideal" in De George, *Soviet Ethics and Morality*, pp. 35–55.

47 For the development of this doctrine see Richard T. De George, *Patterns of Soviet Thought* (Ann Arbor: University of Michigan Press, 1966), pp. 130–1, 191–2, 197–8, 201–2.

48 For a discussion of this point see Richard T. De George, "Philosophy," in *Science and Ideology in Soviet Society,* George Fischer, ed. (New York: Atherton Press, 1967), especially pp. 70–2.

49 Ibid., p. 192; *History of the Communist Party of the Soviet Union (Bolsheviks): Short Course* (Moscow: Foreign Languages Publishing House, 1951), p. 504; Joseph Stalin, *Problems of Leninism* (Moscow: Foreign Languages Publishing House, 1954), pp. 796–7; *The Road to Communism,* pp. 553–8.

50 See for example, Mihailo Marković, "Humanism and Dialectic," in *Socialist Humanism,* Erich Fromm, ed., p. 88; Predrag Vranicki, "Socialism and the Problem of Alienation," Ibid.; Gajo Petrović, *Marx in Mid-twentieth Century,* pp. 150–3; Kenneth A. Megill, *The New Democratic Theory* (New York: Free Press, 1970), p. 94.

51 See for example, Veljko Korać, "In Search of Human Society," in *Socialist Humanism,* Erich Fromm, ed., pp. 1–15, as well as other essays in that volume.

52 See for example, Petrović, "Philosophy and Politics in Socialism," in *Marx in Mid-Twentieth Century,* pp. 154–69. In his article "Marxism versus Stalinism," in the same volume he says (p. 22), " . . . in the Stalinistic conception there is no place for man."

53 See Note 50.

54 Korać, "In Search of Human Society," p. 3–15; Mihailo Marković, "Socialism and Self-Management," *Praxis* 1 (1965): 179.

55 Svetozar Stojanović, "The Statist Myth of Socialism," *Praxis* 3 (1967):176–87; also his "Social Self-Government and Socialist Community," *Praxis* 4 (1968):104–16; Mladen Čaldarović, "Dissolutionary Processes in the System of Self-Management," *Praxis* 1 (1965): 551–61.

56 Petrović, *Marx in Mid-twentieth Century,* p. 161.

57 Ibid., p. 160.

58 Leszek Kolakowski, *Toward a Marxist Humanism* (New York: Grove Press, 1968), p. 140.

59 Ibid., p. 141.

60 Max Horkheimer, *Autoritärer Staat,* as cited in Russell Jacoby, "Towards a Critique of Automatic Marxism," *Telos,* No. 10 (Winter 1971): 146.

61 See for example, Paul Mattick, "Workers' Control" in *The New Left: A Collection of Essays,* Priscilla Long, ed. (Boston: Extending Books, 1969), pp. 376–98.

62 See Herbert Marcuse, *Counterrevolution and Revolt* (Boston: Beacon Press, 1972), p. 46.

63 The anarchist alternative is one that Marx consistently rejected. See Engels, "On Authority," in Marx and Engels, *Selected Works,* 1:35–8; also Herbert Marcuse, "Marx," in his *Studies in Critical Philosophy* (London: NLB, 1972), pp. 128–43.

64 This is the dominant interpretation of Marcuse's position despite his denial of holding this view. See his "Repressive Tolerance," in *A Critique of Pure Toleration* (Boston: Beacon Press, 1969), pp. 81–123.

65 Rudi Dutschke, "On Anti-authoritarianism," in *The New Left Reader,* Carl Oglesby, ed. (New York: Grove Press, 1969), pp 243–53 See also many of the articles and statements in *The New Left of the Sixties,* Michael Friedman, ed. (Berkeley: Independent Socialist Press, 1972), and Theodore Roszak, *The Making of a Counter Culture* (Garden City, N.Y.: Anchor Books, 1969).

2

Marx, liberty, and democracy

LAWRENCE CROCKER

This chapter will present a view of a good society and consider issues of political philosophy arising out of that view. Linking this undertaking with the name of Marx involves two premises, both of which are controversial. The first premise is that utopian speculation is a permissible activity from a Marxist perspective. The second premise goes to the content of Marx's political and social ideal. It is, as a rough formula, that Marx was a revolutionary, libertarian democrat.[1]

Marx's antiutopianism

There can be little doubt that Marx was hostile to attempts either to predict or prescribe the details of the future socialist society. According to one traditional interpretation, Marx's antiutopianism rested on a belief that moral judgments are incompatible with science. We know that Marx considered the theory he developed to be as much a science as chemistry. It is doubtful, however, that he thought normative evaluation to be incompatible with science. If he did, he was guilty of a great many slips of the pen, because indisputably normative evaluations appear frequently in Marx's scientific works.

Moreover, even if Marx did believe science to be nonnormative, that would not explain completely his antiutopianism. Marx was a political activist as well as a theoretician, and there is no plausible argument that political activism can be nonnormative.

A style of Marxist positivism, fashionable earlier in this century, proclaimed that scientific socialists are partisans of the socialist revolution, not because it will bring about a better state of affairs, but because it is inevitable. The hopelessness of this position becomes apparent if one imagines the moment at which the scientific socialist, while studying physics or astronomy, comes to the conclusion that the disappearance of all human life from the universe is inevitable.

There is another variant of Marxist positivism in which the revolutionary is characterized as having simply made a decision to "stand with the working class." It is unlikely, however, that the revolutionary would choose to support working-class activity wherever it may lead. Workers, like members of other classes, can be seduced by nationalism, racism, or fascism. For this reason "standing with the working class" is, in fact, understood as a partisanship for what is in the "true interest" of the working class. But what is in the true interest of the working class is a subject for normative investigation.

Perhaps we cannot make any detailed moral comparisons of socialism with other forms of social organization because we cannot know in any detail what socialism would be like. Marx believed that we can make predictions about the future course of capitalism, or any other class society, because the dynamics of these societies are governed by laws that can be uncovered by observation and theory. After the socialist revolution these laws would no longer apply. We can know something about the socialist society, of course, because we know at least roughly how it would come about. Marx may have believed it possible to know that socialism would be a goal worth struggling for, but that its future course could not be predicted in any detail.

Whether or not Marx adhered to this notion, it seems that we cannot make predictions about postcapitalist societies with a high degree of assurance. But an account of a good society is not a prediction; it is a normative investigation. Ideally it describes the best of all the futures that are compatible with our knowledge of the real possibilities inherent in the present. So the difficulty of making precise predictions is no reason to avoid discussing the good society.

There is little doubt that Marx was optimistic, even uncritically, about the society that would follow the anticapitalist revolution. This optimism may explain why he felt little need to champion one possibility against others. The fact that Marx had not seen a revolution succeed and then go sour largely accounts for this attitude. A Stalinist dictatorship over a nationalized economy was a possibility that simply did not occur to Marx. Whether one calls

33

such societies "state capitalist," "bureaucratic collectivist," or "degenerated workers' states," their very existence requires a revision and expansion of Marx's theories. Sadder but wiser, we now know that not everything that follows an anticapitalist revolution is even an approximation of a good society.

The chief and best reason that Marx had such a low opinion of utopianism was his deep-seated belief that the task of designing and constructing the socialist society properly belongs to those who will create and live in it. The socialist movement is a democratic movement of the "overwhelming majority" and a socialist society would be fashioned democratically with the creativity and unpredictability of free decisions. Organized utopianism, if successful, would tend to restrict democracy in the design of the new society by making agreement with all the details of the founder's blueprint a precondition for membership in the anticapitalist movement. The moralizing tone of utopianism and its tendency to seek top-down solutions through appeals to the rich and powerful stem in part from this same devotion to detail. Even if Marx's other reasons and alleged reasons for opposing the discussion of the good society are no longer persuasive, it seems that any such discussion must violate the democratic intent of the movement. Once one says that a good society would be democratic, perhaps that is all one should say. Commitment to democracy is not, however, commitment to the principle that the way the other details of society *should* be is precisely the way it is democratically decided that they are to be. A democratic decision has some moral force just because it is a democratic decision. It may in other respects be the wrong decision, as one may have argued before the vote and continued to maintain after the vote. Whether it is right or wrong, all things considered, to carry out a democratic decision depends upon the relative moral weight of democracy in the particular case. The majority has a right to be wrong—but not too wrong. One can call democracy a "first" commitment, in the sense that the presumption is on the side of a democratic decision, without denying that other considerations will under certain circumstances take precedence. For example, it is permissible to disobey a democratic decision to undertake a program of genocide or to eliminate fundamental liberties or to replace democracy with monarchy. Thus a commitment to democracy does not commit one to silence about other features of a society.

Marx may have believed it a better exercise in democracy to let the mass movement create alternative conceptions of a good society largely on its own. This was a reasonable idea given Marx's prestige, already considerable in his lifetime, and his optimism about the range of possible results of an anticapitalist revolution. With the wisdom of hindsight, however, that reasonable idea now seems mistaken. A fuller account of the good society from Marx would have prevented the systematic distortion of his views by which they now serve as a justification for oppression. Given the current state of affairs, silence by Marxists about the good society serves not democracy but the broad front from right to left that identifies socialism with nationalized property and central planning.

The grounds for antiutopianism that can plausibly be ascribed to Marx should not then dissuade us from a normative discussion of the good society.

Marx as libertarian democrat

The substantive premise of the following utopian sketch is that Marx was a libertarian democrat. This premise is inconceivable from the standpoint of cold-war treatments of Marxism. The longevity of such studies cannot be explained in terms of their scholarly merit. Largely because of the work of Eastern European dissidents, however, the libertarian and democratic core of Marx's thought is now somewhat more widely recognized – although still by a relatively insignificant minority.

Marx's concepts of freedom and democracy are not precisely those of English-speaking political philosophy, but neither are they unrecognizably foreign. There is no mysterious twist of dialectics by virtue of which Marx's core concept of freedom turns out to be identical to an assent to authoritarianism. Nor is democracy for Marx the rule of the party or unanimous votes by symbolic assemblies.

Instead, Marx's notion of democracy represents an extension of the liberal notion. It identifies additional areas of life as arenas for democratic decision, and is less easily satisfied with democratic forms in which the constituency is passive, uninformed, or faced with less than meaningful choices. Similarly, Marx's notion of freedom extends the liberal concerns about barriers raised directly by human agency – especially by the state. For Marx barriers to freedom include a wide range of limitations on the scope of human choice. Marx was not very sympathetic to the freedoms of free enterprise, but he was sympathetic to those civil liberties that have so frequently been suppressed in his name.

The interpretation of Marx as a libertarian–democrat does not require a subtle reading between the lines – although it does seem possible to miss it, if one reads Marx with the belief that he was reincarnated in Stalin. The key step to understanding Marx's normative theory is to leave behind the vulgarized form of Marxism that is chiefly concerned with justice in the distribution of consumption goods. Marx explicitly warned against this misreading in the *Critique of the Gotha Program:*

[I]t was in general incorrect to make a fuss about so-called *distribution* and put the principal stress on it. Any distribution whatever of the means of consumption is only a consequence of the distribution of the conditions of production themselves. The latter distribution, however, is a feature of the mode of production itself.[2]

In Marx's analysis the mode of production is largely a matter of what class controls production, and in what fashion. In other words, it is a matter of the form of domination.

To say that Marx was not primarily concerned with justice in the distribution of consumption goods is not to say that he was unconcerned with distributional justice in a wider sense. He was vitally concerned with questions of the distribution of power. In his view, the chief goal of a socialist revolution was to end domination and to bring about a society in which each individual has wide-ranging control of his or her own life.

Human emancipation is the central theme for Marx. He did not abandon the concerns with civil liberties of the *Anekdota* and *Rheinische Zeitung;* he simply came to understand that the system of domination extended beyond censorship and state edicts. Domination is the central feature of the entire structure of class society. Exploitation, for example, is fundamentally a matter of domination. The evil of exploitation is not that the capitalist class consumes the surplus. They consume very little of it in percentage terms. The evil is that they *control* the surplus, and through the surplus, the conditions of social life.[3]

The words "emancipation" and "liberation" have lost much of their meaning in the latter part of the twentieth century, but Marx's use of them was intended to convey, not simply a victory for the working class, but a victory with a particular content. That content involves a dramatic increase in the range of decisions that the individual can make about his or her life. Insofar as those decisions are made collectively, "emancipation" means democracy. Insofar as the decisions are purely individual, "emancipation" means liberty. Liberty and democracy are, then, the core of the positive side of Marx's critique of class societies as regimes of domination.

In saying that liberty and democracy are Marx's core ideals, I do not intend to suggest that they are his only goals. Equality, community, self-realization, welfare, artistic and scientific achievement, and any number of other desiderata informed Marx's vision of what a good society would be like. Some of these other values are preconditions for, or the probable results of, a free, democratic society. For example, he envisioned that "Only in community do the means exist for every individual to cultivate his talents in all directions. Only in the community is personal freedom possible."[4] It would be a mistake, however, to think that these other values are exhausted by their relation to the liberty-democracy complex. Marx hated "one-sidedness"; it is to be expected that his view of a good society would be many-sided.

Liberty

Liberty and democracy are closely related ideals that follow from the intuition that people should run their own lives. There are, however, different ways in which people run their own lives. While unanimous collective decision is simply individual decision added up, all other forms of collective decision making are in potential conflict with individual choice. For this reason it is useful to give liberty and democracy separate consideration.

The standard characterization of freedom in English-speaking political philosophy is in terms of the absence of restraint and coercion. Marx's notion of freedom is broader. Nearly anything that restricts what a human being can do, including even the brute facts of our physical existence, count as limitations on freedom. The virtue of capitalism is that it allows man to push back the boundaries of "natural necessity," and thus makes possible an explosive expansion of human freedom. One of the vices of capitalism is that it does not make this explosive expansion of human freedom actual.

Because Marx defines the "preventing conditions" of freedom very broadly, it can be said that for Marx freedom is not the absence of constraint, but rather the presence of alternatives. Anything that enlarges the set of alternatives open to the individual enlarges freedom. By the standard liberal account, release from jail increases freedom, but learning to swim does not. For Marx, both increase freedom.

It is useful to distinguish the two accounts by calling Marx's view, emphasizing the presence of alternatives, "positive," and the liberal view, emphasizing the absence of constraint, "negative." A cautionary note is in order, however. Isaiah Berlin's famous essay "Two Concepts of Liberty," characterizes a notion of "positive liberty" in terms of rational self-determination rather than the presence of alternatives. Although there is a historical connection between the two notions, it is crucial to distinguish them. There is nothing in liberty as the presence of alternatives that would trigger the sinister dialectic that Berlin purports to find in "positive liberty" understood in terms of rational self-determination. "Positive liberty" will be used here exclusively in the "presence of alternatives" sense.

In a society with a high level of positive liberty, each individual would select whatever he or she wanted to do from a long and varied list of alternative activities. Ideally this would include the alternative of doing nothing in the way of material production. "The realm of freedom actually begins only where labor which is determined by necessity and mundane consideration ceases; thus in the very nature of things it lies beyond the sphere of actual material production."[5]

If it is impossible entirely to eliminate labor that would not be elected for its own sake, it should, in Marx's view, at least be minimized. "The free development of individualities . . . the general reduction of the necessary labour of society to a minimum, which then corresponds to the artistic, scientific etc. development of the individuals in the time set free . . . "[6] Under a regime of positive liberty one could devote a lifetime to the study of mathematics or chess or centipedes without ever being expected to make a contribution to the field – or indeed to do very well at it. Moreover one could pursue any such activity with no risk of having to go without a normal level of consumption – better yet without having to give up any consumption good one wanted.

Obviously no society so far has been able to give complete control over one's own time to anyone but members of a small privileged class. There is some question as to how far even socialism could go in eliminating "necessary labor." Marx, of course, expected socialist society to come into existence at a high productive and technical level and to advance those levels still higher. With a great deal of help from machines it should be possible to produce enough to satisfy all reasonable desires with a relatively small input of labor. Marx, at least at times, also expected that in a good society socially useful work would be attractive to most people as a way of spending a significant amount of their time. Still, it seems probable that too few people would elect to work to produce all that society would like to consume. There are three possible ways to adjust the idea of positive liberty to this fact.

The most obvious adjustment is simply to get along with less production than we would otherwise find desirable. Limiting consumption, among its other costs, can be expected to limit the alternative uses of one's time. It may be argued, however, that the freedom not to work is the most fundamental of the positive freedoms because it opens up so many possibilities. For this reason it may be worth sacrifices elsewhere. In addition, limiting consumption would have obvious environmental advantages – perhaps essential to transmitting the benefits of a good society to future generations.

A second sort of adjustment, if there are not enough willing workers, is to adopt a system of incentives, either material or moral. Material incentives might give to those who work a wider range of alternatives in their time off than those the nonworkers enjoy at all times. Marxists have frequently objected to a system of material incentives as a holdover from capitalism and a stimulus to individual acquisitiveness. But such a program would have the advantage of leaving the individual with the choice of two different ways of compromising the ideal of positive liberty. For example, the person who wished to spend all his time reading cookbooks might have to do it in California while the person who was willing to spend a certain amount of time repairing the cookbook press could spend four months of the year on Corfu. Such a scheme maximizes liberty under the conditions of insufficient wholly voluntary labor, but it is important to remember that it falls short of the ideal of positive liberty. The more material incentives have to be used, the farther the scheme falls short of that ideal and the less complete is the individual's control over his or her time.

Moral incentives – the fostering by the society of the desire to do socially useful work – may appear to be the perfect solution. The cookbook reader could elect to do nothing but read cookbooks on Corfu, but instead he agrees to spend part of his time repairing the cookbook press – out of a desire to do his part for the community. The problem with moral incentives is that of determining at what point social reinforcement constitutes unacceptable interference with the individual's freedom of choice. The whole point of moral incentives, after all, is to change the agent's desires. Some manipulations of desires, especially manipulations that an adult would not have agreed to in advance, constitute infringements of liberty. It is desirable, of course, that a nonarbitrary line can be drawn between moral education and moral indoctrination. But whether such a line can be drawn or not, it should be clear that the more work we want moral incentives to do, the greater is the danger of compromising liberty.

The third possible adjustment would be to require a certain amount of labor from everyone – a certain number of hours per year. This would mean less positive liberty than under a material incentives program, but its "equality of sacrifice" and its elimination of marketlike mechanisms might make it more desirable from the standpoint of community. A mandatory rotating system might be especially appropriate for particularly undesirable jobs.

Whether or not one can choose not to work, any society that takes positive liberty seriously must remove all unnecessary barriers to self-realization. Vocations, avocations, and all kinds of education and training should be open to everyone. This does not mean the elimination of such objective requirements as examinations, but it should be possible to attempt any such hurdle at regular intervals and as many times as one wishes – all without the loss of support.

Education and training in all their forms are central to the positive conception of liberty, because in general, the more powers and skills a person has, the wider his or her range of alternative possibilities. Positive liberty makes possible self-realization, and self-realization, as the all-around development of one's capacities, increases one's positive liberty. Marx emphasized all-around development of capacities because of the tendency of other capacities to atrophy when one concentrates too exclusively on one sort of activity. This is obviously true for the factory worker who attains great skill at one endlessly repeated manipulation. It can also occur when the single capacity developed is itself a significant talent. Child prodigies, whether in music, chess, or swimming, often pay a heavy price in the arrested development of other capacities. Although there are times when Marx sounded as if he was opposed to any specialization, it is only pathological specialization that is a threat to positive liberty. Of course a free community does not forbid overspecialization any more than it requires personal development. Individuals would not be forced, but only encouraged, to be free.

Marx used the notion of "praxis" to explain the kind of self-realization that is so closely related to positive liberty. To fashion a society in the understanding that humans are "beings of praxis" is to encourage the development of human capacities, especially the creative capacities.

There is a possible objection that a society that devotes a considerable share of its resources to the development of capacities might produce an overtrained and overeducated citizenry. Too many unskilled or semiskilled jobs would still have to be performed, and there would not be enough challenging jobs to go around. This objection, of course, assumes the the job is still the center of people's lives. Even if undemanding jobs need to be done, they need not absorb so much of anyone's time that it would be better to shrink the worker to fit the job. At the other extreme, we are in no immediate danger of running out of projects demanding creativity. The lists of unsolved problems are not short in mathematics, the sciences, medicine, engineering, or the humanities. In most fields the list grows longer, not shorter, as the field develops. And one can suspect that all these problems will long be solved before the last musical score worth writing is written.

Treating the development of capacities as necessary for *liberty* depends on the principle that alternatives only add to liberty to the extent that they are realizable. No laws forbid me from becoming an Olympic sprinter or starting a company to compete with U.S. Steel. No laws forbid the janitor with a family of seven from spending the spring on Corfu. In one sense these are things we are "free" to do, but, for the most part, these are not freedoms that we should pay much attention to in counting our blessings. I will call a liberty "concrete" for an agent only if it is likely that the agent, through the exercise of a degree of determination reasonable in view of the aim, can do what the liberty makes him or her free to do. The liberty to pursue alternatives that are not realizable or realizable only at a disproportionate cost is "abstract." Because, given the physical facts, no amount of effort will turn me into an Olympic sprinter, that is an abstract liberty. Similarly, in the quite different case of the janitor who would like to vacation on Corfu, the liberty to do so is abstract because the social and economic facts are such that he could get to Corfu only through extreme sacrifice or great good fortune.

Some abstract liberties are of considerable moral importance, such as the liberty to make special achievements in science, culture, or athletics. Naturally, the concrete liberties that open up science, culture, or athletics to the individual are valuable. It would be possible to make tracks available for runners while forbidding anyone to better the previous world records. We might thereby be curtailing only abstract freedom because it is likely that the breaking of world records always requires a disproportionate effort. But, other things being equal, it is best to leave to the individual the choice of whether or not to pay such costs.

The liberties associated with high achievements in business are of a different sort. Obviously the freedom to own industry or to control great wealth is concrete only for the favored few and abstract for the rest of us. But what is of crucial importance is that the system that makes possible such achievements simultaneously makes impossible a great many liberties that could be concrete for all of us – notably control of our own time. Classical liberals defend the largely abstract liberties of business with great energy, while showing little sympathy for a wide range of positive liberties that could be made concrete by a shift in the allocation of resources.

The requirement that alternatives be concrete brings out the connection between positive liberty, on the one hand, and production levels and distributive justice, on the other. Few alternatives are open to the unhealthy and underfed. Many alternatives require material support in the way of special equipment or facilities. Of course possessions are sometimes oppressive, and it has frequently been suggested that we would be freer in a society where there were fewer "things." But while one might have a purer soul on a desert island, one would also have fewer and less varied alternatives. To play music one needs an instrument and to sail one needs a boat. In general in a free society there will be no reason to produce goods that oppress and every reason to produce those that liberate.

Positive liberty also requires the retention and deepening of the traditional civil liberties. In particular it not only entails the absence of bars to expression but encourages the widest possible range of ideas. As a policy this has the defect of insuring publicity to a large number of false, detrimental, and even crackpot ideas. Marx was confident, as were many classical liberals, that good ideas would tend to win out over bad. Subsequent history might lead us to be less sanguine on this count, but Marx would point out that all history so far has been the history of class societies – which have special mechanisms for the protection and promulgation of bad ideas.

Even if we do not fear that bad ideas will become popular, there is still a question of how many resources bad ideas are worth. Prior to the Bolshevik phase of the revolution, Lenin proposed an allocation of resources to the press based on the number of adherents an idea had. Thus a small band of Satanists might be the trustees of a subsidized mimeograph while the major political parties would control daily newspapers. This principle would be extended to other media as well. (Unfortunately this proposal was never put into practice in Russia.)

43

Lenin's method was not intended to filter out dangerous ideas. An idea will usually be dangerous only if it attracts adherents – in which case it is better dealt with openly. The method would limit the resources commanded by the most obviously crackpot ideas, and it would do so while preserving the most important aspects of freedom of expression in a way that would meet the requirements of democracy as well as of liberty positively conceived.

The protection of unpopular ideas in the schools would require a slightly different strategy, because the teachers would be unlikely to represent a full range of opinion on controversial topics even if some attempt were made to provide a mix of teachers throughout the student's career for just that purpose. (All societies have, of course, done their best to maximize the orthodoxy rather than the diversity of teachers.) Some use could be made of books or pamphlets arguing for points of view other than those of the teacher. This might be supplemented by requiring teachers to present the best case for positions that they do not share. Which heterodox positions are to be presented should be a matter of the degree of difference from accepted positions together with degree of plausibility. A theory no one could believe may represent a more diverse alternative but it is not as legitimate an alternative as a reasonably plausible heterodox theory.

Finally there may be some need to restrict especially dangerous ideas, such as racism in the lower levels of school. This is a concession to social values other than liberty and should be made only in cases of clear danger. Any restrictive decision of this sort should be made democratically.

A liberty not included among the traditional civil liberties but without which no society could claim to be really free is the right of secession. In principle any individual as well as any self-selected group should be able to secede from the larger society. The share of land and resources that becomes their sovereign possession should be proportional to their numbers.

The possibility of secession is valuable because it opens up alternative ways of life that would not be otherwise available. The members of the seceded group should be free to create whatever rules they wish for their community up to and including eating only asparagus, living under the dictatorship of a three year old, and practicing human sacrifice. But certain limits are necessary.

The first is that the wider society should enforce the right of any individual in the seceded community to rejoin the wider society. Thus human sacrifice is tolerated only if the victim gives informed consent. The seceded community cannot be allowed to commit aggression against or interfere in any way with the wider society or any other community. Nor can it expand its territory except by agreement with the communities thereby affected. (Growth of population through recruitment might be considered just grounds for expansion of territory, but not growth of population through reproduction.)

Because the wider society enforces the right of secession from a seceded community, either by individuals or groups, the possibility of indoctrination presents a serious difficulty. We would not want people to remain in the seceded community only because they were brainwashed or deceived. Yet to allow the wider society to interfere in education in the seceded community would be a major curtailment of the independence that is its reason for existence. Perhaps seceded children should be bused on occasion to special instructional centers in the wider society where they are informed of the alternative lifestyles available to them. They might also be tested to insure that they really believe that these options are open to them and that they do not believe anything of significance that is false about the other options. Under these circumstances even the individual in an authoritarian community has, in principle, all the alternatives available through the wider society (and so through any other seceded community that would accept him or her). It might also be prudent for the wider society to interfere in the seceded community to the extent of forbidding the existence of any weapon with significant offensive potential.

Apart from these details, the right of secession sketched here could lead to a situation much like the polycentric utopia Robert Nozick recommends in *Anarchy, State and Utopia*. I have included the possibility of independent communities against the background of a "wider society" for which Nozick would have little sympathy. (Any tendency to maximize positive liberty is likely to run into direct conflict with Nozick's "entitlement" theory of distribution.) Of course it is possible that so many people would flee the "wider society" that it would cease to be anything but one community among many. In that case its special role as enforcer of

45

limitations on other communities would have to be taken up by some other agency. We then would arrive at Nozick's utopia of utopias.

Although one may hope that most people would elect to remain within the wider libertarian-democratic society, it is essential to positive liberty that people have the right of secession. It is even a good thing that some people exercise that right – although that might weaken the wider society in certain respects. The actual existence of independent communities makes alternatives concrete that would otherwise be fairly abstract. Moreover these experiments may lead to alternatives we would not otherwise have conceived and will certainly tell us more about those we already can conceive.

Because this sketch of a good society has dealt only with the desirability of maximizing positive liberty, it may need emphasizing that liberty does not always take precedence over other goods. For example, there are times when liberty should be sacrificed to welfare. (We cannot have liberty without a certain level of welfare, but we can have welfare without liberty.) Consider an artificially simple, but for that reason, fairly clear example. Suppose that a is free to cause b a severe but brief pain. It will be so brief that it will not interfere with anything b wishes to do. Weighing the value of this particular freedom against the value of the absence of pain, the moral scales tip decisively against the freedom. Note that this is not a case of conflicting freedoms. B may have a right not to be hurt by a, but that right is not a liberty.

The priority of liberty has sometimes been defended by supposing liberty to have a built-in limitation that excludes from the class of liberties any action having a detrimental effect on others. Any such limitation sufficient to eliminate cases like the one just given will, unfortunately, also eliminate liberties we would like to see protected. For example, suppose that the clashing colors of a's clothes are an irritation to b. This is a detrimental effect but not one serious enough to outweigh the value of a's liberty to dress as he or she pleases. It is always good in itself that one be able to choose, and it is always good in itself that one promote the welfare of others. Which takes precedence on a given occasion depends on the kind of choice and the kind of effect on others.

It would be easier if liberty never had to be weighed against such

46

other goods as welfare, democracy, and community, but the world is morally complex. It should be emphasized, however, that although liberty does not always take priority, in Marx's view it should be given a great deal more weight than it has been in any society to date. In particular, the temptation always to put welfare before liberty should be carefully guarded against. Major and systematic curtailments of liberty of the sort authoritarian regimes require are justifiable only in the most extreme sorts of survival situations.

The conflict between liberty and welfare is the chief point dividing the libertarian from the authoritarian left (based on a sympathetic interpretation of the authoritarian left). The authoritarians are always willing to sacrifice liberty for security, higher levels of consumption, and equality of distribution. The points that divide libertarians of the left from libertarians of the right are disagreements about the content of liberty, about equal liberty, and about the proper balance between liberty and democracy. Right libertarians are concerned with maximizing (other things being equal) negative liberty, that is, with minimizing restraint and coercion. Left libertarians are concerned with maximizing (other things being equal) positive liberty as well, that is, with maximizing the number and variety of concrete alternatives. Right libertarians reject inequalities of negative liberty, that is, societies in which some are coerced in ways others are not – paradigmatically, slaveholding societies. Left libertarians reject, in addition, inequalities of positive liberty – societies in which some have more concrete alternatives and opportunities than others. These differences are already enough to make possible a great divergence between the right and left libertarian visions of a good society. Only a society that makes high levels of positive liberty a major social goal is likely to have high levels of positive liberty. Certainly no society in which there are significant differences in wealth will have equal concrete positive liberty.

Part of the greater positive liberty of the wealthy – for example, their greater command over consumer goods – can be distributed so as to increase the individual positive liberty of those less well off, simply by redistributing incomes and liquid assets. But the positive liberty that the wealthy enjoy by virtue of their ownership prerogatives in productive land and factories is not entirely

47

redistributable in this way. We cannot give each individual control over part of a factory. What we can do is substitute democratic social control for the owner's private control – gaining thereby the power for individuals collectively to control their own productive activity and its uses. This would equalize both positive liberty and social power by transferring power from the domain of the owner's individual liberty to that of collective democratic decision-making. The left libertarian believes both these equalizations to be demands of justice. Although transfers of wealth and power require some constraints on ownership, they should increase overall concrete positive liberty, because the liberties of ownership of the means of production are so abstract for most of us.

Democracy

In an 1843 letter Marx wrote:

Freedom, the feeling of man's dignity, will have to be awakened again in these men. Only this feeling, which disappeared from the world with the Greeks and with Christianity vanished into the blue mist of heaven, can again transform society into a community of men to achieve their highest purposes, a democratic state.[7]

Marx would not have expressed himself in these terms later in his career. In his later analysis all states are instruments of coercion. Far from being mankind's highest purpose, the democratic state is something to be overcome. It is, however, the highest form of state, and the form of state that the revolution itself will make use of as a transitional measure. That is, what Marx on a few occasions called the "dictatorship of the proletariat,"[8] would, in fact, be a highly democratic state, in the majoritarian sense of "democratic."

There are any number of places in Marx's works where one can find evidence of the democratic nature of the workers' state. *The Communist Manifesto* is the most persuasive source in the corpus for any political question rising above the level of detail. The *Manifesto* was intended as a major political statement of program for a wide readership. It was carefully drafted and published and republished during Marx's lifetime. It is significant, then, that the *Manifesto* characterizes the working-class movement as a movement of the "immense majority," and speaks of "the raising of the proletariat to the position of a ruling class" as "winning the battle of democracy."[9]

That the dictatorship of the proletariat was to be democratic is made even clearer in *The Civil War in France,* in which Marx expressed approval for the political institutions of the Paris Commune. They were, according to Marx, "really democratic institutions."[10]

The Commune was formed of the municipal councillors, chosen by universal suffrage in the various wards of the town, responsible and revocable at short terms . . . The Commune was to be a working, not a parliamentary body, executive and legislative at the same time . . . The police was at once stripped of its political attributes and turned into the responsible and at all times revocable agent of the Commune. So were the officials of all other branches of the Administration . . . Like the rest of public servants, magistrates and judges were to be elective, responsible, and revocable.[11]

The idea that judges should be revocable may strike some as carrying democracy too far. But then, Marx was not a moderate. The dictatorship of the proletariat, more thoroughly democratic than parliamentary democracies, would be a radical democracy.

If it is clear that the transitional workers' state would be democratic, it is somewhat less clear, or at least less obvious, that the stateless society of victorious communism would be democratic. Marx did not, in his later works, link the notion of democracy with the stage following the workers' state. This is because the word "democracy" for Marx could not be properly applied to a nonstate. Democracy is majoritarian *rule (Herrschaft,* domination). Majoritarian decision making in a society without an apparatus of coercion simply could not be called "democracy."

Given current usage it is probably more convenient to disregard Marx's terminological preferences and call "democratic" any majoritarian decision procedure. In these terms, was Marx's vision of a good society democratic? The best way to pursue this question is to consider the alternatives to democratic decision making – bearing in mind Marx's strong preference for democratic decision in the transitional phase.

Among egalitarian social-decision procedures that guarantee a decision, universal majoritarian democracy minimizes the number of people whose wishes are frustrated. This does not make it the best procedure in all circumstances, but it is the best procedure in a wide range of circumstances.

The other alternative for social decision making that Marx might have approved is unanimous consent. Unanimous consent, when achieved, leaves no one frustrated. Unfortunately, in the real world, it is rarely achieved. The coerced or manipulated "unanimity" of authoritarian regimes is, of course, no unanimity at all. Only slightly better was the unanimity of some New Left organizations whose procedure was to talk all night if necessary until there was agreement. The actual result of this procedure was to give effective power to the most committed.

When a unanimity principle is adopted and no genuine agreement can be reached, nearly everyone's wishes may be frustrated. Some supporters of unanimity principles ask us to be optimistic that we will always reach agreement in a free community. One might, however, be optimistic that a free community will often be capable of generating more than one alternative course of action with supporting arguments plausible enough to attract votes. Moreover, where self-interest is involved, votes are likely to be nonunanimous, because interests vary. The town hall should be painted fuchsia, automobiles should be banned from the shopping district, and the national (or international) anthem should be played before sports events if and only if more people like it that way. In more serious cases, where we hope people will take the general welfare into account, individual preference still plays a legitimate, even essential role. Should we devote resources to medical or space research? If most people were more interested in satisfying their extraterrestrial curiosity and sense of vicarious adventure than in an increased life expectancy and decreased risk of suffering and disability, we would want that to emerge through the vote. Social decisions are frequently matters of selecting among competing ends, and in such cases what we are after is the expression of individual preferences. The unanimity optimist must either construe all social decisions as decisions about means or believe that people in a good society would not have any significant differences in interests, tastes, desires, or preferences. The latter possibility seems both unlikely and depressing. In any event, majoritarian democracy becomes equivalent to unanimous democracy if these "optimists" are right in their predictions, while retaining its superiority if they are wrong. So these considerations give us no reason to adopt the principle of unanimity in favor of the principle of majority, and they make it difficult to believe Marx could have favored any social decision procedure other than democracy.

The desirability of majoritarian democracy as a means of making social decisions is today widely accepted at least in name. Marx would depart from liberalism first with respect to the range of decisions that should fall within the scope of democracy. Should it be a matter of democratic social decision how national (or international) resources are to be allocated and how the economic life of society is to be organized? Should it be a matter of democratic social decision how the smaller institutions of everyday life – the shop floor, the school, the neighborhood, avocational groups – are to be organized and to carry out their activities? The affirmative answer to the first question might be called "planning democracy," and that to the second "participatory democracy." The two together constitute "socialism" in the sense I will use that term.

The arguments for both principles are straightforward. First it is *prima facie* better that decisions be made by human beings rather than by default, at random, or through the play of impersonal mechanisms. The greater the field we make subject to our decision making, the wider the range of alternatives we collectively have. The second half of the argument simply cites the considerations in favor of democracy in decision making – the equality of power and the minimization of frustrated choices.

One major counterargument is that either impersonal mechanisms such as the market, or talented and specially placed individuals are likely to make *better* decisions that we would collectively. However, the evidence for this is ambiguous at best. The international and national markets have frequently brought us to the brink of economic chaos or beyond, and rarely seem to work very well. And neither the interventions of experts in the economy nor the management of foremen on the shop floor have produced enviable records. But even if it were true that socialism would entail lower production and hence lower consumption, that might be a price worth paying to gain more control over our lives and the destiny of our society.

51

The first departure that a good society would make from classical liberal democracy is, then, the extension of that democracy into more of the institutions of society. A second possible departure might be called "participatory weighting." People should have a voice in making decisions in proportion to the degree to which they are affected by the decision. To take a simple example, in a chess club the yearly business meeting is conducted giving each member a number of votes equal to the numbers of evenings he or she spent in the club during the previous year. In the more difficult case of school board elections everyone in the community might receive one vote as a token of the general impact of the schools, while parents have one extra vote per child and teachers have five additional votes. In general the weighting process can be thought of as having two stages. First the constituency is divided into groups so that within each group the individuals are as nearly equally affected by the issue as is possible with any practical division procedure. The degree-affected ratios are computed by comparing representative members from each of the groups. These become the basis for the distribution of votes. This procedure is not sensitive to the number of members of the various equally affected groups, and so does not itself insure a balance of power among groups. In particular it does not guarantee minority rights because the highly affected minority with heavily weighted votes may still be insufficiently numerous to outvote the majority. All the procedure does insure, unlike classical democracy, is that we have more say on what affects us more, at the price of less say on what affects us less. Working properly this seems a worthwhile gain. Participatory weighting need not lead to unmanageable complexity. In many elections on national issues and on the shop floor one person one vote would remain appropriate. In other cases, as in that of the chess club or the school board, at least rough participatory adjustments can be made without severe practical difficulties.

The best set of mechanisms for realizing a socialist democracy should be determined by experimentation and debate in the process of creating a good society. One of the most difficult of the issues that will have to be settled in this fashion is the exact mix between the centralization of planning democracy and the decentralization of participatory democracy. At the participatory, local end of the spectrum, voting units should be small enough to allow full discussion. As the size of the unit increases such direct mechanisms as initiatives and referenda (facilitated by electronic gadgetry) assume a key role. Where representative bodies are needed they should be subject to such semidirect controls as easy recall and the instruction of delegates. It would be desirable to have antibureaucratization policies, such as short terms for those such as technical advisors or official policy makers, who might accumulate any sort of direct or indirect power. Subsidized alternative groups of technical advisors is another device that Yugoslav experience suggests would be valuable.

Indispensable to liberty as well as democracy is the right to form any sort of caucus or political party either around single issues or around entire social programs, without restriction of the content of that program. Even the organized advocacy of violence should be protected, although not violence itself. Without the protection of alternative political caucuses and parties there is no reason to believe that heterodox policies will be systematically developed and vigorously argued for.

The one party that should not exist after the revolution is the party that is identified in people's minds with the revolution. If there is a single mass revolutionary party, that party should dissolve itself. If there is a smaller party that worked within the mass movement, perhaps alongside other parties, but whose proposals for strategy and tactics were accepted by the mass movement at crucial junctures, that party too should be dissolved. Anyone perceived as a leader in the process of the revolution should retire from politics with the success of the revolution. The purpose of these measures is to prevent subsequent political decisions from being influenced by the prestige that attaches to successful revolutionary parties and their leadership.

Libertarian, democratic community

A community is a group of people joined by some sense of common purpose and feelings of belonging. The members care about, trust, and respect each other, and give each other aid and comfort. Sometimes communities have been rigidly stratified, authoritarian, and unified by common assent to a body of dogma. According to Marx's left libertarian vision, however, a community will not count as a good community unless it is free of elites of power or status as well as the compulsion of orthodoxy.

Because community is more a matter of the heart than of legal and institutional relations and mechanisms, there is no very exact recipe for the making of a good community. We can be reasonably sure that education will play a large part in bringing about the commonality of values on which community depends. Obviously there is a potential conflict with the ideal of liberty. But a libertarian educational system need not abstain from all teaching of values. After all, children, not having their own developed value systems, inevitably learn values from adults one way or another. That values be consciously taught is surely no worse than that they be absorbed unconsciously from the culture. Moreover, good schools might teach alternative value systems without the population's ending up with values differing so widely that community would be impossible – especially if the community is, as a free community must be, reasonably tolerant. The more fundamental the value at issue, presumably the more our similar genetic and environmental background will tend to lead us to similar conclusions. A value that could be inculcated only with techniques that infringe upon libery, such as strong motivation-altering techniques, is probably a value so at odds with our nature that it should be rejected in any event.

The question of whether it is possible for people to acquire a reasonably strong spirit of community in a libertarian educational system is essentially empirical. One is not likely to believe that it is possible if one believes that the individualistic elements of human personality structure are considerably stronger than the side of human nature that tends to produce ties among people. If, on the other hand, our inherent tendencies toward community are at least on a par with our individualistic tendencies, then there is no reason that education for community need be seriously manipulative or otherwise infringe liberty.

Marx had more to say about the elimination of classes, elites, stratification, and grasping individualism than he did about the problems of shared values and education. Radical democratization, if successful, would eliminate the elites of power. The key structural reform in undermining undue selfishness and elites of privilege and status is, in Marx's view, the elimination of the money economy.

Marx believed that scarcity could be largely overcome through the democratic management of the economy. Goods and services could be distributed solely on the basis of need. Early on, health care would be fully provided. At a later stage the check stands would disappear from supermarkets. One would simply pick up what one wanted and take it home. If all consumption were put on this basis, it would eliminate avarice and elites of privilege. It would also undercut a chief motivation for achieving membership in a status elite.

There would always be some goods and privileges that are scarce, of course, such as ocean-going yachts or the right to camp in a particular wilderness area. These scarcities could be distributed through such devices as sign-up waiting lists or lotteries, or they could be kept on a money system or quasimoney system. For example, everyone might get ten demand certificates per year with a sophisticated stereo costing four demand certificates, a week in a wilderness one, a car nine, and so forth. The advantage of such a scheme is, again, that it maximizes liberty in the context of scarcity. I can opt to have less than my share of one scarce good in exchange for having more than my share of another. If everyone has such options, society might differentiate somewhat according to inclinations, but it will not be a differentiation by status. Notice that this remains true if leisure is thought of as a scarce good, and so there is a limited material incentives program as previously described.

If there is a money system for scarce goods (mostly luxury goods), should people be allowed to save money, give it away, and inherit it? If they are, the possibility arises that some people will accumulate a fortune. Avarice, envy, and feelings of inequality might then undermine community, and private power might arise to undermine democracy. One partial solution would be to eliminate long-term savings by having demand certificates valid only during a given period. On the other hand, it is by no means certain that even the unrestricted use of money within a socialist framework would be destructive of left libertarian values. Suppose that there are no limitations or taxes on savings, gifts, and inheritance. A fortune might be accumulated but it would not grow on its own if there is no opportunity for investment. Private fortunes then would presumably rarely be very great, and they would not represent significant social power. One who could afford to consume more this year *really would* only be able to do so because he or his family or friends consumed less in the past.

I am not arguing that there should be no restrictions on savings or transfers. This does, however, seem to be another matter best left to experimentation. If there is money, the general presumption should be that savings and transfers be as little restricted as possible compatible with continued equality of power and the avoidance of significant long-term inequalities in the ability to obtain consumer goods. To think that freedom to do what one wants with money is not, other things equal, desirable is as much a mistake as to believe that the freedom to do what one wants with money is absolutely desirable. It is better that I be able to choose between a sailboat and a wilderness vacation, given that I cannot have both. It is not better that I be able to choose between a large diamond and a small factory, because with the latter alternative I acquire a power over others that is better divided among them. This objection does not, of course, apply to forms of investment that are carefully restricted so that the investor acquires no power but only a return on his or her investment – government bonds or, conceivably, nonvoting stock in worker-controlled enterprises. These forms of investment are compatible with socialism because they do not represent social power. Some other objections to them fall away if avarice and envy vanish in the good society. Still, such investment should probably either be forbidden or strictly regulated so as to rule out the possibility of significant long-term differences among people in their ability to obtain consumer goods. Reasonable equality of ability to obtain consumer goods is an independent desideratum of justice. As such it does not require justification in terms of such other goods as liberty or democracy.

Assuming that socialism and the elimination or curtailment of the money economy have put an end to elites of power and privilege, there might still be elites of status based on accomplishment. The danger of these elites becoming hereditary is lessened by the self-selection system in education and vocations. But even a non-hereditary status elite is a threat to a left libertarian community, because it destroys feelings of equality of worth. It is possible, of course, that in a good society everyone will achieve equally brilliantly. This, although it would create interesting problems of its own, is probably the best of possible worlds. Unfortunately it seems improbable. So it is to be hoped that there will be some way of having different levels of achievement without engendering feelings of differences of worth. Again, most of this task falls to education. More mechanically, we can insure that the achiever has no special privileges. A good community must, however, make arrangements to insure that special achievements are made best use of. This will often involve treating the author of the achievement in some respects differently from other people. We will want the best pianists to make tours. For this same reason a good society cannot avoid praising achievement, nor would that be desirable. That we want a given pianist to tour is already praise, and for socialist concert halls to be silent at the end of a performance would serve no useful purpose.

Conservatives have feared that "collectivism" must breed conformity. Marx thought the opposite to be the case. A close community is in an ideal position to stimulate innovation and creativity. It can encourage effort and applaud success while providing the psychological insurance of continued acceptance in case of failure. There is evidence that people can derive more strength from each other than an individual can muster alone; so the proper sort of close community should provide the basis for more individuality and less conformity than would a highly individualistic society. Of course, the close community may pay the price of seeing produced a good deal more of the ridiculous as well as more of the sublime.

Probably nothing else contributes to community so much as a commitment to a common project – as evidenced by societies at war or facing a natural catastrophe. The project of creating a good society would itself provide such a focus, at least in the initial stages.

A society formed on the basis of Marx's vision of a democratic and libertarian community would probably seem to many people to have a good deal more to recommend it than do existing societies, including those societies that pay homage to Marx's name. For this reason it is to be expected that official and unofficial spokespersons for regimes both East and West will continue to resist the interpretation of Marx as a revolutionary, libertarian democrat.

There is certainly evidence in the Marx corpus against the interpretation, although the preponderance of the evidence, I believe, clearly favors it. In the end, of course, the more important question is not what Marx thought would be a good society, but what really would make a society a good one. That is, the more important question is normative, not historical. A left libertarian perspective deserves careful examination whether or not Marx is properly placed in its genealogy. There are, however, tactical, rhetorical advantages in laying claim to Marx for the left libertarian perspective – especially because that claim is thoroughly defensible.

Notes

1 David Crocker, Robert Coburn, Jane English, and members of the University of Washington Colloquium in Social Theory made helpful comments on earlier drafts of this paper.

2 Marx and Engels, *Selected Works,* vol. 2 (Moscow: Foreign Languages Publishing House, 1962), p. 25; Marx and Engels, *Werke,* vol. 19 (Berlin: Dietz Verlag, 1959), p. 22. See also Marx, *A Contribution to the Critique of Political Economy* (New York: International Publishers, 1970), pp. 201–2.

3 See Lawrence Crocker, "Marx's Concept of Exploitation," *Social Theory and Practice* 2 (1972): 201–15.

4 Marx and Engels, *The German Ideology,* reprinted in *Writings of the Young Marx on Philosophy and Society,* Loyd Easton and Kurt Guddat, eds. (Garden City: Doubleday Anchor, 1967), p. 457.

5 Marx, *Capital,* vol. 3 (Moscow: Foreign Languages Publishing House, 1959), pp. 799–800.

6 Marx, *Grundrisse* (New York: Vintage Books, 1973), p. 706.

7 Letter to Ruge, reprinted in Easton and Guddat, *Writings of the Young Marx on Philosophy and Society,* p. 206.

8 This phrase was used to distinguish a dictatorship *of* the proletariat from a (Blanquist) dictatorship *over* the proletariat. See Hal Draper, "Marx and the Dictatorship of the Proletariat," *New Politics* 1 (1962): 91–104.

9 Marx and Engels, *Selected Works,* 1:53; Marx and Engels, *Werke,* 4:481. See also the "first draft" for the *Manifesto* by Engels. "What will be the course of this revolution? Above all, it will establish a *democratic constitution* and thereby, directly or indirectly, the political rule of the proletariat." Engels, *Principles of Communism* (New York: International Publishers, 1971), p. 180. Marx and Engels, *Werke,* 4:372.

10 Marx and Engels, *Selected Works,* 1:522; Marx and Engels, *Werke,* 17:342.

11 Marx and Engels, *Selected Works,* 1:522; Marx and Engels, *Werke,* 17:339.

3

Marx's early concept of democracy and the ethical bases of socialism

NORMAN FISCHER

Kreuznach: between liberalism and socialism

Karl Marx's stay in the small town of Kreuznach, during the summer and early fall of 1843, represented a lull in the public sphere of his life. His editorship of the *Rheinische Zeitung* was over – the paper had been suppressed by censorship – and his move to Paris, a plunge into economic studies, and new political associations would not come till late fall of that year. Undoubtedly the young Marx reflected during this time on the impossibility of expressing the liberal political ideals of the *Rheinische Zeitung* in the reactionary Germany of the day. He was also in the process of testing two ways of thought against each other. He engaged himself in the study of political philosophy and the history of the modern state, reading Machiavelli, Montesquieu, Rousseau, and Hegel. He also concerned himself with the ontological critique of Hegel that had appeared in Feurbach's *Essence of Christianity* and in a work that appeared shortly before his move to Kreuznach, the *Preliminary Theses on the Reform of Philosophy*.[1] These two ways of thought produced new concepts of democracy in the two works composed at Kreuznach: *The Critique of Hegel's Doctrine of the State (Critique)* and the essay *On the Jewish Question*. These works hover between liberalism and socialism. Furthermore, fragmented and inconsistent as they may be, they give unique suggestions for distinguishing between which actions should and should not be mandated in socialism.

In the *Critique* Marx uses three types of argument against Hegel to construct his notion of democracy. Part of his concept of democracy simply states positively his negative attitude toward institutions. When they are gone, then democracy exists. This is part of Marx's Feuerbachian argument against Hegel's ontology. Second, Marx wants democracy in the sense of more participation by members of civil society in state affairs, which include the economy and other aspects of man's social but not specifically political life. This is Marx's political argument against Hegel's stress on the state as an elite group that represents the masses of civil society. Third, Marx maintains that in modern times there is separation between the state and civil society and that the negation of this separation, as in medieval and ancient society, represents democracy. This is Marx's economic argument against Hegel. Each of these arguments develops at least a tentative characterization of democracy, and these characterizations are in conflict with each other. Each is too fragmentary, however, to be seen as a complete definition of democracy. Nevertheless, they point toward a complete and unified definition of democracy. It is because they have this potential that it is important to show the inconsistencies in the characterizations that prevent them from realizing this potential.

The ontological concept of democracy in The Critique of Hegel's Doctrine of the State

The first argument arises out of Marx's encounter with Feuerbach's ontology, an encounter that highlights, whether intentionally or not, an ambiguity in Rousseau's concept of democracy. This ambiguity occurs when Rousseau argues that in order for there to be a justified state there must not only be majority rule; the members of the state must also have common principles. What common principles? It seems that Rousseau was most concerned with equality. Thus, democracy could not be achieved unless the people were committed to the principle of equality. However, when Rousseau describes these common principles he is sometimes quite vague, which leads some commentators to think that he had a great deal more in mind than just equality.[2] The extension of the idea of commitment to principles other than equality also characterizes early nineteenth-century German philosophy. Both Hegel and Feuerbach expanded the idea of commitment beyond equality to include what they call community. Feuerbach quarreled with Hegel over what this community meant, but their debate presupposes that it is more than political equality; Marx's comment on the debate in the *Critique* presupposes this as well.

Hegel had held that much of man's reality is in his institutions. For Hegel this could be positive or negative, depending on whether the institutions allowed man to realize himself or not.[3] Feuerbach, writing within the context of the debates over religion following Hegel's death, argued that Hegel's strong defense of such institutions as the state reflected a fault both in his religious view and in his views of knowledge and reality. For Feuerbach, man must find himself in himself, not in the state or in God. Furthermore, when he finds himself he does not so much retrieve his individual ego as the common powers that belong to him and other members of the species. All energy that had previously gone into politics and religion should now go into the search for man's common species powers, experienced directly, rather than indirectly through the state and religion. This directness includes finding oneself in ordinary experience, which becomes something superior to the abstract realms of the state and religion.

So when Marx takes up the Feuerbachian cudgel against Hegel, two doctrines that sound like Rousseau's theory of democracy emerge.[4] First, man must experience his own powers directly rather than through a representative state. This sounds like Rousseau's notion that all men should legislate, that they cannot allow representatives to do this for them, and that the executive is unimportant in relation to the legislature. Second, when man experiences these powers he understands them in relation to the common powers of all men. This sounds like Rousseau's insistence that for true democracy there must be acceptance of common principles. But for Feuerbach, and Marx insofar as he follows him, the basic principle is not equality. Rather, the primary principles are such things as accepting that there must be a passive as well as an active element in love, and accepting that an individual's activities must be complemented by the activities of all other human beings.[5]

These ideas place the early Marx in a very peculiar relationship to the anarchist tradition. Probably the two concepts most associated with anarchism are hatred of institutions and stress on the individual. It seems that Marx affirms the first and denies the second. He stresses social liberation without institutions. There may be other than Feuerbachian reasons for this hatred of institutions. For Marx does not see how liberation is possible in the state and he does not yet understand how it could be possible in the economy. Hovering between knowledge of a state that he does not like and ignorance of an economy that he does not yet understand, Marx advocates return to men bereft of institutions.

The question of which common principles there should be is also connected with another topic that might define Marx's relation to anarchism: the question of what an institution should make its members do; that is, the problem of mandation. If there are no institutions, however, then the problem does not arise. It is Marx's disbelief in institutions that prevents him from addressing this question.

Marx's theory of democracy of this time may seem strange to some. Like Rousseau's, it stresses commitment to principles, but, as with Feuerbach, the commitment is to the principle of community; a community, however, without what we ordinarily think of as institutions. Marx's political argument against Hegel continues this stress on commitment to community, but at the expense of giving up some of the animus against institutions.

The Critique's political concept of democracy

Hegel placed himself in the middle of two constitutional traditions. One he identified as Rousseau's and saw as the theory that would destroy all social traditions in order to make things better. The other is the theory that simply accepts traditions as they are without figuring out which are more basic or what the connections between them are.

Hegel seems to have desired a median way, so that the traditions could be evaluated in the light of rationality and rationality in the light of traditions. All of Western Europe had to find some such median way as the formation of modern states was achieved. The result was the creation of codes of law, which Hegel defends. Hegel expresses his median position when he notes that "a constitution is not just something manufactured; it is the work of centuries, it is the Idea, the consciousness of rationality so far as that consciousness is developed in a particular nation."[6]

By placing himself in this median tradition, Hegel can take the emphasis on common principles, so essential to Rousseau's theory of democracy, and apply it in a transformed way to the liberal doctrine of the separation of powers, which also becomes transformed. Hegel can then talk about how the various powers in the state accept or are committed to various principles. The state as a whole will have the task of connecting these principles and showing how they are connected. In Hegelian terms it has the task of mediating between the principles. It is the concept of *mediation* of principles that separates Hegel from Rousseau. It is not the case that all people in the same way simply accept some common principles. Some adopt some, other people others, and the state as a whole brings them together. But it is the concept of mediation of *principles* that ties Hegel to Rousseau and differentiates him from other separation-of-powers theorists. By stressing the necessity of mediating between the separate powers, Hegel adopts the content of the liberal political philosophy of Locke and Montesquieu. By stressing the concept of common principles, Hegel adopts the spirit of the political philosophy of Rousseau. Hegel's position is expressed practically in his notion that various groups in the state should choose their own representatives, and that these representatives would then meet to achieve a sense of national interest.

Marx argues that each person should vote directly on a national ballot, and against Hegel's median position. Marx defends universal suffrage and the notion that all the people make the constitution against what he regards as Hegel's more elitist and feudalistic view. Against Hegel he says that, " 'Not *all, as individuals* should share in deliberating and deciding on political matters of general concern,' for 'individuals' do share in deliberating and deciding on *matters of general concern* as 'all,' i.e. within society and as the members of society. Not all as individuals but the individuals as all."[7] Marx is siding here with both Rousseau and Hegel against the position that it is simply quantities of self-seeking individuals that make up the justified state; that is, the position of Locke and Hobbes who then can be said to hold at most that all as individuals participate in the state. When Marx counterposes to this individualistic concept of democracy the notion that the state is also made up of the individuals as all, he is stressing, as did Hegel and Rousseau, that in order for there to be a state, the individuals must have some common principles. This emerges clearly when Marx says, "When people speak of the 'general concerns of the state,' the impression is given that the 'general concerns' are one thing and the 'state' is another. However, the *state* is the 'matter of general concern,' and in reality by 'matters of general concern' we mean the state."[8]

"The individuals as all" as a defining concept of democracy really implies three things for Marx: first, *all the individuals,* the empirical test of whether all are participating; second, the *individuals as all,* the question whether all these individuals have common principles; third, that they all have the same common principles as opposed to Hegel's view that they have different common principles that are mediated by the state. Thus, once again, Marx is following Feuerbach in arguing that there must be an immediate and direct unity between the species and the self. This concept is also applied in Marx's economic argument.

The Critique's economic concept of democracy

Marx's economic argument is that for Hegel the modern state and economy are separate and should be so. This is unfair to Hegel who tried to show essential connections between what appeared to be separate in modern society.[9] Marx's basic ethical point is that the various aspects of man's life should be harmoniously connected. Marx finds this harmonious connection only in precapitalist societies. Presumably in order to show this Marx would have to define separation as well as harmonious connection. Separation could mean (1) that ontologically the state and the economy can exist without each other, (2) that the rules and actions of each are truly characterized in much different ways. Marx does not develop the first definition at all systematically. In considering the second, he is unclear and even contradictory on how to characterize the rules and actions of the state and the economy. Usually he suggests that in the state the actions are primarily self-regarding and the rules facilitate this. But he is unclear about the rules and actions of the economy. At one point he says they are individualistic: "The civil society of the present is the principle of *individualism* carried to its logical conclusion." Elsewhere he suggests that they are nonindividualistic: "the communistic entity, in which the individual exists, civil society, is separated from the state." Once he admits that he does not know whether they are individualistic or not: "Even though this atomistic point of view vanishes in the family and perhaps (??) also in civil society."[10] These vacillations, however, do not affect his basic definition of democracy in terms of the unitary socialness of the state and economy in precapitalist societies.

The three concepts of democracy considered together

The three concepts of democracy – ontological, political, and economic – intertwine in the following passages:

(1) Democracy is both form and content . . . Hegel proceeds from the state and conceives of man as the subjectivized state; democracy proceeds from man and conceives of the state as objectified man . . .

(2) Just as religion does not make man, but rather man makes religion, so the constitution does not make the people, but the people the constitution . . .

(3) Hitherto, the *political constitution* has always functioned as the *religious* sphere, the *religion* of the life of the people, the heaven of its universality as opposed to the earthly existence of its actual reality. The sphere of politics has been the only real state-sphere in the state, the only sphere in which both form and content was that of the species, i.e. truly universal . . . It is self-evident that the political constitution as such is only developed when the private spheres have achieved an independent existence. Where commerce and landed property are unfree, where they have not yet asserted their independence, there can be no political constitution. The Middle Ages were the democracy of unfreedom.[11]

The very juxtaposition of these different characterizations of democracy, however, shows their inconsistency.

The conflict between the political and economic concepts of democracy

According to the third passage, in medieval society the political and the economic are not separated, which can be interpreted to mean they are ontologically interdependent and/or that the political and economic rules and actions are homologous. Furthermore, the rules and actions of each are nonindividualistic. Marx then characterizes this state of nonseparation and harmoniousness as sufficient for democracy. It is the democracy of unfreedom. But this view is inconsistent with the political notion of democracy that the people all vote and make the constitution. For the economy and state may be interdependent in fascism; and neither there nor in medieval society did the people make the constitution and all have the right to vote. Marx seems to recognize this problem when he steps back and notes that with his new definition democracy is compatible with nonfreedom. For medieval society is "the democracy of unfreedom."

The conflict between the economic and ontological concepts of democracy

It is easy to show the conflict between the political and economic concepts of democracy. For the economic assumes that democracy is compatible with institutions whereas the ontological assumes that it is not. The first passage reflects Marx's ontological opposition to Hegel. How could democracy be both form and content? It was Feuerbach who had distinguished between the form and content of man's species powers. The content is the powers themselves, the form their expression through the belief in God.

Because Feuerbach's idea was for men to experience the species powers directly, it can be said that he too wanted to merge form and content. For he wanted to deny that the powers should be expressed through religion, which is a form that distorts the content. But presumably he held that there must be some form or way of expressing the species powers in a natural way.[12] So too, Marx denies that the species must express itself through the distorting form of the state, and argues that it should find a more direct natural form beyond the realm of institutions. We do not know what that natural form is but it seems incompatible with the democracy of unfreedom. It also seems incompatible with Marx's political argument.

The conflict between the political and ontological concepts of democracy

Is Marx's characterization of democracy that "the people make the constitution" not an acceptance of the reality of the state? This implies that Marx is giving a positive role to institutions. Marx even notes that when, as in the French Revolution, the legislature made the constitution, this represented the activity of the species will.[13] Marx seems to be taking a position here that falls on two sides of Rousseau. Rousseau's position itself stands between one that says that all political institutions, legislative or executive, de-form man, and one that could accommodate liberation in almost any institution, legislative or executive. For Rousseau, the general will, which is analogous in certain respects to the Feuerbachian species, must express itself through a legislative body that is not representative.[14] Marx, however, first claims that the species must not express itself through any institutions. Thus, he is more anarchistic than Rousseau. Then he claims that it can express itself through a representative legislature such as the one that existed during the French Revolution. Thus, he is less anarchistic than Rousseau. Marx's Feuerbachian opposition to Hegel, then, leads in a contradictory direction to his political opposition to Hegel.

Marx's tendency to move to both sides of Rousseau can also be seen in his analysis of voting. We saw that Marx stressed that the species showed its direct unity when all voted on the same issues. This was in opposition to Hegel's notion that the various groups expressed their own local principles and then were united by the state. Marx's most extended praise of universal suffrage suggests that what he is really after in the vote is the way it signifies the unity of the species. But if voting is only symbolic of the unity of the species, then presumably that unity could be manifested with-out that particular symbol.

Marx notes that as soon as universal suffrage is achieved, then the political state is transcended: "Only when civil society has achieved *unrestricted* active and passive *suffrage* has it really raised itself to the point of abstraction from itself . . . But the perfection of this abstraction is also its transcendence. By really establishing its *political* existence as its authentic existence, civil society insures that its civil existence, insofar as it is distinct from its political existence, is *inessential*. And with the demise of the one, the other, its opposite, collapses also."[15] As soon as universal suffrage is achieved, then the distinction between the state and civil society is broken down. The state and civil society are distinct as long as there is a representative body. The universal suffrage that Marx talks about includes the representative body. Therefore, it must be concluded that as soon as there is universal suffrage then there is no longer any need of universal suffrage. This suffrage is only a symbol of the species essence. When there is direct expression of the species essence then universal suffrage is no longer needed.

Thus, if Marx accepts universal suffrage as itself liberation, then he accepts the representative state. But if he thinks of the attainment of universal suffrage as ending the need for universal suffrage, then he accepts no state at all. Marx seems to hover between both positions.

The Critique, the essay On the Jewish Question, and Marx's later writings

Although the specific characterizations of democracy in the *Critique* may be inconsistent, they contain several larger themes that can be integrated into a coherent theory of democratic socialism. These are (1) community, (2) stress on common principles, (3) stress on the importance of harmony in the various things that people do, (4) stress on ruling oneself directly, and (5) a distrust of institutions. The last two themes have been used by Lucio Colletti to show the continuity between Marx's early writings and the attack on bureaucracy in *The Civil War in France*. Freed from some of their conflict with other aspects of the *Critique* these points can indeed be connected with Marx's attack on bureaucracy and statism in his defense of the Paris Commune. However, and here I disagree with Colletti, they also must be freed of their Feuerbachian tendency to negate rather than to preserve politics, a characteristic that they lack in *The Civil War in France* formulations. It is the absolutist negation of politics that causes most of the inconsistencies in the *Critique*. [16]

The first three points – community, commitment to principles, and harmony – are developed further in the essay *On the Jewish Question*. This development constitutes its major advance over the *Critique*, much of the rest of its content simply carrying on the *Critique's* stress on direct self-rule and its attack on institutions. The concepts of community, commitment to principles, and harmony, however, are developed in such a way that they shed light on several important questions about what socialist society should be like. To how many principles should people be committed? Should socialism stress rights, equality, or community or some combination or hierarchy of these values? In the *Critique* and the essay Marx avoids connecting these questions to another: "Which actions should and should not be mandated in a socialist society?"

68

This is because of his anarchistic attack on all institution and thus, by implication, on the concept of mandation. However, it seems that many socialists, including Marx in most of his writings, were not so opposed to all institutions; and acceptance of institutions in socialism seems to imply some concept of mandation. For how could workers run the economy if there were not some way of telling themselves what they can and cannot do in order to make that economy work? Presumably, later in his life Marx thought that the institutions of workers' groups that control the economy would have to mandate certain aspects of social production.[17] But just because they could demand y does not mean that they could demand z, even though z is desirable. Just because they could demand liberation through social production does not mean that laws could be passed forcing artists to create group art projects, even though that social activity could be justified as good.

The problem in understanding Marx's position on this question is that the only general basis that he gives for answering it is found in these early writings on democracy, community, harmony, and commitment to principles. But in these writings Marx does not have any clear understanding of the importance of distinguishing between the mandated and the nonmandated. When we find in Marx's later writings more concrete evidence about what should and should not be mandated, it is cut off from those very themes of the early writings that could have formed the basis for the distinction. For this reason I am now going to evaluate the essay in terms of the question of mandation.

The essay On the Jewish Question

Some contemporary debate about which actions should and which should not be mandated revolves around a conceptual framework that might broadly be called the theory of totalitarian democracy. This term was first used by J. L. Talmon but the idea is older and broader than his presentation of it.[18] The argument assumes the following general form. Suppose institution A requires that its citizens do y but not z. Y is justified as being good for the citizens, but z is also. Nevertheless, y is justly required of the citizens but z is not. If an institution requires z, then it has the characteristic of being a totalitarian democracy, and of acting unjustly. The injustice does not come from the fact, if fact it be, that z is demanded by a minority. It may be demanded by a majority. It does not come from the fact, if fact it be, that z is not good. Z may be better than y. The injustice comes in the mandating of z. What type of theory mandates activities of type z? According to the theory of totalitarian democracy, it is one that holds that men can be legally forced to do things that are too far removed from their self-interest. Certain ways of committing oneself to moral principles, whatever their consequences, are seen as leading to this path away from self-interest. This involves mandating a nonbasic as opposed to a basic morality. Basic morality can be mandated, but nonbasic morality cannot be. To mandate nonbasic morality is not to go beyond simple goodness but to go beneath it. The problem, of course, is to define basic morality, nonbasic morality, and their connection with commitment to principles. Here the totalitarian democracy theory becomes fragmented into many paths. But one point always emerges out of most of them. Commitment to equality in property goes beyond basic morality. It involves commitment to principles that move far enough away from self-interest that actions according to those principles could not justly be mandated. Marx's discussion of rights in the essay *On the Jewish Question* provides a framework opposed to that of the totalitarian democratic theorists.

Marx argues that acceptance of unequal property in modern constitutional law betrays the lack of concern with general moral principles in the modern state. This argument is made in the context of a new perspective on the positive aspect of the state. For the essay repeats the Feuerbachian idea that even though the state is distorted, nevertheless just as religion, however distorted, expresses the species, so too the state, however distorted, does the same thing. Whereas in the *Critique* civil society was more likely to express the species than the state, in the essay the state is more likely to express the species than civil society. Marx is accordingly more consistent in his praise of political democracy in the essay. Political democracy is seen as the best way that has yet been found of expressing the species essence. However, political democracy makes the mistake of continuing to allow the opposition between the idea of the species and the actuality of selfish autonomous individuals:

Political democracy is Christian inasmuch as it regards man – not just one man but all men – as a *sovereign* and supreme being; but man in his uncultivated, unsocial aspect, man in his contingent existence, man just as he is, man as he has been corrupted, lost to himself, sold, and exposed to the rule of inhuman conditions and elements by the entire organization of our society – in a word, man who is not yet a true species-being. The sovereignty of man – but of man as an alien being distinct from actual (*wirklich*) man –, is the fantasy, the dream, the postulate of Christianity, whereas in democracy it is a present and material reality, a secular maxim.[19]

There is one concept, however, that straddles both the ideal of the species in democracy and the stress on the individual person: the concept of rights. In its former aspect it is the rights of the citizen. In its latter aspect it is the rights of man. Equality has two aspects also, one connected with the species and the rights of the citizen, the other connected with the individual and the rights of man.[20] When it plays the second role it defines the equal liberty of all to be as unequal as they want. How about when it plays the first role? Unfortunately, Marx does not follow out his idea that a certain type of rights, the rights of the citizen, expresses even in bourgeois society a nonindividualistic aspect of man. If he had, his notion of the positive aspect of political democracy could have led to an analysis of the connecting points between (1) the bourgeois notion of the rights of the citizen and the equality that is entailed by those rights and (2) the concept of rights and equality in social-ism. But this path is not followed and Marx's emphasis in the essay is on the individualistic aspects of the concepts of rights and equality, connected with the rights of man as opposed to the rights of the citizen.

This tendency in the essay to stress the individualistic aspect of rights can lead Marx's defenders to construct the following argu-ment. There is an opposition between the concept of rights, which gives too limited a notion of democracy, and the concept of community, which gives an adequate definition of democracy. The theoretical opponent of totalitarian democracy would then reply that this position does not distinguish between basic moral-ity, which should be based on rights, and nonbasic morality, which can be based on community. For him it is unjust to legis-late the aims of community even though they may be good in themselves. Our hypothetical Marxist would then respond that it is wrong not to legislate for something so clearly good as community. The problem with this position, however, and the essay in general, is in the failure to distinguish between two separate positions. Position (1) holds that only the concept of community resolves the issue of mandation and that any conception of rights would lead to an incorrect way of dividing the mandated and the nonmandated. Position (2) denies this. It holds that it is correct to distinguish between basic and nonbasic morality, the one that can be mandated and the other that cannot be; it holds that some conception of rights, connected, for example, with the rights of the citizen, may allow us to make the proper distinction between the mandatable and the nonmandatable. It would also hold that the distinction between the mandatable and the nonmandatable is not done correctly by the opponents of totalitarian democracy, because they mandate too little, in particular because they mandate too little property equality. Position (2) would hold that even though there is a distinction between the mandated and the nonmandated there is still a way of unifying the two in a total ethical conception of man. The concept of rights is not adequate for this total conception. But position (2) differs from (1) in that it holds that some conception of rights can be adequate for the less total ethical vision connected with the realm of the mandated.

I will argue that if the essay is to be a tool for analyzing the ethical and legal bases of socialism, the second position is useful but not the first. I will argue for a conception of community, part of which is bound up with the concept of rights, and part of which goes beyond it. The first is mandatable, the second is not. Furthermore, in the moral consciousness, the unity that ties the two concepts of community together is just as important as their differentiation into the mandated and the nonmandated. In opposing position (1), which holds that the concept of rights necessarily makes the wrong distinction between the mandated and the nonmandated, I will take up the nonindividualistic interpretation of rights. I will argue that it entails that more must be mandated than the opponents of totalitarian democracy imagine, but that it also entails that less must be mandated than those thinkers have nightmares about. The first task is to analyze the connection between rights, equality, and community.

Equality, rights, community, and mandation

In an ethics of rights the individual has certain justified claims on another's things. In an ethics of community it is a positive good for individuals to share moral rules. In an ethics of equality similar problems must be treated in similar ways.

Sometimes theoreticians of rights and community both want to minimize equality. Suppose, for example, that both want to defend inequalities of property. The rights theorist could claim that people have equal rights to own property, but that specific rights can exist as claims to unequal property. The community theorist could claim that although all property owners follow the same moral rules, nevertheless those rules do not have to lead to equality. All could follow the same rules, rules that stress inequality. Even the most individualist rights theorists, however, would admit that there is some equality of rights, even though it may be only potential equality. Similarly, even the most hierarchical community theorist would have to admit that there is some equality simply in the fact that all people participate in the moral rules. Does equality then belong primarily to the rights theorist or to the community theorist? I argue that both the concept of rights and the concept of community, if interpreted in an active as opposed to a passive way, lead to the same concept of expanded equality. It is only when they are both interpreted passively, or one passively and the other actively, that equality can be said to belong primarily to one rather than the other.

The passive concept of rights and community holds that (1) what the individual claims as rights and (2) the moral rules that the community follows are determined for them or given to them. As opposed to this, with the active concept of rights and community the individual or community chooses, respectively, the rights and the rules. On the passive interpretation the only thing that leads to equality on the side of rights is the fact that all people are at least passively given some rights; and on the side of community the fact that all people are equal in following the rules that are given to them. Because both rights and rules are given, they may be given arbitrarily. There may be no strong conceptual connection between community and rights. One may exist without the other.

There may be a great deal of equality connected with the one and not with the other.

With the active conception of rights and community it is different. The active seeker of rights becomes of necessity the active seeker of community and vice versa. Furthermore, both seek an expanded equality.

Suppose someone claims to have a right to x, x being some object or action or omission of an action. Thus, he might claim that he has the right to a piece of land, or to have someone give him medical aid, or to have someone refrain from murdering him. He either assumes that others will accept these rights, or he does not. Suppose that he does not. Then the right just involves his belief that he should have the land, the medical aid, or the security from murder. Nobody else may agree and he may never actually have them. This lack of acceptance is either contingent or necessary. If it is necessary, then the right becomes cut off forever from the community of people who accept the right. If it is only contingent then the community can at most be held together contingently. Neither case gives the claimant of the right any stable expectations about his claim. It might as well be based on raw power. Therefore there must be some necessary connection between someone's claim to have a right and the acceptability of that claim. Acceptability of the claim implies acceptance of moral rules.

Such acceptance, however, does not imply that everyone is treated equally within the moral rules. Each person may have very different claims and consequently very different kinds of rights. Still, these differences must be justified. Perhaps they are justified in different ways. There would, nevertheless, have to be some general rules that would allow each justification to be evaluated. Perhaps, however, the move to these general rules is only done for pragmatic purposes. Then the right would still be primary and the rule would only be a means of attaining the end that is the right. But this pragmatic use of the general rule would not entail the active creation of the rule by everybody using it, and thus would not entail the active creation of community. For the active creation of the rule assumes that all who follow it have equal consciousness of it and equally helped make it. One of the easiest ways to get others to accept the rule would be precisely to hide its origins from them. Thus, the pragmatic use of the rule could be achieved with passivity. But for the seeker of rights to promulgate this passive acceptance of the rule would be to make his freedom to seek for rights necessarily conflict with the freedom of others to consciously create and understand the rule that would allow him those rights. This is not the contingent conflict with the freedom of others that may come when individual rights conflict. Rather, it is a necessary conflict between the freedom of the seeker of rights and the freedom of those that are to accept those rights, that is, the community that follows the moral rules.

For passive acceptance entails lack of deliberation and full consent on the part of those who are accepting. To avoid the consequences of passive acceptance there must be commitment to the rule and to making sure that the others who follow the rule are actively involved in making it work. This, however, represents the kind of commitment to principle to which the antitotalitarian democrat objects. He does not deny that the seeker of rights commits himself to principles. He is not necessarily an ethical egoist. He simply does not hold that the seeker of rights must commit himself to helping ensure that these principles are created equally by all. Passive community he can commit himself to, but not active community. He can commit himself to following rules and in that sense is committed to equality. But he is not committed to making sure that those rules are a living expression of the community. For him that type of commitment leads to unjust mandation.

I have argued, however, that stress on commitment to principles, and making sure that all are actually involved with them, is not inimical to freedom but its only guarantee. For the antitotalitarian democrats such commitment to principles could lead to the individual being forced too far away from his self-interest. That is possible. But what they failed to see is that rights, without such commitment to principles, would mean either the negation of those rights through lack of acceptance or achievement of the rights through passive, unfree acceptance. If the totalitarian democratic theorists had been consistent in stressing that there was no acceptance of rights then they could have claimed that their system emphasized the freedom, although the somewhat nihilistic freedom, of the individual. Instead, they often tend to blend an active seeking of rights with a passive acceptance of rules, a view that stresses freedom with one hand, only to deny it with the other.

The connection can now be shown between the general principles of the antitotalitarian democratic theory and its espousal of inequalities in property. Passive acceptance of rules can be buttressed with the idea that certain rules are embodied in institutions and passively accepted there. This institutional passivity allows inequalities of property to be generally accepted with certain limitations perhaps put on these inequalities by active seekers of rights. On the contrary the active conception of rights and rules demands that all such institutions be consciously accepted or rejected by all. For an individual then to justify his ownership of property, he would have to get the community to freely and consciously make certain rules about property. Property would be based neither on individual self-seeking nor on tradition but on the conscious creative act of the community. It is this concept of property that the totalitarian democratic theorists must reject. They try to draw the line between commitment to principles that are mandatable and those that are not, by arguing that great property equalities fall on the latter side. I have argued against them that the line that they draw on property is not between the mandatable and the nonmandatable, but between what is mandatable through passive acceptance versus what is mandatable through active acceptance.

I have argued that the active conception of rights entails committing oneself to moral rules of the community in a way that leads away from justifying property inequalities. Thus, this concept of rights, foreshadowed by Marx's notion of the rights of the citizen, entails more equality than the antitotalitarian democrats think. I now must show that this extended conception of equality and rights does not become swallowed in a concept of community where all things can be mandated and all good moral acts demanded of the individual by the community. If the concept of rights has become extended to reach socialist equality, the concept of community must, at least in relation to mandation, limit itself to that socialist equality.

Consider Feuerbach's notion that the activity of each individual should complement the activities of others.[21] Certainly egalitarian activity in the sense that we have been defining it would do this.

For the active rule must be created and consciously followed by many. Thus, in following the rule each would complement the activity of others. However, this activity could take place both at the level of a person's role in social production and at the level of the image that parents might help their children have of their grandparents.[22] Should both of these be objects of mandation? The active conception of communal rules can help answer this.

The family can be brought into socialist politics only if it can be shown that it has been politicized so as to interfere with equality and can be shown to be capable of change in the direction of equality. But what types of equality? Equality is bound up with the active creation of rules. But rules can be actively created by a community only if they are capable of public comparison. To see this point a new characterization of anarchism must be introduced. There is a kind of anarchism that argues that all liberation must be put at the same level. Personal, family, and political problems are ultimately resolvable by the same tools. The strength of this theory, which was exemplified in some of the movements toward social liberation in the late 1960s, is that it tries to present a unified image of human beings and their liberation. Its weakness is that by blurring the distinction between the private and public realms of morality, the problems of achieving liberation are made to appear overwhelming. Suppose it is claimed that family members are taught to perceive in a certain way that parallels the way in which members of the state are taught to perceive. Still, does the problem of deciding what an institution can make its members do, that is, the problem of mandation, work the same in both? There are too many mysteries in the family situation for norms to be too generally applied to it. On the other hand, some of the ways in which family members are taught to perceive certainly do lead to continuance of the mode of social production; and changes in modes of production may be mandatable. For it is possible to get enough agreement about them from the human community. It is possible for the active seeker of rights to commit himself to ensuring that the rules of social production are consciously created by all. It may be possible for him to commit himself to rules changing the family structure that are entailed by changes in the rules of social production. It is not possible to commit himself to changing personal and interpersonal dreams – the ones we have at night and the ones that tell children how to think of their grandparents. This impossibility is partly moral, but there are factual elements as well. The possibility of commitment to ensuring that rules accepting rights be consciously created breaks down when we talk about rules of family and interpersonal meanings that simply are not generally comprehensible to the human community.

Neither the extended notion of rights nor the limited notion of community leads to legislation of dreams. If dreams, however, themselves have been mandated in such a way as to prevent equality, and if that prevention is manifested in actions that are publicly comparable, then the abolition of those actions can be mandated. Equality or inequality in the realm of social production can be publicly compared. The family that produces socially but that hides this, so that the work of women is never publicly evaluated, can have this public evaluation. Changes in the way in which this family relates to social production could conceivably be legislated. Nevertheless, family dreams and the images of grandparents given to children can never be evaluated or compared in this way, even though they may change after the advent of socialism.

The extended idea of equality, then, with its stress on public practice, can prevent such things as basic changes in the family structure, other than those relating to social production, from being mandated. Therefore, the idea of community can limit itself and merge with the extended concept of rights. It distinguishes itself from the larger Feuerbachian theory of community, which could be said to deal with public dreams. But a public dream can no more be mandated than a private one can. If in the future more of our dreams were to become public and if that publicity were put into action, then perhaps some would think of justly extending the realm of mandation in socialism. Conscious public participation in dreams, however, has usually only happened in the realm of play, the Greek theater or the Italian Renaissance city as a work of art in itself; and the spirit of play is perhaps inconsistent with the very notion of mandation.

To say this, however, may give rise to another objection. "Won't socialism as a whole in its playfulness rise above the spirit of mandation? Perhaps Marx was right when he railed against institutions in these early writings. When free people are controlling the economy perhaps there is no need for institutions." I have argued elsewhere that the antiinstitutional emphasis of the early writings on democracy is carried over into the attacks on bureaucracy in Marx's later elaborations on socialism. Institutions, however, will continue to exist in socialism in so far as there are laws.[23] These laws are not necessarily made by rigidly defined groups or legislatures. Indeed, socialism tries to break down the opposition between professional men of the law and ordinary people. Laws are publicly observable and codified moral rules. They must be capable of gaining the assent of all, unlike family dreams. Furthermore, their codification is a positive end in itself rather than just a means to an end. The codification of certain types of moral rules allows each individual to extend himself beyond his immediate circumstances and perceptions.

Socialist consciousness and mandation

It may be that the consciousness that moves toward socialist society does not know the difference between the mandated and the nonmandated. It may be aiming at a perfection that is denied by the distinction. For perfect beings all virtues would be on the same level. They would not divide moral tasks into those that they had to do and those that were supererogatory.

An example of an ideal of perfection is human nature. Here each individual finds perfection by understanding his role in the human community. He understands that his actions by themselves are limited, but that if they are seen in the context of another's reaction, or vice versa, then the perfection of action is understood. The aim, ultimately, is to see as many of the contextual aspects of the action as possible. X's judgments about whether to do the action or not are determined by x's ability to understand these contexts. Perfection arises out of thought about the total meaning of action. Religion shows, although in a distorted way, the concern that men have to understand the meaning of their action in its widest possible context. If the false total picture of meaning that was given by religion were ever destroyed, then perhaps that desire to look at the total context of action would switch to an explicitly socialist consciousness.[24] The importance of Marx's essay is that he moves beyond Feuerbach in showing that religious

79

consciousness has already been mediated by the state and now must be mediated again in the liberated society. I have argued that this causes Marx to fail to make the necessary distinctions between the mandated and the nonmandated. This distinction is important for the theory of socialism. But for the theory of the consciousness that moves toward socialism and liberation perhaps this criticism does not hold as much. Why? Because it may be that the meaning of the whole range of actions, mandated and nonmandated, is what draws a person in the direction of socialism. Again, religion gives us a clue about this process. Religion attempts to tie the meaning of actions and rituals into the largest possible context. It may be that all people attempt to fit the meaning of their actions into the largest and most all-encompassing context possible. However, each way of integrating actions has a history – a beginning, a middle, and an end. Could it be that the idea of socialism has the task of helping people to see the conflicts in the old way of seeing meaning and then gradually drawing them to a rupture with that old system of meaning so that they switch to the gestalt of the new meaning system?

Socialism, then, would be split into two ideals: socialism as the production and distribution of goods and the basic ethical actions that correspond to this, and socialism as the production of total meaning and the nonbasic ethical actions that would correspond to this. The danger is that these ideals would come to be confused with each other. This danger is particularly important to consider because implementation of nonbasic ethics in some socialist regimes has often worked to institute the cult of the censor, or of the religious duties of the citizen, or of the supererogatory worker who went beyond justice and worked himself to death.

It should be noted, however, that there would never be any hope at all of adequately blending basic and nonbasic ethics in a given social situation, if there were not some overall connection between them. There is a connection between the basic ethics of social production and the less basic ethics of meaning, because both are bound up with commitment to free acceptance of principles. Of course the opponents of totalitarian democracy would probably reply that this common link between basic and nonbasic morality is dangerous and makes it too easy to confuse them.

Nevertheless, if there were not a common link between the ideals, then although they may not be confused, they may be so far apart that they could never be gotten together. The man who performed both would be divided and lacking harmony.

The overall significance of the Kreuznach writings

"The world has long dreamed of possessing something of which it has only to be conscious in order to possess it in reality."[25]

Marx's Kreuznach writings hover between liberalism and socialism, between religious, political, and economic analysis. They present an account of the world's dream, but fail precisely in their analysis of how to put that dream into practice. Different images of how men achieve community and democracy by committing themselves to principles intermingle in the writings. The community or species life exists when people create a constitution, or when they vote, or when they realize their powers without institutions, or when all institutions are harmonious, or when they exist in the state, or when they move beyond the state. Many of these points conflict, mainly because of a tension between liberation viewed as within or without institutions. The problem of how to minimize the bureaucratic nature of institutions is worked out later in writings such as *The Civil War in France*. The themes of harmony, community, and commitment to principles require to be elaborated in a way consistent with Marx's later belief that there must be some institutions in socialism. How much harmony, commitment, and community should be mandated in socialism and how much is an integral part of socialist consciousness? I argued that an analysis of the active conception of rights reveals that for there to be equality much more community and commitment to principles must be mandated than antitotalitarian democratic theorists usually imagine; however, much less must be mandated than they sometimes fear. Nevertheless, the mandated and the nonmandated may work together in harmony in the consciousness that draws people toward socialism. There is more in the world's dream than can be possessed in reality. Yet although the active application is less than the dream, it still depends on the dream.

Notes

1 For the relevant historical background see especially Maximilien Rubel and Margaret Manale, *Marx without Myth* (New York: Harper and Row, 1976), pp 28–31

2 See Jean-Jacques Rousseau, *Du Contrat Social* (Paris: Editions Social, 1968), especially Books One and Two; J. L. Talmon, *The Origins of Totalitarian Democracy* (New York: Praeger, 1960); Sergio Cotta, "La Position du Problème de la Politique chez Rousseau," in *Études sur le Contrat Social de Jean-Jacques Rousseau* (Paris: Socíeté les Belles Lettres, 1964), pp. 177–90.

3 See especially G. W. F. Hegel, *Hegel's Philosophy of Right,* trans. T. M. Knox (Oxford: Oxford University Press, 1942).

4 For Feuerbach see especially the *Vorläufige Thesen zur Reform der Philosophie,* in Ludwig Feuerbach, *Kleine Schriften* (Frankfurt: Suhrkamp, 1966), p. 128 and throughout. Richard Hunt, *The Political Ideas of Marx and Engels: Marxism and Totalitarian Democracy* (Pittsburgh: University of Pittsburgh Press, 1974), p. 68, has commented on the relation between the young Marx, Feuerbach, and Rousseau.

5 See Ludwig Feuerbach, *Das Wesen des Christentums* (Berlin: Akademie Verlag, 1956), especially Chapters 2 and 6.

6 *Hegel's Philosophy of Right,* pp. 286–7.

7 Karl Marx, *Early Writings,* trans. Rodney Livingston and Gregor Benton (New York: Random House, 1975), p. 186; *Die Frühschriften* (Stuttgart: Alfred Kröner Verlag, 1953), p. 137.

8 Ibid., p. 187, 138.

9 See Norman Fischer, *Economy and Self: Philosophy and Economics from the Mercantilists to Marx* (Westport and London: Greenwood Press, 1979), Chapter 5.

10 Marx, *Early Writings,* p. 147, 145; *Die Frühschriften,* p. 98, 95.

11 Ibid., pp. 87–90; pp. 47–50.

12 Feuerbach, *Vorläufige Thesen zur Reform der Philosophie,* pp. 143–4.

13 Marx, *Early Writings,* pp. 119–20; *Die Frühschriften,* p. 67.

14 Rousseau, *Du Contrat Social,* Book Three, Chapter One.

15 Marx, *Early Writings,* p. 191; *Die Frühschriften,* p. 143.

16 See Norman Fischer, "Lucio Colletti on Socialism and Democracy" in *Varieties and Problems of Twentieth Century Socialism,* Jack Thomas and Louis Patsouras, eds. (Chicago: Nelson-Hall, forthcoming).

17 See my *Economy and Self,* pp. 175–8.

18 See J. L. Talmon, *The Origins of Totalitarian Democracy.* Richard Hunt's *The Political Ideas of Marx and Engels* is organized around the confrontation between Talmon's totalitarian democracy thesis and the early writings of Marx. I do not restrict my usage of the concept of totalitarian democracy to Talmon's work. Rather, I use it as a generalization of a type of attack that has appeared on Marx. Examples of what I consider to be the totalitarian democracy framework would include Karl Popper's *The Open Society and Its Enemies*

(London: G. Routledge and Sons, 1945) and Sergio Cotta's *Etudes sur le Contrat Social de Jean-Jacques Rousseau* (Paris: Societé les Belles Lettres, 1964), which explicitly mentions totalitarian democracy (p. 189).

19 Marx, *Early Writings*, pp. 225–6; *Die Frühschriften*, p. 108.
20 Ibid., pp. 228–31, 234, 191–6, 199. Although Marx recognizes throughout this discussion that the rights of the citizen present a less individualistic ideal than the rights of man his skepticism about the political realm of citizenship seems to undercut this recognition. He also thinks that the rights of citizens usually become simply used to attain the rights of man.
21 Feuerbach, *Das Wesen des Christentums*, pp. 65–6.
22 R. D. Laing has discussed the topic of how parents make children perceive in certain ways in *The Politics of the Family* (New York: Random House, 1971).
23 See Fischer, "Lucio Colletti on Socialism and Democracy."
24 See Marx's comments in a letter to Ruge from Kreuznach in Marx and Engels, *Collected Works*, vol. 3 (New York: International Publishers, 1975), p. 144. Also see Marx's letter to Feuerbach August 11, 1844, Ibid., p. 354.
25 Ibid., p. 144.

4

The necessity of revolution

JOHN P. BURKE

At the end of Part I of Marx and Engels's *The German Ideology*, one finds the statement that a revolution is necessary not only to overthrow the ruling class of capitalists but also to overthrow the "muck of ages" attached to the revolutionary class and to fit such a class for founding a new society. Because the new society of interest to Marx and Engels was communism, it seems clear that for them a revolution was a necessary condition for communism. Strictly speaking, they conceived of a "revolutionary transformation period," which they termed the "revolutionary dictatorship of the proletariat" and "the first phase of communist society," between capitalist society and communist society.

This chapter will refocus attention on an aspect of Marxism that has occasionally been neglected – Marx's revolutionary thesis. I argue that Marx consistently held that a revolution was a necessary condition for communist society, and I attempt to show the importance of Marx's concept of the *revolutionary process* for his belief in the necessity of revolution. There are some properties of that process that are necessary to and partly constitutive of communist society. Marx's concept of the revolutionary process can be shown to be present from his early writings through *Capital*. I contend that attention to this concept demonstrates that the necessity of revolution was not the dogmatic assumption for Marx that some have maintained it was.

In addition, this chapter will examine the several apparent admissions by Marx (and Engels) that there might be nonrevolutionary paths to communist society. These admissions have periodically received undue emphasis. The emphasis is unwarranted because the usually cited passages do not support the claim that Marx sometimes relaxed his revolutionary thesis. What these passages show is that Marx held that nonrevolutionary measures might be sufficient to achieve certain reforms, but not communist society. Nor does Engels's much-cited 1895 "Introduction" to *The Class Struggles in France* support the contention that Engels, if not Marx, modified or abandoned the revolutionary thesis in favor of some doctrine of a peaceful, legal evolution toward communism.

Finally, I suggest that if there were any clear admissions by Marx (or Engels) that communist society might be achieved without a revolution, such statements deserve to be treated as empirical claims and assessed accordingly. For example, if Marx believed that universal suffrage might suffice to usher in communism, then the history of western liberal democracies since the nineteenth century suggests his belief was false. Alternatively, perhaps Marx thought that universal suffrage and the revolutionary process shared certain important properties and thus that communism could come about in either way. This is quite speculative for in general both Marx and Engels were acutely aware of the limited function and value of universal suffrage in capitalist democracies. The conclusion that emerges is that neither Marx nor Engels gave up the view that revolution was necessary for communist society.

Marx's concept of revolution

What did Marx mean by "revolution"? He nowhere defined it in precise terms, and it seems doubtful it can be so defined. The concept can be given meaning by identifying certain typical or characteristic properties. The French Revolution surely served as both a precedent and a model for Marx, but his sense of historical variability made him reluctant to apply that model rigidly. The contexts in which he used the term "revolution" suggest that his concept embraced the following: A revolution is any substantial political transformation effected by a social class or movement, which takes the form of overthrowing the established government and assuming state power, with the objective of bringing about profound changes in the social, economic, and political institutions of a society.

This concept stipulates nothing whatsoever about the span of time involved nor about the amount and degree of force and violence, if any, present in a revolution. Such stipulations would be presumptive. The use of force and violence is not conceptually

85

required for Marx, although he appears to have believed there was historical justification for expecting that revolutions would be marked by some violence. For revolutions, in his view, are at least partly defensive responses to oppression and exploitation, which may themselves be violent. It is not unreasonable to expect oppressors and exploiters to resist, and thus force and violence may be resorted to by both sides. In any event, whether a revolution is violent, causing damage to property and injury to persons, was for Marx not a conceptual but an empirical matter.

The Marxian concept of revolution as characterized is rough and abstract, but sufficient to distinguish revolution from legal reform and "evolution" of a social system, as well as from insurrections, palace revolts, *coups d'état,* colonial revolts, preventative counter-revolutions, and so forth.

In *The German Ideology* the concept of revolution is characterized concretely as follows: Revolution is working-class appropriation of the means of production in capitalist society; it is overthrow of the capitalist class, capitalist relationships of production, and the state; revolution is the seizure and transformation of the resources of production in order to usher in a better stage of social relations, human development, and technical and human progress. Such a communist revolution is thought of as a collective effort to replace the capitalist mode of production and the social institutions of capitalism with rational social control of the productive capacities of society. It is maintained that not only would such a revolution introduce a technically improved society, but because of democratic social control, it would be normatively better as well.

Marx's theory of revolution

Marx's theory of revolution was first sketched in an early essay that set out to determine the conditions for a partial, "merely political" revolution and the probability that such conditions would be fulfilled in Germany. The French Revolution is analyzed to conclude that for a merely political revolution it is necessary that the prominent social problems be attributed to the dominant class in a particular society and that another social class succeeds in representing its own interests to the rest of society as general interests. When such a "revolutionary situation" occurs, the latter class may be able to command the attention and political energies of a significant stratum of the population, overthrow the rule of the dominant class, and seek to reorganize society in accordance with its own class interests. Marx terms such revolution merely "partial" or "political" because the new society is still a class society.

Marx claimed no class in Germany was capable of representing its interests as general social interests, and thus no political revolution analogous to France's could occur in Germany at that time. But he did note that the proletariat was beginning to develop in Germany and asserted, without a very convincing argument, that the proletariat was potentially the agent of a liberation effort that would far exceed a partial revolution.[1]

The German Ideology presents a more complex theoretical account of revolution embedded in the general theory of historical materialism. Human history, according to Marx and Engels, supports the generalization that various ruling classes, by virtue of their ownership and control of the resources of production, exercised a progressive role in the development of productive capacity and the exploitation of nature. Those ruling classes, however, periodically failed to adapt the prevailing mode of production. They sought to sustain a mode of production consistent with their own ruling-class interests and tended to reject any innovations and reorganization of social production when those threatened their position as a ruling class. But there occurs a need, which is prompted by such factors as increased population, changing needs of the people, availability of resources, developments in technology, alterations in the environment, and so on, to revolutionize production. Thus refusal to transform production often brought on a crisis in societies, which had sometimes been exploited by new and rising classes. Whether such crises in the history of human production had as their outcome a fundamental change of the mode of production, a new ruling class, and corresponding changes in social institutions depended on such factors as the stage of development of the resources of production and the numbers of people concerned to bring about profound social change.

Our immediate interest is the specific application of this theory to capitalist society. The capitalist mode of production, Marx and

87

Engels claim, will continue to be subject to crises because of the irrationality of capitalist production, the effort by the capitalist class to sustain a mode of production favorable to increasing accumulation of capital, and the resistance to growing tendencies toward socialized production and social control of resources. Thus, although the capitalist class, as the *Communist Manifesto* states, was the most progressive and "revolutionizing" ruling force in history, that class too would come to represent an obsolete mode of production committed to the preservation of capitalist class rule and production for profit. As we know, Marx and Engels concluded that the working class must become the revolutionary class.

The proletariat as revolutionary class

The claim that the working class can and will make a revolution against capitalist society remains one of the more arresting claims of Marxism, particularly in light of how commonly political theorists of the modern period believed that significant social change, if it occurred at all, originated from the upper classes. Moreover, the identification of the working class as a revolutionary agent is not obviously plausible, even if one grants that such a class might constitute a majority in society and that it lacks control over production.

Whereas some writers have held that Marx and Engels gave entirely too little attention to the revolutionary motivation of the working class, others think that too much was said, for what was said was false or absurd. T. B. Bottomore seems to have treated the idea of a revolutionary working class as a mere assumption: "There had been bourgeois revolutions, therefore there would be proletarian revolutions."[2] David McLellan stated the same thesis more elaborately when he asserted that Marx's espousal of the working class was an application of the earlier analysis of the French Revolution: "The proletariat was now in the position the French bourgeoisie had occupied in 1789."[3] Plamenatz has asserted, "The idea of an organized, united, and enlightened revolutionary class is, surely, unrealistic to the point of absurdity."[4]

Robert Tucker holds that what Marx did say on this subject is false: "And he believes – wrongly as it turns out – that a proletarian

88

revolution will be necessitated by the impossibility of fully developing the productive potentials of modern machine industry within the confines of wage labor as the mode of production."[5] Tucker does not say why Marx was wrong to hold such a belief,[6] yet he emphasizes an important point. It is not suffering or poverty per se that prompts the proletariat to become revolutionary, but rather "the source of revolutionary energy in a class is the frustration of man in his capacity of producer, his inability to develop new powers of production to the full within the confines of an existing mode of production or socioeconomic order."[7] This is a correct, but incomplete, explanation of revolutionary motivation.

Alienation cannot be treated as the central motivation. If, as Marx held, the growth of capitalist society would produce increasing alienation of the workers from the state, from their jobs, and from their working relationships, conceivably workers might try to eliminate such alienation and assume control over the state and production. But alienation does not seem to provide sufficient stimulus for transforming the proletariat into a revolutionary class.

One must consider how Marx views the proletariat as a class and as individuals. The proletariat will make a communist revolution because in the history of classes it is faced with a unique and distinctive problem: Any revolution it comes to make is a revolution it cannot make in its own interest *as a class,* or, not *merely* as a class. It is the view of Marx and Engels that previous social classes had an interest in revolutionizing society in order to legitimize, enhance, and extend their class interests and advantages. Such rising classes sought to guarantee the optimal conditions for their existence as a class. For example, the bourgeoisie sought economic freedom from feudal constraints. In capitalism, the prime condition for the existence of the proletariat is the ability to find jobs, the continuous sale of labor. But the sale of labor power is something that the proletariat as a class cannot guarantee in capitalist society. The conclusion offered in *The German Ideology* is that the proletariat, if it is to launch a revolution and not just reform society, must aim at the elimination of its status as the laboring class of society, must attack class society itself, and abolish the state, which acts as a coercive power to preserve and consolidate capitalist class society.

Thus, while the refugee serfs only wished to be free to develop and assert those conditions of existence which were already there, and hence, in the end, only arrived at free labor, the proletarians, if they are to assert themselves as individuals, will have to abolish the very condition of their existence hitherto . . . , namely, labour.[8]

Not to become more secured proletarians, but to throw off the proletarian yoke altogether, becomes the revolutionary motivation distinguishing this from past revolutions.

To Tucker's point, that the proletarian revolution is theoretically required by the failure of capitalism to exploit fully the productive potential of industrial society, we must add that a working-class revolution is needed for the self-development of individuals as beings of various productive potentials themselves. The view is that working-class revolution would be prompted not only by the need for more progressive economic development but also the need for progressive development of talents and capacities of human beings.

The necessity of revolution

Marx believed that a working-class revolution was necessary for the formation of communist society. Why did he hold this belief? Without denying the influence of the French Revolution on Marx's thinking, nor minimizing the importance of the general theory of historical materialism, nor discounting the special analysis of capitalist society, I argue that Marx entertained a conception of the revolutionary process, a conception that was to become firm in his mind, and that led him to think a working-class revolution was a necessary condition for communist society.

Some support for this claim is found in the final point of a summary of the historical materialist position in *The German Ideology*.

Both for the production on a mass scale of this communist consciousness, and for the success of the cause itself, the alteration of men on a mass scale is necessary, an alteration which can only take place in a practical movement, a *revolution;* this revolution is necessary, therefore not only because the *ruling* class cannot be overthrown in any other way, but also because the class *overthrowing* it can only in a revolution succeed in ridding itself of all the muck of ages and become fitted to found society anew.[9]

The necessity of revolution is argued for on two grounds. The ruling class cannot be overthrown without a revolution. This seems to be derived from general considerations of the theory of historical materialism. Second, only a revolution transforms human beings in their thinking and their practice, freeing them from "all the old muck," and readying them for communist society. The "old muck," one may suppose, includes ideology, powerlessness, alienation, and so forth. Not only would the revolution fail without the transformation of a working class no longer characterized by particularistic interests and ideas, but the new society requires people modified by their revolutionary experience. These are people who perceive the possibility that work can be a means of self-determination, that the advanced technology of capitalist society could become the means for the creation of "complete" individuals, but, above all, who contest the naturalness or inevitability of class society and private property.

Involvement in the practical movement, the revolutionary process, provides an indispensable education or development of the working class, without which it could not cope with a new social order (if, indeed, such a social order could come about). This education is both a liberation from past conceptions and ways of acting and a preparation – a practice – for new thinking and activity. Self-determination through rationally organized social life is the feature of the revolutionary process that would carry over into communist society.

Perhaps the best-known source for the idea that the revolutionary process is educational is *The Communist Manifesto*. Organized trade union activity, together with the political struggles against the capitalist class are not just "features" of capitalist society but are thought of as anticipatory practice for popular participation in a self-managing society, especially a populous society. "The bourgeoisie itself . . . supplies the proletariat with its own elements of political and general education . . ."[10] One may even see the role of the communists as a "unique" working-class party in this light, for the communists are claimed to (1) combat nationalism in the working class and (2) uphold the interests of the working-class movement as a whole – two features that would plausibly characterize postrevolutionary communist society.

Marx and Engels conceive of a revolutionary praxis that is not

91

only crucial for the success of the revolution but that is a preparation for the maintenance of the new social order. This conception
of revolutionary praxis has a much more significant role in original Marxism than as an aphoristic thesis on Feuerbach. I refer, of
course, to the justly famous Third Thesis on Feuerbach.

The materialist doctrine concerning the changing of circumstances and
upbringing forgets that circumstances are changed by men and that it is
essential to educate the educator himself . . . The coincidence of the
changing of circumstances and of human activity or self-changing can be
conceived and rationally understood only as *revolutionary practice*. [11]

This concept of revolutionary practice is found not only in the
"early writings" of Marx. The sociohistorical writings of the
1850s are lengthy testimonies not only to the need for maturation
of objective economic conditions and political struggle before
proletarian revolution can succeed, but also to the necessity of the
learning process in the revolutionary practice. Revolution is analyzed as a complex process with advances and reverses, but even
the failures are held up as lessons for the working class. Marx
intends his writings to be both records of and contributions to
revolutionary praxis.

Proletarian revolutions . . . criticize themselves constantly, interrupt
themselves continually in their own course, come back to the apparently
accomplished in order to begin it afresh, deride with unmerciful thor-
oughness the inadequacies, weaknesses and paltrinesses of their first attempts, seem to throw down their adversary only in order that he may
draw new strength from the earth and rise again, more gigantic, before
them, recoil ever and anon from the indefinite prodigiousness of their
own aims, until a situation has been created which makes all turning back
impossible, and the conditions themselves cry out: *Hic Rhodus, hic salta!* [12]

Nineteen years later, in his autopsy of the Paris Commune, Marx
still adhered to his conception of the *process* involved in revolutionary praxis, with much the same optimism and patience.

The working class did not expect miracles from the Commune. They have
no ready-made utopias to introduce *par décret du peuple*. They know that in
order to work out their own emancipation, and along with it that higher
form to which present society is irresistibly tending by its own economical
agencies, they will have to pass through long struggles, through a series of
historic processes, transforming circumstances and men. They have not
ideals to realize, but to set free the elements of the new society with which
old collapsing bourgeois society itself is pregnant. [13]

It was Marx's view that revolutionary practice emerged not only from political struggle but from the work process itself. In *Capital* he presents the idea of an evolution in praxis, from laboring activity to revolutionary activity to self-managing activity in postcapitalist society. Not only is the evolution a natural and historical development of capacities of human nature, but certain features of capitalist society facilitate this evolution. To put it somewhat crudely, in capitalism the working class receives some on-the-job training in revolution and communism!

Influenced by Hegel's theory of the historical function of human labor in transforming the human species, Marx wrote: "By thus acting on the external world and changing it, he at the same time changes his own nature. He develops his slumbering powers and compels them to act in obedience to his sway."[14] The meaning and function of human labor is of course obscured and compromised in the phenomenon of alienated labor. But Marx believed that capitalism's own "long and painful process of development" transformed labor and the working class itself, schooling the class for a form of productive activity that transcends alienated labor. Evidence of his belief is found in his chapter "Co-operation."

When numerous labourers work together side by side, whether in one and the same process, or in different but connected processes, they are said to co-operate, or to work in co-operation . . . Not only have we here an increase in the productive power of the individual, by means of co-operation, but the creation of a new power, namely, the collective power of masses. Apart from the new power that arises from the fusion of many forces into a single force, mere social contact begets in most industries an emulation and a stimulation of the animal spirits that heighten the efficiency of each individual workman . . . The reason of this is that man is, if not as Aristotle contends, a political, at all events a social animal.[15]

Cooperation among laborers changes the character of the work process, increases the productive power of labor, heightens efficiency, but it also transforms the laborers. "When the labourer co-operates systematically with others, he strips off the fetters of his individuality, and develops the capabilities of his species."[16] Marx suggests that an approximation of workers' self-management can emerge from generalized cooperation in the production process.

That Philistine paper, the *Spectator,* states that after the introduction of a sort of partnership between capitalist and workmen in the "Wirework Company of Manchester," "the first result was a sudden decrease in waste, the men not seeing why they should waste their own property any more than any other master's, and waste is, perhaps next to bad debts, the greatest source of manufacturing loss." This same paper finds that the main defect in the Rochdale co-operative experiments is this: "They showed that associations of workmen could manage shops, mills, and almost all forms of industry with success, and they immediately improved the condition of the men, but then they did not leave a clear place for masters." Quelle horreur![17]

Not only does the capitalist mode of cooperation produce a change from individualized to social labor, but resorting to technology contributes to the evolution of human praxis. It does so by dissipating the air of specialization surrounding particular trades and occupations and by requiring modern laborers to become versatile in many types of work. Marx argues that advanced capitalism is *technically* revolutionary, but that it revolutionizes laborers too, equipping them for a variety of tasks. Technology

is continually causing changes not only in the technical basis of production, but also in the functions of the labourer, and in the social combinations of the labour-process. At the same time, it thereby also revolutionizes the division of labour within the society, and incessantly launches masses of capital and of workpeople from one branch of production to another . . . Modern Industry, by its very nature, therefore necessitates the variation of labour, fluency of function, universal mobility of the labourer . . .[18]

Marx does not pass over the destructive consequences of a technology subordinated to capitalism's priorities (economic insecurity, unemployment, poverty, the squandering of human labor power) – "this is the negative side." But he does insist that the industrial development of capitalism forces people to recognize "as a fundamental law of production, variation of work, consequently fitness of the labourer for varied work, consequently the greatest possible development of his varied aptitudes."

Modern Industry . . . compels society . . . to replace the detail-worker of to-day, crippled by life-long repetition of one and the same trivial operation, and thus reduced to a mere fragment of a man, by the fully developed individual, fit for a variety of labours, ready to face any change of production, and to whom the different social functions he

94

performs, are but so many modes of giving free scope to his own natural and acquired powers.[19]

Marx does not focus only on the technical versatility of the worker, for he thinks that the socialization of labor is of the highest importance for future communist society. He sees the introduction of women, young persons, even children into the production process as establishing an economic basis for "a higher form of the family and of the relations between the sexes." The fact that the collective working group is increasingly composed of people of both sexes and all ages he sees as becoming a "source of humane development."[20]

Admittedly, Marx is not explicitly discussing revolution conceived as the political struggle between capital and labor, a struggle that might embrace violence. Instead, technology is termed revolutionary, the labor process is revolutionized, the capacities and activities of the working class are transformed, and social and personal relationships are radically changed. But he does imply that the working-class revolution overthrowing capitalism is an extension of such revolutionary tendencies within capitalist development, and he suggests that the transformations experienced by workers produce in them qualities that render them increasingly fit for social control of the means of production in communist society. It was also his view that the revolutionary tendencies within capitalism could not be contained indefinitely within the capitalist mode of production.

There is also no doubt that such revolutionary ferments, the final result of which is the abolition of the old division of labour, are diametrically opposed to the capitalistic form of production, and to the economic status of the labourer corresponding to that form.[21]

There is considerable evidence from Marx's writings testifying to the need for a revolution as precondition of communist society, pointing to specific features of the revolutionary process that prepare the working class for self-managing society and social control of the means of production, and locating the initial elements of this revolutionary process within certain identifiable tendencies of advanced capitalist society.

We know that to work well the new-fangled forces of society, they only want to be mastered by new-fangled men—and such are the workingmen. They are as much the invention of modern time as machinery itself. In the signs that bewilder the middle class, the aristocracy, and the poor prophets of regression, we do recognize our brave friend Robin Goodfellow, the old mole that can work in the earth so fast, that worthy pioneer – the Revolution.[22]

Nonrevolutionary avenues to communism?

A major objection to the Marxian thesis on the necessity of revolution apparently comes from Marx and Engels themselves in some remarks traditionally interpreted as addressing the possibility that communist society might be achieved, at least in some countries, through nonrevolutionary means. I will examine some of the cited remarks about peaceful, legal methods and argue that the traditional interpretation is mistaken. The standard passages cited do not contradict the claim that revolutionary means are necessary for a communist society to come about.

In the "Address of the Central Committee to the Communist League" (March 1850),[23] Marx advises that the revolutionary workers' party should cooperate with the petit-bourgeois democratic party against their common foe, but oppose that party when it tries to consolidate its own position. There is need, he states, for an independent workers' party that will aim for a "permanent revolution," rather than the temporary one in which the petit-bourgeois party is interested. There is also need for the armed organization of workers to counteract the petit-bourgeois party. Marx endorses the running of workers' candidates alongside petit-bourgeois party candidates when the latter are in power, and suggests that the function of workers' candidates is to radicalize petit-bourgeois demands and proposals. This address sanctions electoral activity and limited cooperation, but it does nothing to withdraw the revolutionary thesis.

Marx's discussion of the Chartists in London (August 10, 1852)[24] has been cited as an instance where he allowed for nonrevolutionary avenues to socialism. Marx identifies the Chartists, with their central demand for universal suffrage, as the politically active portion of the British working class.

But Universal Suffrage is the equivalent for political power for the working class of England, where the proletariat forms the large majority of the population, where, in a long, though underground civil war, it has gained a clear consciousness of its position as a class, and where even the rural districts know no longer any peasants, but only landlords, industrial capitalists (farmers) and hired laborers. The carrying of Universal Suffrage in England would, therefore, be a far more socialistic measure than anything which has been honored with that name on the Continent. Its inevitable result, here, is the *political supremacy of the working class*.[25]

Three points should be made here. First, Marx does not deny the necessity of revolution even in Britain (much less anywhere else). Second, universal suffrage (should it be extended to the working class) is considered a "more socialistic measure" relative to other measures on the continent. Finally, universal suffrage is claimed to result in political power wielded by the working class. Such political power could thus be at most the "dictatorship of the proletariat" and not yet communist society.

The Yugoslav philosopher Marković[26] has identified two passages as evidence of Marx's relaxation of the revolutionary thesis. The first is in an interview of Marx in *The World* (July 3, 1871) in which Marx is reported to have said that in England "a rebellion would be a stupidity since the goal could be attained more quickly and more surely by peaceful agitation." The second is found in a speech at the London Congress of the International (September 21, 1871) in which Marx is reported to have said that workers would rise against governments peacefully whenever possible or with arms if necessary.

Lenin commented on such remarks of this period of Marx's thought:

The argument that Marx in the seventies allowed for the possibility of a peaceful transition to socialism in England and America is completely fallacious, or, to put it bluntly, dishonest in that it is juggling with quotations and references. Firstly, Marx regarded it as an exception even then. Secondly, in those days monopoly capitalism, i.e., imperialism, did not exist. Thirdly, in England and America there was no militarist clique then—*as there is now*—serving as the chief apparatus of the bourgeois state machine.[27]

Whether or not what Lenin says is correct, one point to be made is that Marx's claim must be evaluated in light of conditions present in England in 1871. Furthermore, Marx does not identify the "goal" in his remark with communist society, and there is no reason to assume that is what he meant. Finally, whether or not the "goal" could be reached better through peaceful agitation or rebellion in England is surely an empirical issue whose truth or falsity depends on observations of what actually occurred or could have occurred. The second passage cited by Marković also seems to be an empirical claim, and it does nothing to deny the necessity of revolution for communist society.

The "Inaugural Address of the Working Men's International Association" (October 1864)[28] might seem to some to tolerate reforms at the expense of revolution, but it does not. In the address, Marx praises the Ten Hours Bill because he thinks it demonstrates that the political economy of the working class is superior to that of the middle class, in that capitalist industry can shorten the workday without collapsing. Marx then praises the cooperation practiced in capitalist industries because it shows the dispensability of the masters, yet he denounces it as an end in itself because it neither arrests monopolies nor eases the misery of workers. He ends by counseling a "foreign policy" of solidarity among all workers.

The much-cited Amsterdam speech (September 8, 1872)[29] must have been read out of context frequently to treat Marx as a gradualist reformer. Marx there reaffirmed the need for workers to fight the old society politically and socially. Against groups that advocated an abstention from politics, Marx claimed that workers must seize political power "to build a new organization of labor." The ways to achieve *that goal* are not everywhere the same. He allows that in America, England, and possibly Holland workers may attain their goal peacefully. Initially, however, he clearly implies that in most countries a revolution will be necessary. Moreover, his remarks do not even show that he thought a revolution unnecessary to usher in communism in America, England, and Holland. He concludes this speech by saying that the revolution must be carried out with solidarity!

Two passages by Engels have often been cited as proof that Engels, if not Marx, abandoned the insistence upon revolution to embrace nonrevolutionary avenues to communism. The first quotation, from *Capital*, needs only to be quoted in full to demonstrate that it cannot support such a claim.

Surely, at such a moment of economic crisis in England the voice ought to be heard of a man whose whole theory is the result of a life-long study of the economic history and condition of England, and whom that study led to the conclusion that, at least in Europe, England is the only country where the inevitable social revolution might be effected entirely by peaceful and legal means. He certainly never forgot to add that he hardly expected the English ruling classes to submit, without a "pro-slavery rebellion," to this peaceful and legal revolution.[30]

Finally, Engels's 1895 "Introduction" to Marx's *Class Struggles in France*[31] has, by its repudiation of some of the tactics of 1848 in light of social democracy's growth by 1895, suggested to some that Engels repudiated revolution as necessary for communism. Engels's argument supports no such conclusion. In 1848, he claims, conditions were not yet ripe for advancing beyond bourgeois gains to proletarian power, for there was still room for capitalist expansion. Therefore, surprise attacks were not sufficient in 1848 to defeat capitalism. Even in 1871, the Commune showed that the working class was not mature enough to take power. Universal suffrage in Germany allowed, however, the Socialist Party access to workers and some political visibility. In such a situation, the streetfighting of 1848 had become obsolete, although, he says, it may once again prove necessary. On the whole, he continues, the time of surprise attacks and of conscious minorities leading unconscious masses (1848 Europe) is past (for 1895 Germany). The masses must be conscious politically, socially, and economically to be able to reorganize society, and propaganda and parliamentary activity aid their consciousness. Other comrades, he adds notably, need not forego their right to revolution. But, he concludes, German Social Democracy in 1895 is succeeding best with legal, elective means.

But he nowhere denies that revolution is necessary for most countries in Europe, nor does he deny that revolution is appropriate at some point for Germany. And what has been little noticed is how he later treated this 1895 "Introduction" in a letter to Kautsky: "My text had to suffer from the timid legalism of our friends in Berlin, who dreaded a second edition of the anti-socialist laws – a dread to which I was forced to pay attention at the existing political juncture."[32] Robert Michels did notice this qualification by Engels, and concluded that the doctrine of a parliamentary road to socialism thus came into existence out of fear that the socialist party organization might suffer at the hands of the state.

Although at the time Engels was alternately praised as a realist and denounced as a pacifist utopian, it seems wise to agree with Michels's assessment: "Engels would seem to have been the victim of an opportunist sacrifice of principles to the needs of organization, a sacrifice made for love of the party and in opposition to his own theoretical convictions."[33]

There may be other passages from Marx (and Engels) that might appear to allow for nonrevolutionary paths to communism, but I have considered the ones that are traditionally cited.

That Marx would not have ruled out the possibility of nonrevolutionary avenues to communism would be evidence of good sense in a theorist opposed to dogmatism and alive to historical specificity and variations in empirical conditions. Thus, if clearcut allowances could be found in his writings, one might want to regard the revolutionary thesis as a probability statement to be considered in the light of other probability statements concerning peaceful and legal approaches to communism. But, as I have tried to show, there are not any clear-cut statements that jeopardize the revolutionary thesis.

Marx does seem to be optimistic about a peaceful and legal transition to some political power for workers through the vote in some countries. But where he speaks of this, the context makes it clear that he is discussing *immediate* goals of workers, not the long-range objective of building communism. In addition, he never offers a blanket allowance for the peaceful, legal route for all countries and clearly implies in just these passages that such a route will not be the rule. Moreover, both he and Engels were skeptical, to say the least, about the function and value of universal suffrage in bourgeois democracies.

In the *Civil War in France*, Marx contrasted universal suffrage as envisioned by the Paris Commune with voting in bourgeois England.

Instead of deciding once in three or six years which member of the ruling class was to misrepresent the people in Parliament, universal suffrage was to serve the people, constituted in Communes, as individual suffrage serves every other employer in the search for the workmen and managers in his business. And it is well known that companies, like individuals, in matters of real business generally know how to put the right man in the right place, and, if they for once make a mistake, to redress it promptly.[34]

Engels too had a critical eye for the vote in capitalist societies. In his *Origin of the Family, Private Property and the State* he maintained that although modern democratic republics represent the "highest form of the state," they, like other historical states, are based on property distinctions. Wealth actually governs such republics through the direct corruption of officials and the collusion between government and stock exchange. And he identifies the vote as an instrument for ruling the people.

And lastly, the possessing class rules directly through the medium of universal suffrage. As long as the oppressed class . . . the proletariat, is not yet ripe to emancipate itself, it will in its majority regard the existing order of society as the only one possible and, politically, will form the tail of the capitalist class, its extreme Left wing. To the extent, however, that this class matures for its self-emancipation, its constitutes itself as its own party and elects its own representatives, and not those of the capitalists. Thus, universal suffrage is the gauge of the maturity of the working class. It cannot and never will be anything more in the present-day state; but that is sufficient. On the day the thermometer of universal suffrage registers boiling point among the workers, both they and the capitalists will know what to do.[35]

Finally, in Engels's 1891 "Introduction" to the *Civil War in France,* he claimed that in democratic republics as well as in hereditary monarchies, the state is a machine for the oppression of one class by another. He singles out the United States for special complaint.

Nowhere do "politicians" form a more separate and powerful section of the nation than precisely in North America. There, each of the two major parties which alternately succeed each other in power is itself in turn controlled by people who make a business of politics, who speculate on seats in the legislative assemblies of the Union as well as of the separate states, or who make a living by carrying on agitation for their party and on its victory are rewarded with positions. It is well know how the Americans have been trying for thirty years to shake off this yoke, which has become intolerable, and how in spite of it all they continue to sink ever deeper into this swamp of corruption. It is precisely in America that we see best how there takes place this process of the state power making itself independent in relation to society, whose mere instrument it was originally intended to be. Here there exists no dynasty, no nobility, no standing army, beyond the few men keeping watch on the Indians, no bureaucracy with permanent posts or the right to pensions. And nevertheless we find here two great gangs of political speculators, who alternately take possession of the state power and exploit it by the most corrupt means and for the most corrupt ends – and the nation is powerless against these two great cartels of politicians, who are ostensibly its servants, but in reality dominate and plunder it.[36]

These would not seem to be the words of a person who is naively optimistic about voting in capitalist democracy, nor, still less, of a person who would replace revolutionary activity by electoral activity in achieving communism.

If one attends to the particular contexts of passages where Marx and Engels appear to allow that revolution may not be necessary, one finds that revolution may be unneccesssary for workers to achieve some immediate goals, may be unnecessary even then in only some countries, whereas in other countries revolution will be necessary for both the improvement of the conditions of workers and certainly for communist society. One also finds that although Marx and Engels had a high estimation of the political prospects for the working class where universal suffrage could be enjoyed, they did not identify political supremacy of the working class with full communist society. Nor, more importantly, did they regard universal suffrage in capitalist democracies as a panacea.

If Marx (or Engels) really did think that universal suffrage, in some countries at least, could be a substitute for the revolution, I am led to make two responses. First, they were mistaken on the empirical matter of whether bourgeois democratic processes suffice to institute communist society. The history of the western liberal democracies since the nineteenth century provides considerable evidence against that claim. Second, it may be that in seriously endorsing universal suffrage, parliamentary activity, propaganda, and legal and peaceful agitation as ways to achieve communism, Marx may have thought that basic elements of the revolutionary process – class-consciousness, political organization, trial-and-error learning, political self-determination, and so on – were likely to be present in a nonrevolutionary form. If that were so, then the allowance for nonrevolutionary paths to communism might not be incompatible with the requirement that revolution precede and prepare for communism. It might not be incompatible because it is at least conceivable that the essential elements of the revolutionary process would be identical or crucially similar to those of the democratic process. It should be stressed, however, that in the absence of decisive evidence that Marx and Engels ever allowed that revolution was unnecessary, this latter interpretation is most speculative.

The revolutionary thesis today

What is the status of the Marxian revolutionary thesis today? This question deserves separate treatment, but several points can be made. The requirement of a revolution for the creation and maintenance of a communist society today may appear utopian. This is partly because revolution of a scale that might introduce communism in no way appears imminent, in the United States, or perhaps in any major capitalist country. However, in evaluating the Marxian theory of revolution it must be remembered that Marx and Engels themselves witnessed periods in nineteenth-century western Europe in which even limited revolutions did not appear to be, and in fact were not, imminent and in which revolutionary upheavals fell short of the scope of revolutionary praxis discussed in this chapter. Yet their insistence on revolution as a precondition for communism was not withdrawn.

Finally, if I am correct in reaffirming the necessity of revolution for communist society as a central Marxist theoretical tenet, we have available in that tenet another means of confirming the truth or falsity of Marxist theory. By "confirmation," I do not mean to suggest quiescent waiting for the fulfillment of a prediction. Rather, we can test the social world, both to determine if revolutionary praxis can appear and be sustained within advanced capitalist societies and to ascertain whether a genuinely communist society can be brought about without revolutionary praxis.

Notes

1 Karl Marx, "Toward the Critique of Hegel's Philosophy of Law: Introduction" in *Writings of the Young Marx on Philosophy and Society*, Loyd D. Easton and Kurt H. Guddat, eds. and trans. (New York: Anchor Books, 1967), pp. 249–64.

2 T. B. Bottomore, *Classes in Modern Society* (London: Allen and Unwin, 1966), p. 93.
3 David McLellan, *Marx Before Marxism* (London: Macmillan, 1970), pp. 154–7.
4 John Plamenatz, *Karl Marx's Philosophy of Man* (Oxford: Clarendon Press, 1975), p. 179.
5 Robert C. Tucker, *The Marxian Revolutionary Idea* (New York: W. W. Norton, 1969), p. 18; See also p. 61.
6 He thus remained open to David Braybrooke's pointed criticisms in the forum where Tucker's discussion first appeared: Carl J. Friedrich, ed., *Revolution*, Nomos viii (New York: Atherton Press, 1969) pp. 240–6. Tucker, in his later book, does not attempt to deal with the criticism.
7 Tucker, *The Marxian Revolutionary Idea*, p. 18.
8 Marx and Engels, *The German Ideology*, (New York: International Publishers, 1970), p. 85.
9 Marx and Engels, *The German Ideology*, pp. 94–5.
10 Marx and Engels, *The Communist Manifesto* in Marx and Engels, *Selected Works*, vol. 1 (Moscow: Foreign Languages Publishing House, 1962), p. 43.
11 Marx, "Theses on Feuerbach," no. 3 in Marx and Engels, *The German Ideology*, p. 121.
12 Marx and Engels, *Selected Works*, 1:250–1. See also ibid., pp. 116–17 (Address of the Central Committee to the Communist League"); Marx and Engels, *Werke*, 8: 598–601, cited in Shlomo Avineri, *The Social and Political Thought of Karl Marx* (Cambridge: Cambridge University Press, 1971), pp. 195–6; see also Marx and Engels, *Werke*, 7: 273–4 cited in Avineri, p. 201.
13 Marx and Engels, *Selected Works*, 1: 523.
14 Marx, *Capital: A Critique of Political Economy*, vol. 1 (New York: International Publishers, 1967), pp. 177–8.
15 Ibid., pp. 325–6.
16 Ibid., p. 329.
17 Ibid., p. 331.
18 Ibid., p. 487.
19 Ibid., p. 488.
20 Ibid., p. 490.
21 Ibid., p. 488.
22 Speech at the Anniversary of the *People's Paper*, April 14, 1856, in *Karl Marx on Revolution*, Karl Marx Library, vol. 1, Saul K. Padover, ed. and trans. (New York: McGraw Hill, 1971), p. 60.
23 Marx and Engels, *Selected Works*, 1:106–17.
24 Marx, "The Chartists," in *Karl Marx and Frederick Engels on Britian* (Moscow: Foreign Languages Publishing House, 1962), pp. 358–69.
25 Ibid., p. 361.
26 Mihailo Marković, *From Affluence to Praxis: Philosophy and Social Criticism* (Ann Arbor: University of Michigan Press, 1974), pp. 183, 261–2.
27 Lenin, "The Proletarian Revolution and the Renegade Kautsky," in Lenin, *Selected Works* (Moscow: Progress Publishers, 1975), p. 466.

28 Marx and Engels, *Selected Works*, 1:377–85.

29 Padover, *Karl Marx on Revolution*, pp. 63–5.

30 Marx, *Capital*, 1:6.

31 Marx and Engels, *Selected Works*, 1:118–38.

32 Cited in Robert Michels, *Political Parties: A Sociological Study of the Oligarchical Tendencies of Modern Democracy* (Glencoe, Ill.: Free Press, 1949), p. 370.

33 Ibid.

34 Marx and Engels, *Selected Works*, 1:520–1.

35 Marx and Engels, *Selected Works*, 2:322.

36 Marx and Engels, *Selected Works*, 1:483–4.

5
Marx and Engels on the future communist society
DAVID MCLELLAN

It was not until the composition of *The German Ideology* – in Brussels in 1845–46 – that Marx arrived at the materialistic conception of history that was to be the "guiding thread" for the rest of his studies. During the previous decade Marx's writings show a development through the successive stages of idealism – romantic and then Hegelian – to liberal rationalism and an extended criticism of Hegel's philosophy that yielded many of the major themes of Marxian socialism. Engels said that Marx's ideas were based on a synthesis of German idealist philosophy, French political theory, and English classical economics: The early writings show Marx assimilating all three influences – although not, as yet, integrating them.

The intellectual background of Marx's home and school was the rationalism of the Enlightenment – a pale Protestantism incorporating the virtues of reason, moderation, and hard work. A radically different perspective was opened up by his future father-in-law, Baron von Westphalen. Marx's daughter Eleanor wrote that the Baron "filled Karl Marx with enthusiasm for the romantic school and, whereas his father read Voltaire and Racine with him, the Baron read him Homer and Shakespeare – who remained his favourite authors all his life."[1] During his early student days in Bonn, therefore, Marx gave himself up to the current romanticism although his move to Berlin in 1836 brought about a decisive change: Previously, Hegel's conceptual rationalism had been rejected by Marx, the follower of Kant and Fichte, the romantic subjectivist who considered the highest being to be separate from earthly reality. Now, however, it began to appear as though the idea was immanent in the real. Previously, Marx had "read fragments of Hegel's philosophy, but I did not care for its grotesque and rocky melody."[2] Now he embraced Hegelianism in a conversion that was as profound as it was sudden. It was probably the most important intellectual step of his whole life. For however much he was to criticize Hegel, accuse him of idealism, and try to stand his dialectic "on its feet," Marx was the first to admit that his method stemmed directly from that of his master of the 1830s.

Hegel started from the belief that, as he said of the French Revolution, "man's existence has its center in his head, i.e., in Reason, under whose inspiration he builds up the world of reality." In his greatest work, *The Phenomenology of Spirit,* Hegel traced the development of Mind, or Spirit, reintroducing historical movement into philosophy and asserting that the human mind can attain to absolute knowledge. He analyzed the development of human consciousness from its immediate perception of the here and now to the stage of self-consciousness, the understanding that allowed man to analyze the world and order his own actions accordingly. Following this was the stage of reason itself, understanding of the real, after which Spirit, by means of religion and art, attained to absolute knowledge, the level at which man recognized in the world the stages of his own reason. These stages Hegel called "alienations," insofar as they were creations of the human mind, yet thought of as independent and superior to the human mind. This absolute knowledge was at the same time a sort of recapitulation of the human spirit, for each successive stage retained elements of the previous ones at the same time as it went beyond them. This movement that suppressed and yet conserved Hegel called *Aufhebung,* a word that has this double sense in German. Hegel also talked of "the power of the negative," thinking that there was always a tension between any present state of affairs and what it was becoming. For any present state of affairs was in the process of being negated, changed into something else. This process was what Hegel meant by dialectic.

Hegel's philosophy was ambivalent: Although he himself preferred to talk of philosophy painting gray with gray and owl of Minerva only rising at dusk, emphasis on the negative and dialectic side of philosophy could obviously give it a radical bent – a development associated with a group of intellectuals known as the Young Hegelians. They embarked on a process of secularization, progressing from a critique of religion to one of politics and society. It is important to note that in his early writings Marx worked out his ideas in interaction with the other members of this close-

knit movement. His doctoral thesis clearly reflected the Young
Hegelian climate: Its field – post-Aristotelian Greek philosophy –
was one of general interest to the Young Hegelians. Marx's proc-
lamation in the preface that "Philosophy makes no secret of it.
Prometheus' confession 'in a word, I detest all Gods,' is its own
confession, its own slogan against all Gods in heaven and earth
who do not recognize man's self-consciousness as the highest di-
vinity,"[3] was typical of the Young Hegelians' antireligious idealism. The way forward for Marx lay in an application of the principles that Hegel had discovered to the "real" world.

But Marx did not immediately have the leisure to work on this
line of thought: Deprived of the possibility of an academic career
by repressive government measures, his contact with the real
world came through his work as a journalist for the *Rheinishe
Zeitung*. In his seven major articles for the paper, he seldom made
his own ideas explicit, because he gave his articles the form of
critical exegesis by exposing the absurdities in his opponents'
ideas. For this he used any weapon at hand, usually combining a
radical Hegelianism with the simple rationalism of the Enlightenment. In October 1842, now editor of the paper, Marx had to
reply to the accusation that his paper was flirting with communist
ideas. "The *Rheinische Zeitung*," he wrote, "does not even concede
theoretical validity to communist ideas in their present form let
alone desires their practical realization."[4] and he promised a fundamental criticism of such ideas. Soon, however, Marx had to
write on such sociopolitical matters as the law on the thefts of
wood and the poverty of the Moselle Winegrowers – subjects, as
he said later that "provided the first occasions for occupying myself with economic questions"[5] and impressed on him how closely
the laws were formed by the interests of those who were in
power.

The eighteen months following the suppression of the *Rheinische Zeitung* were to be decisive in forming Marx's ideas: In his
assault on the metaphysical fog that engulfed not only Hegel but
also Young Hegelian writing, Marx was helped by two influences. First, he was reading a lot of politics and history: He read
French socialism even before he went to Paris and his reading on
the French Revolution was extensive. Indeed, his writing of this
period can be viewed as an extended meditation on the question of

why the French Revolution, which started out with such excellent principles, had failed to solve the fundamental problem of the redistribution of social wealth. Second, there was the influence of his young Hegelian colleague Ludwig Feuerbach. Although Engels exaggerated when he said later that "we all became Feuerbachians"[6] this influence was profound. Feuerbach was fundamentally interested in religion, and his main thesis was that God was merely a projection of human attributes, desires, and potentialities. If men once realized this, they would be in a position to appropriate these attributes for themselves by realizing that they had created God, not God them, and thus be in a position to restore to themselves their alienated "species-being" or communal essence. What interested Marx was the application of this approach to Hegel's philosophy, which Feuerbach regarded as the last bulwark of theology, in that Hegel still started from the ideal instead of the real. Feuerbach wrote: "The true relationship of thought to being is this: being is the subject, thought the predicate. Thought arises from being – being does not arise from thought."[7]

This view of Feuerbach was incorporated into a long manuscript that Marx composed in the summer of 1843. Here, by means of a critique of Hegel, Marx's views on democracy and the abolition of the state began to take shape. According to Hegel's political philosophy, human consciousness manifested itself objectively in man's juridical, social, and political institutions that alone permitted man to attain to full liberty. Only the highest level of social organization – the state – was capable of uniting particular rights and universal reason. Hegel thus rejected the view that man was free by nature: On the contrary, for him the state was the only means of making man's freedom real. In other words, Hegel was aware of the social problems created by a competitive society in which there was an economic war of all against all – a state of affairs that he summed up under the term "Civil Society"; but he believed that these conflicts could be harmonized by the organs of the state into some "higher" unity. Following Feuerbach, Marx's fundamental criticism of Hegel was that, just as in religion men had imagined God to be the creator and man to be dependent on Him, so Hegel mistakenly started from the idea of the state and made everything else – the family and various social groups – dependent on this idea. Applying this general approach to particular issues, Marx declared himself in favor of democracy: "Just as religion does not create man, but man creates religion, so the constitution does not create the people but the people the constitution."[8] Marx was especially concerned, in a few pages of brilliant analysis, to reject Hegel's view that the bureaucracy performed a mediating function among different social groups and thus acted as a "universal class" in the interests of all. Marx believed that bureaucracy encouraged the political divisions that were essential to its own existence and thus pursued its own ends to the detriment of the community at large. Toward the end of his manuscript, Marx described how he expected universal suffrage to inaugurate the reform of civil society. Marx saw two possibilities: If the state and civil society continued to be separate, then all as individuals could not participate in the legislature except through deputies, the "expression of the separation and merely a dualistic unity."[9] If civil society became political society, then the significance of legislative power as representative would disappear, for it depends on a theological kind of separation of the state from civil society. Hence, what the people should aim for was not legislative power but governmental power. Marx ended his discussion with a passage that makes clear how, in the summer of 1843, he envisaged future political developments:

Only in unlimited voting, active as well as passive, does civil society actually rise to an abstraction of itself, to political existence as its true universal and essential existence. But the realization of this abstraction is also the transcendence of the abstraction. By making its political existence actual as its true existence, civil society also makes its civil existence unessential in contrast to its political existence. And with the one thing separated, the other, its opposite, falls. Within the abstract political state the reform of voting is a dissolution of the state, but likewise the dissolution of civil society.[10]

Thus Marx reached the same conclusion as in his discussion of "true democracy." Democracy implied universal suffrage, and universal suffrage would lead to the dissolution of the state.

It is clear from this manuscript that Marx was adopting the fundamental humanism of Feuerbach and with it Feuerbach's reversal of subject and predicate in the Hegelian dialectic. Marx considered it evident that any future development was going to involve a recovery by man of the social dimension that had been lost ever since the French Revolution leveled all citizens in the political state and thus accentuated the individualism of bourgeois society. He was explicit that private property must cease to be the basis of social organization, but it is not obvious that he was arguing for its abolition, nor did he make clear the various roles of classes in this social evolution.

The manuscript on Hegel was never published, but the embryonic ideas it contained received a clearer formulation when Marx got to Paris. During the winter of 1843–4 Marx wrote two essays for the *Deutsch-Französische Jahrbücher* – both as clear and sparkling as the Hegel manuscript had been involved and obscure. In the first, entitled "On the Jewish Question," Marx reviewed the opinions of his old mentor Bruno Bauer on Jewish emancipation. According to Bauer, for Jewish emancipation to be effective, the state had to cease to be effective and the state had to cease to be Christian. Otherwise discrimination against the Jews was inevitable. But for Marx, Bauer had not gone far enough: The mere secularization of politics did not entail the emancipation of men as human beings. The United States had no established religion, yet was notorious for the religiosity of its inhabitants. "But since the existence of religion," Marx continued, "is the existence of a defect, the source of this defect can only be sought in the nature of the state itself. Religion for us no longer has the force of a basis for secular deficiencies but only that of a phenomenon. We do not change secular questions into theological ones. We change theological questions into secular ones. History has for long enough been resolved into superstition: we now resolve superstition into history. The question of the relationship between political emancipation and religion becomes for us a question of the relationship of political emancipation to human emancipation."[11] In Marx's view this problem arose because "man has a life both in the political community, where he is valued as a communal being, and in civil society, where he is active as a private individual, treats other men as means, degrades himself to a means, and becomes the plaything of alien powers."[12]

Bauer had argued for a state based exclusively on the universal rights of man as proclaimed by the French Revolution and the American Declaration of Independence. For Marx, however, the rights of man were only the rights of the atomized, mutually hostile individuals of civil society. Thus

the right of man to freedom is not based on the union of man with man, but on the separation of man from man . . . The right of man to property is the right to enjoy his possessions and dispose of the same arbitrarily, without regard for other men, independently of society, the right of selfishness. It is the former individual freedom together with its latter application that forms the basis of civil society. It leads man to see in other men not the realization but the limitation of his own freedom.[13]

After pointing out that the society inaugurated by the French Revolution had forfeited many of the social and communal dimensions present in feudal society, Marx sketched his goal of bridging the gap between the individual viewed as a citizen member of a community and as an isolated egoistic member of civil society: "Human emancipation will only be complete when the real, individual man has absorbed into himself the abstract citizen; when as an individual man, in his everyday life, in his work, and in his individual relationships, he has become a species-being; and when he has recognized and organized his own powers (*forces propres*) and social powers so that he no longer separates this social power from himself as political power."[14]

The article "On the Jewish Question" had set the goal of full human emancipation; in his second article for the *Jahrbücher* Marx identified the means to achieve it. This article was intended as an introduction to his critique of Hegel that was to be written up for publication. The article began with Marx's famous epigrams on religion:

The foundation of irreligious criticism is this: man makes religion, religion does not make man. But man is no abstract being squatting outside the world. Man is the world of man, the state, society. This state, this society, produces religion's inverted world themselves. Thus the struggle against religion is indirectly the struggle against that world whose spiritual aroma is religion . . . Religion is the sigh of the oppressed creature, the feeling of a heartless world, and the soul of soulless circumstances. It is the opium of the people . . .[15]

But the role of religion having been exposed, the duty of philosophers was now to direct their attention to politics, a particularly appropriate activity in a Germany that was, according to Marx, still pre-1789. The one hope for Germany lay in its political philosophy, which was very progressive: The Germans had thought what other nations had done.

Therefore, to criticize this philosophy and progress beyond it would show, at least theoretically, what the future of society was to be. And although Marx was clear that "the criticism of religion ends with the doctrine that man is the highest being for man, that is, with the categorical imperative to overthrow all circumstances in which man is humiliated, enslaved, abandoned, and despised,"[16] the difficulty obviously lay in finding "a passive element, a material basis" necessary to revolution. He proclaimed the solution in a passage that has given much support to the view of Marx as a messianic, prophetic figure. The solution lay

in the formation of a class with radical chains, a class in civil society that is not a class of civil society, of a social group that is the dissolution of all social groups, of a sphere that has a universal character because of its universal sufferings and lays claim to no particular right, because it is the object of no particular injustice but of injustice in general. This class can no longer lay claim to a historical status, but only to a human one. It is, finally, a sphere that cannot emancipate itself without emancipating these other spheres themselves. In a word, it is the complete loss of humanity and thus can only recover itself by a complete redemption of humanity. This dissolution of society, as a particular class, is the proletariat . . .[17]

Thus the vehicle of revolution was clear to Marx: The proletariat was destined to assume the universal role that Hegel had misleadingly assigned to the bureaucracy. And there is also adumbrated here the idea that it is precisely the backwardness of Germany that offered Germany the opportunity to come to the forefront of the European revolutionary movement – an idea that was destined to reappear continually in less "orthodox" variants of Marxism. But hitherto Marx's writings had been almost exclusively political, although he had come to realize that politics was not enough. His interest in the essential economic dimension was sparked by an essay published in the *Deutsch-Französische Jahrbücher* alongside his own two. It was by Engels and entitled "Outlines of a Critique of Political Economy." In it, Engels indicted private property and its concomitant spirit of competition. Growing capitalist accumulation necessarily entailed a lowering of salaries and accentuated the class struggle. Uncurtailed growth of the economy meant recurrent crises, and the progress of science only served to increase the misery of the workers. This "sketch of genius" (as he later called it) made a great impression on Marx, and his notebooks during the summer of 1844 begin with extracts from it. These notes (unpublished by Marx) were entitled by their first editors "Economic and Philosophical Manuscripts" and represent a radical critique of capitalism based partly on Engels, partly on the antiindustrial ideas of such German romantics as Schiller, and partly on Feuerbach's humanism. On their first full publication in 1932 they were hailed by some as Marx's most important single piece of work.

The "Economic and Philosophical Manuscripts" consist of three main sections: a critique of the classical economists culminating with a section on alienated labor; a description of communism; and a critique of Hegel's dialectic.

The first section contains lengthy quotations from the classical economists – in particular Adam Smith and David Ricardo – to demonstrate the increasing polarization of classes and the deleterious effects of private property. Although he believed that the economists faithfully reported the workings of capitalist society, Marx criticized their approach on three main grounds: First, while admitting that labor was fundamental to the working of the economy, they acquiesced in assigning to it an increasingly poverty-stricken role; second, they did not view the economic system as one of interacting forces, that is, they took the laws of capitalism to be immutable and could not explain the origins of the system they were describing; and third, they took a one-sided view of man simply as a cog in the economic wheel and did not consider him "in his free time, as a human being."[18]

At this point Marx began a new section headed "alienated labor" that contained a description of the general impoverishment and dehumanization of the worker in capitalist society. Alienated labor consisted of four aspects. First, the worker was related to the product of his labor as to an alien object; it stood over and above him, opposed to him as an independent power. Second, the worker became alienated from himself in the very act of production; the worker did not view his work as part of his real life and did not feel at home in it. Third, man's "species-life," his social essence, was taken away from him in his work, which did not represent the harmonious efforts of man as a "species-being." Fourth, man found himself alienated from other men.

In an extended note to James Mill written about this time (unfortunately not included in most editions of the "manuscripts"), Marx attacked the notion of credit, which he called "the economic judgment on the morality of a man. In credit, man himself, instead of metal or paper, has become the mediator of exchange but not as man, but as the existence of capital and interest."[19] In contemporary society, according to Marx, men were increasingly producing with the sole object of exchanging and thus "you have no relation to my object as a human being because I myself have no human relation to it . . . our mutual value is the value of our objects for us."[20] The passage toward the end of the note constitutes a positive counterpart to the description of alienated labor:

Supposing that we had produced in a human manner; each of us would in his production have doubly affirmed himself and his fellow men. I would have: (1) objectified in my production my individuality and its peculiarity and thus both in my activity enjoyed an individual expression of my life and also in looking at the object have had the individual pleasure of realizing that my personality was objective, visible to the senses and thus a power raised beyond all doubt. (2) In your enjoyment or use of my product I would have had the direct enjoyment of realizing that I had both satisfied a human need by my work and also objectified the human essence and therefore fashioned for another human being the object that met his need. (3) I would have been for you the mediator between you and the species and thus been acknowledged and felt by you as a completion of your own essence and a necessary part of yourself and have thus realized that I am confirmed both in your thought and in your love. (4) In my expression of my life I would have fashioned your expression of your life, and thus in my own activity have realized my own essence, my human, my communal essence.[21]

The second main section of the "Manuscripts" contained Marx's solution to the problem of alienation in communism. Although while still in Germany he had rejected communism as a "dogmatic and one-sided abstraction," the impact of Paris had made him a swift convert. But Marx's communism was not the "crude" kind, inspired by "universal envy," which aimed to negate all culture in a leveling-down process. He summarized his ideas in an almost mystical passage:

. . . communism as the positive abolition of private property and thus of human self-alienation and therefore the real reappropriation of the human essence by and for man. This communism as the complete and conscious return of man himself as a social i.e., human being. Communism as completed naturalism is humanism and as completed humanism is naturalism. It is the genuine solution of the antagonism between man and nature and between man and man. It is the true solution of the struggle between existence and essence, between objectification and self-affirmation, between freedom and necessity, between individual and species. It is the solution to the riddle of history and knows itself to be this solution.[22]

In the following sections (in many ways the key passage of the "Manuscripts"), Marx expanded on three particular aspects of his conception of communism. First, he stressed that communism was a historical phenomenon whose genesis was "the entire movement of history." At the present stage, the essential problem was an economic one – in particular, the abolition of private property: "the positive abolition of private property and the appropriation of human life is the positive abolition of all alienation, thus the return of man from religion, family, state, etc., to his human, that is, social being."[23] Second, Marx stressed that everything about man – starting with his language – was social. Even man's relationship to nature was included in this social dimension:

thus society completes the essential unity of man with nature, it is the genuine resurrection of nature, the fulfilled naturalism of man and humanism of nature . . . For not only the five senses but also the so-called spiritual and moral senses (will, love, etc.), in a word, human love and the humanity of the senses come into being only through the existence of their object, through nature humanized. The development of the five senses is a labor of the whole previous history of the world.[24]

Nevertheless, Marx emphasized, thirdly, that the stress on man's social aspects only served to enhance the individuality of communist, unalienated man, whom he described as "total" or "all-sided." For just as the state of alienation vitiated all human faculties, so the supersession of this alienation would be a total liberation. It would not just be limited to the possession and enjoyment of material objects: All human faculties would, in their different ways, become means of appropriating reality. This was difficult to imagine for alienated man, because private property had so blunted men's sensibility that they could only imagine an object to be theirs when they actually possessed it: All physical and intellectual senses had been replaced by the single alienation of having. And, finally, the reciprocal relationship between man and nature would be reflected in a single all-embracing science: "natural science will in time comprise the science of man, as the science of man will embrace natural science: there will be one single science."[25]

The third and final section of the "Manuscripts" was devoted to a critique of Hegel's dialectic as found in his most famous work, *The Phenomenology of Spirit.* Marx began by praising Feuerbach for having shown that Hegel's philosophy was no more than a rationalized theology and having discovered the true materialist approach by starting from the social relationship of man to man. But Marx's attitude to Hegel was far from being wholly negative: "The greatness of Hegel's *Phenomenology* and its final product, the dialectic of negativity as the moving and creating principle is on the one hand that Hegel conceives of the self-creation of man as a process, objectification as loss of the object as externalization and the transcendence of this externalization. This means, therefore, that he grasps the nature of labor and understands objective man, true because real man, as the result of his own labor."[26] On the other hand, this whole dialectic was viewed from an idealist standpoint: "The appropriation of man's objectified and alienated faculties is thus first only an appropriation that occurs in the mind, in pure thought, i.e., in abstraction."[27] Marx, however, started from the "real man of flesh and blood, standing on the solid round earth and breathing in and out all the powers of nature"[28] and defined his position as a consistent naturalism or humanism that avoided both idealism and materialism. Hegel saw man as a disembodied consciousness and the world as necessarily inimical to man's fulfillment, but Marx considered that it was only man's present relationship to the world that was askew: Man needed to interact with external objects in order to develop or "objectify" himself. For Hegel, all objectification was alienation; for Marx, man could overcome alienation only if he objectified himself by using nature in cooperation with his fellow men.

With his move to Brussels in 1845, Marx's writings take on a systematic form – albeit an open-ended system – that is not present in his early writings. These early writings document Marx's struggle to conclude, from very idealistic beginnings, that the fundamental activity of man was one of productive interchange with nature; that this activity was vitiated by the class divisions of capitalist society with its institutions of private property and the division of labor; and that this present alienation could be overcome by a proletarian revolution inaugurating communism.

What Marx's writings up to 1844 failed to deal with was the nature of historical change. It would not, of course, be fair to say that the "Manuscripts" had no developmental view of society. That view, however, was vague and although Marx had used Hegel against Feuerbach to demonstrate the importance of man's self-creation through labor, this still remained very abstract. Marx, now working in close cooperation with Engels, devoted himself to clarifying his materialist view of history by "setting accounts with our erstwhile philosophical consciousness"[29]–and principally with Feuerbach, whose static materialism was pithily criticized in the short *Theses on Feuerbach*. This criticism expanded into the lengthy polemic against the whole Young Hegelian school in *The German Ideology*. Here Marx and Engels outlined their basic position: "The way in which man produces his food depends first of all on the nature of the means of subsistence that he finds and has to reproduce. This mode of production must not be viewed simply as reproduction of the physical existence of individuals. Rather it is *a* definite form of their activity, *a* definite way of expressing their life, *a* definite mode of life. As individuals express their life, so they are. What they are, therefore, *coincides* with what they produce, and how they produce. The nature of individuals thus depends on the material conditions which determine their production."[30]

They went on to state that "how far the productive forces of a nation are developed is shown most evidently by the degree to which the division of labour has been developed."[31] They showed how the division of labor led to the separation of town and country and then to the separation of industrial from commercial labor and so on. Next they summarized the different stages of ownership that had corresponded to the stages in the division of labor: tribal ownership, communal and state ownership, feudal or estate ownership. Marx and Engels summarized their conclusions:

The fact is, then, that definite individuals who are productively active in a specific way enter into these definite social and political relations. The social structure and the state continually evolve out of the life-process of definite individuals, but individuals not as they may appear in their own or other people's imagination but rather as they really are, that is, as they work, produce materially, and act under definite material limitations, presuppositions, and conditions independent of their will.[32]

They then reiterated their general approach, stating that "consciousness does not determine life, but life determines consciousness,"[33] and showed how the division of labor, leading to private property, created social inequality, class struggle, and the erection of political structures.

The materialist conception of history outlined in *The German Ideology* formed the theoretical basis for Marx's political activities in the late 1840s and particularly his work in the Communist League. Large sections of the *Communist Manifesto* are simply trenchant summaries of *The German Ideology*. With the failure of the 1848 revolutions, Marx concentrated more on the study of economics, and, in his work on the production process of capitalist society – *Capital* – brought to a conclusion the research he had begun in Paris in 1844.

Notes

1 Eleanor Marx, "Karl Marx," *Die Neue Zeit* (1883), p. 441.
2 Karl Marx, "Letter to his Father," *MEGA* (Marx-Engels Gesamtausgabe): Marx-Engels Verlagsgesellschaft, I (2), p. 218.
3 Marx, "Doctoral Thesis," *MEGA*, I i (i), p. 10.
4 Marx, "Communism and the Augsburger Allgemeine Zeitung," *MEGA*, I i (2), p. 263.
5 Marx, "Preface to a Critique of Political Economy," in Marx and Engels, *Selected Works*, vol. 1 (Moscow: Foreign Languages Publishing House, 1962), p. 36.
6 Engels, *Ludwig Feuerbach and the End of Classical German Philosophy* (Moscow: Foreign Languages Publishing House, 1946), p. 20.
7 Ludwig Feuerbach, *Anthropologischer Materialismus; Ausgewählte Schriften* (Stuttgart: Fromann Verlag, 1967), p. 95.
8 Marx, "Critique of Hegel's Philosophy of Right," *MEGA*, I i (i), p. 434.
9 Ibid., p. 542.
10 Ibid., pp. 543 ff.
11 Marx, "On the Jewish Question," *MEGA*, I i (i), pp. 581 ff.
12 Ibid., p. 584.
13 Ibid., p. 594.
14 Ibid., p. 599.
15 Marx, "Introduction to a Critique of Hegel's Philosophy of Right," *MEGA*, I i (i), p. 607.

16 Ibid., pp. 614 ff.
17 Ibid., pp. 619 ff.
18 Marx, *Frühe Schriften,* vol. 1, ed. Hans-Joachim Lieber and Peter Furth (Stutt-
    gart: Alfred Kroener Verlag, 1962), p. 518.
19 Marx, *Texte zu Methode und Praxis,* vol. 2, ed. Günther Hillman (Hamburg:
    Rowohlt Verlag, 1966), pp. 170 ff.
20 Ibid., pp. 178 ff.
21 Ibid., pp. 180 ff.
22 Marx, *Frühe Schriften,* pp. 593 ff.
23 Ibid., pp. 594 ff.
24 Ibid., p. 601.
25 Ibid., p. 604.
26 Ibid., p. 645.
27 Ibid., pp. 643 ff.
28 Ibid., p. 649.
29 Marx and Engels, *Selected Works,* vol. 1 (Moscow: Foreign Languages Pub-
    lishing House, 1962), p. 364.
30 Marx and Engels, *The German Ideology* (Moscow: Foreign Languages Pub-
    lishing House, 1968), p. 31.
31 Ibid., p. 32.
32 Ibid., p. 32.
33 Ibid., p. 38.

6

Alienation and justice in the market

ARTHUR DIQUATTRO

"Communists preach no morality at all," say Marx and Engels (1964a, p. 267), but if Marx and Engels fail to preach morality, or lack an ethical *theory*, they steadfastly display an ethical sense or commitment which, as Ollman indicates (1971, Chapter 4), is "internal" to their explanation of capitalist reality. This chapter will elucidate Marx's sense of justice in more explicitly theoretical terms and critically evaluate the Marxian ideas of justice and alienation by distinguishing between the class structure of capitalism and the use of the market as a mode of resource allocation. It will show that the social relations of production, not the market mechanism, are primarily responsible for exploitation and alienated labor under capitalism.

The Marxian sense of justice and the market system

Cambridge controversies

In her *Essay on Marxian Economics,* Joan Robinson draws a distinction between the productivity of capital goods and the productive contribution of capitalists. "Whether we choose to say that capital is productive or that capital is necessary to make labor productive, is not a matter of much importance. What is important to say is that *owning* capital is not a productive activity" (Robinson, 1966, p. 18). Since characterized as a touchstone of the "Cambridge controversy," this elementary distinction brings neatly together the composite features of the Marxist idea of exploitation and reveals the reasoning, not often explicitly couched by Marx and Engels, behind the Marxian sense of distributive justice. The Cambridge controversies in the theory of capital bear on the distributive issue by focusing on the inability of neoclassical marginal theory to account for profit as the marginal product of capital.

According to the neoclassicists the rate of profit is the "equivalent" of the marginal product of capital. But this cannot be the case because, as two Cantabrigian critics put it, "it is necessary to know the rate of profit in order to aggregate capital into a single quantity to determine the effect on output of varying it by a unit amount, i.e., its marginal rate of return" (Hunt and Schwartz, 1971, p. 19). In other words, "attempts to relate the return to capital to its contribution are based on circular reasoning, since it is impossible to conceive of a quantity of capital independent of the profit rate" (Lebowitz, 1974, p. 387). Hunt and Schwartz elicit the likely conclusion that the distribution of the wage and profit shares of total income must be determined by something other than capital's marginal productivity; such as the distribution of relative market power or conflict between workers and owners (1971, p. 20; also see Hunt and Sherman, 1972, p. 41). And Lebowitz, seeing the connection between the demise of the marginal explanation and the neoclassical "justification" of income distribution delivers the upshot: "the theoretical nexus between the returns to the owner of capital and the contribution of means of production has been shattered" (1974, p. 387). After all, if it makes no conceptual sense to assert that the level of the rate of profit is calculable as the return on capital investment, than how can it be claimed that the owners of capital merit their income as a consequence of their investment?

The force of this criticism should not be underestimated, but the general point established by Robinson strikes deeper. For it suggests that even if the marginalists *could* make good on their argument, and apparently their argument holds in very special cases (cf. Nell, 1972a, p. 13), the critical point about income distribution would still stand firm. It does not follow that because capital, understood as "capital goods" (produced means of production) *or* as a "fund of value" (the value of property), is productive, that the owners of capital (defined in either sense) deserve their profit income. Additional argument is required to demonstrate that, and it is here that the neoclassicists have virtually *nothing* to say. Indeed, modern neoclassicists delight in saying nothing explicit about the issue of distributive justice, an issue they locate outside of their "scientific" purview and place instead in the realm of ethics and value judgments.[1] But if the neoclassicists refrain from dealing openly with the ethical issue, they nonetheless proceed to explain the world in such a way that cultivates an evaluative attitude, and it is precisely its implicit defense of capitalist inequality that prompts Marxists to dub neoclassical theory a species of "vulgar economy," a mode of analysis that paints a distorted picture of capitalism as the best of all possible worlds. Certainly one of the reasons that the neoclassicists want to save the idea of the marginal productivity of capital is that they believe the answer to key ethical questions turns on its truth or falsity.

The relevant ethical issue is: Do capitalists deserve their profit income as a consequence of their ownership of capital? The answer must be no, and not just because the marginalists' theory has been riddled by its Cantabrigian critics. Marginal theory purports to *explain* the distribution of income in the capitalist market as a species of exchange according to which each productive factor contributes to production. This explanation suggests, but does not constitute, an ethical justification, so that even if the theory were true it would not follow that the owners of capital deserve their profit income. In the same way, the labor theory of value purports to *explain* distribution under capitalism according to which labor is ultimately the only productive factor; profit income is the surplus yielded by the labor factor and its size depends on the class struggle in both its economic and political dimensions. But even if the labor theory of value is true, while it suggests where an ethical argument might lie, it does not constitute one. It is logically possible for the labor theory of value to hold true and for the defenders of capitalist inequality to maintain their defenses. Someone could agree that the value of commodities is determined by socially necessary labor but go on to argue that people should be rewarded according to some politically designed distributive scheme, or according to luck, religious scripture, or a variety of other distributive criteria. There is a sense in which the controversies in the theory of capital and the labor theory of value, relating as they do to *explanatory* theories, cannot resolve the controversies surrounding the ethical issue of distributive justice. The explanatory theories bear on theories of distributive justice, but the former do not contain sufficient information to imply ethical conclusions.

Labor theory of value not a theory of exploitation

This point deserves expansion because it is mistakenly assumed by many Marxists and neoclassicists that the Marxian theory of exploitation stands on the truth of the labor theory of value. On the Marxist side: "the Marxian doctrine of surplus value is based . . . on his teaching of value. That is why it is important to keep the Marxian theory of value free from all distortion, because the *theory of exploitation* is built on it" (Leontiev, n.d., p. 89). From a non-Marxist perspective: "[Why do Marxists] bother with the labor theory of value? [Because] a labor theory of value is necessary to Marx's theory of class exploitation" (Gordon, 1968, p. 137). Neither of these claims can be substantiated. The classical labor theory of value states that in a competitive exchange economy individual prices are proportionate to the socially necessary quantity of labor expended in the production of commodities. Adam Smith provided his familiar deer-beaver illustration to prove that in a simple market system the ratio at which commodities exchange must correspond to labor-time ratios.

If among a nation of hunters, for example, it usually costs twice the labor to kill a beaver which it does to kill a deer, one beaver should naturally exchange for or be worth two deer. It is natural that what is usually the produce of two days' or two hours' labor should be worth double of what is usually the produce of one day's or one hour's labor. [Smith, 1910, pp. 41–42]

If deer and beaver were to sell for the same price, the hunters would lack the incentive to continue catching beaver and would switch to hunting deer. The supply of deer would saturate the market, lowering their price until once again beaver would sell for twice the price of deer. This particular exchange ratio, one corresponding to labor-time ratios, would signal the point of equilibrium because neither beaver nor deer hunters would any longer have an incentive to shift from one type of hunting to the other.

Sweezy (1942, p. 46) notes that for Smith to get this result he must assume implicitly utility maximization and mobility; that is, conditions guaranteeing perfect mobility so that the hunters can freely maximize their advantages. But in order for the labor theory to work, additional assumptions are required, including at least the following. First, labor must be treated as a cost; only if individuals are compensated for their labor will they be moved to expend it. Second, and more importantly, the provision must be included that commodities *ought* to exchange at prices proportional to labor time embodied in them. One beaver exchanges for two deer not because it is "natural," but because the hunters are operating on the belief that they *should* be compensated in proportion to labor expended. Exchange is a matter of social convention incorporating a complex corpus of beliefs about rights, obligations, fairness, and so forth, and certain distributive principles must therefore be included as a presupposition of the labor theory of value. This does not make the labor theory "a conception of the 'just price,' " as opposed to a theory of markets, as claimed by Joan Robinson (1962, p. 29; 1973, p. 20), but it does mean that only if the economic actors whose behavior the theory seeks to explain adopt the distributive maxim "to each according to labor expended" can the theory work. The theory, then, does not propose any first-order normative recommendation (the theorist need not *advocate* any distributive principles), but it does assume that those whose activity is up for explanation do adopt distributive principles of the specified kind. It is the task of a theory of justice, not the labor theory of value or the marginal theory of productivity, to morally assess these operative distributive principles. Recognizing this distinction between normative and explanatory theories, Oskar Lange emphasizes the point that "the fact of exploitation can be deduced without the help of the labor theory of value" (1968, p. 77). He bares the exploitative character of capitalist institutions while adhering simultaneously to the marginal theory of productivity.

If interest is explained by the marginal productivity of capital, it is only because the workers do not own the capital they work with that interest is the personal income of a separate class of people. If interest is regarded as due to a higher valuation of present than future goods it is only because workers do not possess the subsistence fund enabling them to wait until the commodities they produce are ready that the capitalist advancing it to the workers gets the interest as his personal income. Just as in Marx's case it is because the workers do not possess the means of production that the surplus value is pocketed by the capitalist. [Lange, 1968, p. 78]

Exploitation as a result of class structure

As theories of the market, both the labor and marginal accounts are consistent with the Marxian theory of exploitation. This is so because what makes capitalism exploitative is not the market mechanism *per se,* but the unique class features of its social environment; that is, the "institutional datum" that separates labor from capital, subordinates labor to capital, and locates economic and political power in the hands of the owners of the means of production.

Marx distinguishes between simple commodity production and commodity production under capitalism. In the former, production and allocation of commodities are regulated by the market, but because each producer possesses and works with his/her own means of production, labor power is not itself a market commodity. Exchange values and the prices that approximate them are determined by socially necessary labor and competition between buyers and sellers, and these prices determine how individuals allocate their work among various kinds of production. The market is self-regulating in that competitive prices select the goods to be produced and allocate resources to their production in such a way that there would be no way to improve upon the resulting economic configuration (for elaboration, see Mandel, 1968, Chapter 2; Sweezy, 1942, pp. 45–7; O'Connor, 1976).

The central identifying feature of a *capitalist* market system is the separation of labor and capital and the coincident subordination of workers to capitalists (see Marx, 1909, p. 1025; Dobb, 1947, p. 7). Besides possessing a quantitative dimension, capital is a historically specific social relation in which ownership confers and solidifies domination of owners over workers who have been deprived of free access to the means of making a living. In a capitalist market system, where labor power assumes the form of an alienable commodity that workers are compelled to sell to capitalists, the market functions to facilitate exploitation. It does so by automatically and continuously transferring from wage workers to capitalists the surplus created by productive labor. Given the separation of labor and capital, the market provides the means whereby capitalists are enabled to take systematic advantage of workers. It is not, however, the market *per se* that involves exploitation, but rather the use of the market against the background of the class relations peculiar to capitalism. It is the *capitalist* market that entails the exploitation and domination of workers by capitalists.

This argument can be clarified by distinguishing between the allocative and distributive aspects of market prices:

The price of a commodity or factor of production is a determinant both of the use which will be made of that commodity or factor of production and of the real income which the owner of the commodity or factor of production will receive as a result of its sale. [Meade, 1965, p. 11]

With respect to efficiency, Meade argues that it is necessary to attach prices to the various factors of production and to final goods and services in order to effectively allocate resources; that is, if high prices are levied for scarce goods and low prices for abundant goods, the users of these goods will be informed automatically as to how to satisfy their wants in the most efficient manner possible. Meade's argument, which is familiar enough, is that the use of competitive prices will accomplish a Pareto-optimum allocation of economic resources. But, Meade continues, prices used for this efficiency purpose may result in an extremely undesirable distribution of wealth and income. He refers to this as the distributional aspect of the price mechanism and makes use of the case of international trade relations to show that a reliance on competitive prices results in a grossly unequal distribution of benefits. Meade's point is that an efficient capitalist market may, and often does, lead to an undesirable distribution of wealth and power. As Vickrey indicates in his consideration of the idea of competitive equilibrium, this potential conflict between efficiency and distribution should come as no surprise because the theorem of optimal competition "takes no account of the distribution of income and an allocation of resources would be considered to satisfy this optimum properly even though half of the population were starving while the other half were enjoying great luxury" (1964, p. 214; see also Vickrey, 1973). Following Tawney (1920, Chapter 5), we can refer to capitalist control and revenue as the price workers must pay as a condition of gaining access to the means of making a living. This is the core of the distributional aspect of the price mechanism in the capitalist market system.

It should be clear by now that the distribution of wealth and income in capitalist society proceeds according to the class relations of the capitalist market system and not the market itself. It is quite possible to abstract the market (as a method of allocating resources) from its capitalist context (as a method of distributing wealth and power). To paraphrase Paul Sweezy (1942, p. 56), "the market does not imply capitalism." This is evident in the case of the simple market and, as we shall see, is also true in the case of market socialism. The market as an allocative device can be put to work against the backdrop of dissimilar institutional forms; its distributive operation is a function of the specific class structure of its social environment.

Thus far we have seen that labor and marginal theories purport to *explain* how goods get allocated and rewards distributed; the theory of exploitation seeks to *evaluate* the fairness of the distribution so explained, and it does so by focusing on the class structure of capitalism. Lange derives the Marxian conception of exploitation by "contrasting the personal distribution of income in a capitalist economy (irrespective of whether monopolistic or competitive) with that in an 'einfache Warenproduktion' (simple exchange economy) in which the worker owns his own means of production" (1968, p. 78). Exploitation is the consequence not of the market but of the differences in class structure between these two systems. C. B. Macpherson provides a similar account of the nature of exploitation in a possessive (capitalist) market society:

When land and capital are all owned by one set of people, there is a permanent change in the distribution of the whole product between persons, to the disadvantage of the persons without land and capital. Since the latter cannot resort to independent production, they cannot demand in wages an amount equal to what would be the product of their labor on land or capital of their own. Those who have the capital and land, therefore, by employing the labor of others, get a net transfer of the powers (or some of the products of those powers) to themselves. [1962, p. 56]

Compensatory principles of socialist justice

It might be objected that this "net transfer" does not entail exploitation. The profit transferred to capitalists by workers could be interpreted as payment for services rendered. If it could be demonstrated that capitalists merit or deserve their income and power by virtue of their contribution to production, and if justice requires giving each his/her due, then the charge that capitalists exploit (take systematic advantage of) workers would be difficult to sustain. The Marxian incrimination must therefore stand on the proposition that "profits as a whole are paid for nothing at all" (Hollis and Nell, 1975, p. 18). As Sherman states: "What we mean by exploitation is that, under capitalism, capitalists own resources but put forth no effort, yet receive a large share of the national income" (1972, p. 58). It is true enough that capital *goods* contribute to production, that workers need access to them, and that machines typically increase worker productivity, but it is not at all clear that capital as private property contributes to anything except the pocketbooks of the owners of capital goods. This is the essence of Robinson's distinction between the productivity of capital and the productivity of capitalists. Profit is yielded by workers and equipment produced by workers, but it is appropriated by captialists simply because they own the means of production, and "owning capital is not a productive activity."

This conception of exploitation implies basic normative principles of a compensatory sort: In a society defined by moderate scarcity, the distribution of income should proceed according to one's contribution to production, or more generally, the acquisition of rewards should be contingent upon the discharge of social obligation. This principle is implicit in Sherman's definition of exploitation as it is in Edward Nell's treatment of the concept. Nell criticizes the well-known introductory text diagram used by Samuelson and other neoclassicists to explain exchange under capitalism:

The flow of profit income is not an exchange in any sense. The Samuelson diagram is fundamentally misleading: there is no "flow" from "household supply" to the factor market for capital. The *only* flow is the flow of profit income in the other direction. And this, of course, leads straight to that hoary but substantial claim that the payment of wages is not an exchange either, or at any rate, not a fair one. For Wages plus Profits adds up to the Net Income Product; yet Profits are not paid for anything, while wages are paid for work. Hence the work of labor (using the tools, equipment, etc., replacement and depreciation of which is already counted in) has produced the entire product. *Is labor not therefore exploited?* Does it not deserve the whole product? [1972b, p. 47]

Note that Nell's conception of desert implies the acceptance of compensatory principles of distributive justice. The same is true of Marx and Engels, who speak of capitalists "extorting" a surplus from workers, "pumping booty out of the laborer," and living in idleness off the unpaid labor of the working class (Marx, 1909, vol. 1, p. 653; Engels, 1967, pp. 98–100, 113–16). Stated simply, Marx and Engels argue that, given the separation of labor and capital, workers are compelled to work for capitalists and, finding themselves in this subordinate position, must surrender to capitalists (1) their surplus product and (2) control over their work lives. This is the dual price workers must pay in order to gain access to the means of production.[2] Do capitalists *do* anything productive to merit this payment? No. As far as productive contribution is concerned, capitalists constitute a "superfluous" class of coupon clippers that has long ceased to perform a useful function. It is people in their capacity as managers or paid employees who supervise the workplace and carry on the business of investment, leaving people *qua* capitalists in the position of "pretending to earn" (Engels, 1967, p. 115; see also Marx, 1909, vol. 3, pp. 449–59). The only labor performed by capitalists is the "labor of exploitation" (Marx, 1909, vol. 3, p. 450). And capitalists are joined by managers in this "labor" to the extent that the latter have as their task the *control* of workers, a function that "arises out of the specific form of capitalist production" and that will disappear after economic organization has stripped off its capitalist integument (Marx, 1971, vol. 3, pp. 496–97).

The best demonstration of this are the cooperative factories built by the workers themselves. They are proof that the capitalist as functionary of production has become just as superfluous to the workers as the landlord appears to the capitalist with regard to bourgeois production. [Marx, 1971, vol. 3, p. 497]

Marx goes on to dispose of the other defenses erected by apologists of capitalist distribution. The justification of private profit as a payment for "abstinence" lacks any evidential backing, because there exists no discoverable connection between alleged abstinence and profit making. Marx "had only to contrast the profit and the 'abstinence' of a Rothschild to feel that the so-called 'explanation' required no further refutation" (Dobb, 1960, p. 137). If anyone undergoes abstinence from consumption in order to generate capital accumulation, it is the enforced abstinence of the working class. The idea that capitalists take risks can be handled with similar facility. First, there is a paucity of evidence that capitalists take significant risks, especially in developed capitalist countries where the highest rates of profit are realized in the most stable and secure (oligopolistic) sectors of the economy (Sherman, 1972, Chapter 8). If we define risk-taking as measuring risk in terms of rates of success and failure over time, we find little evidence pointing to the downward mobility of capitalists. The structured inequalities of capitalist society make extensive movement on the stratification scale highly unlikely (see Mayer and Buckley, 1970, Chapter 7). Second, if the risk-taking argument is used to justify profit income, simple equity requires that the principle be impartially applied. What about risks undertaken by workers as measured by deaths and injuries on the job, unemployment, occupational disease, and so forth?[3] Rewarding the supposed risks of capitalists and not the real risks of workers is a very peculiar sort of fairness, "yet according to the political economy of the capitalist class, that is the very pink of fairness" (Engels, 1967, p. 99).

Having demonstrated the indolent and parasitic character of the capitalist class, Engels concludes that "the capitalist class can no longer lay claim to its profits" (1967, p. 116).

What is morally fair, what is even fair in law, may be far from socially fair. Social fairness or unfairness is decided by one science alone – the science which deals with the material facts of production and exchange, the science of political economy.

According to what we may call common fairness, the wages of labor ought to consist in the produce of his labor. But that would not be fair according to political economy.

The fairness of political economy, such as it truly lays down the laws which rule actual society, that fairness is all on one side – on that of Capital. [Engels, 1967, pp. 98–100]

Engels here employs compensatory principles of justice, included in the conception "moral or common fairness," to negatively evaluate the operative distributive norms ("social fairness") of capitalist political economy.[4] During the transition period from capitalism to communism these principles come into their own. Marx and Engels see socialism as a cooperative social union in which each individual (who is able) is expected to do his/her share of work, and in which, as Engels puts it, "no individual can throw on the shoulders of others his share in productive labor" (Engels, 1947, p. 438). The distribution of rewards is contingent upon the execution of social obligation.[5]

The classic statement on distribution under socialism appears in the *Critique of the Gotha Programme,* in which Marx posits the compensatory principle: To each according to the duration or intensity of his/her work, from each according to his/her ability (1955, vol. 2, pp. 21–5). Marx advocates this principle even while regarding it as "defective." The principle is defective when compared with the distributive maxim under communism, the imperfection stemming from the limited, slightly structured, inequalities that result from its implementation. Only under communism, where there are more goods available than there are claims for these goods, can individuals equally satisfy their unequal needs. Although defective from the vantage point of communism, compensatory principles find an appropriate place under socialism, a society defined by moderate scarcity. These principles are *compensatory* in that they justify limited inequalitites by awarding larger incomes to workers who undergo disproportionate disutility in the course of working for the common advantage. These inequalities, however, require containment at the point where they tend to foster the development of a class-divided society. Only if workers who bear greater burdens receive greater compensation can other workers avoid the charge that they are taking advantage of their harder-working comrades.[6] The use of material incentives governed by compensatory principles of distributive justice is both consistent with socialist morality and necessary to evince the willing cooperation and maximum productive effort of everyone participating in socialist society.

Lange's postulation of a scheme of distribution comes close to the theory of justice just sketched. Assuming that the same demand price offered by different consumers must represent an equal urgency of need, he calls for a distribution of equal incomes. At the same time, "the distribution has to lead to such apportionment of the services of labor between the different occupations as to make the differences of the value of the marginal product of labor in the various occupations equal to the differences in the marginal disutility involved in their pursuit." This requires a differentiation of incomes because "to secure the apportionment of labor services required, differences in the marginal disutility of the various occupations have to be compensated by differences in income." There is no contradiction here.

By putting leisure, safety, agreeableness of work, etc., into the utility scales of the individuals, the disutility of any occupation can be represented as an opportunity cost. The choice of an occupation offering a lower money income, but also a lower disutility, may be interpreted as the purchase of leisure, safety, agreeableness of work, etc., at a price equal to the difference between the money income earned in that particular occupation and others. Thus the differences of incomes required by condition 2 are only apparent. They represent prices paid by the individuals for different conditions of work. Instead of attaching different money incomes to the various occupations the administration of a socialist economy might pay all citizens the same money income and charge a price for the pursuit of each occupation. It becomes obvious not only that there is no contradiction between both conditions, but that condition 2 is necessary to satisfy condition 1. [Lange, 1938, pp. 101–2]

By way of concluding this discussion of compensatory principles, two difficulties with Marx's account of distribution during the transition period should be brought out. First, contrary to Marx's characterization in *Critique of the Gotha Programme,* there is nothing peculiarly "bourgeois" about a conception of distributive justice based on proportionate equality. Second, rewarding workers solely according to "quantity and intensity" of labor is an insufficient criterion because it ignores the varying degrees of disutility attached to different kinds of labor. Some work, although it takes considerable time and effort, may confer ample enjoyment, providing its own reward, in contrast to less satisfying work of equal duration and intensity that needs to be redressed by additional income.

The bourgeois principle of distribution is "To each according to what he and the instruments he owns produces" (Friedman, 1962, pp. 161–2). The principle assumes the institution of capitalist property and sets no limits on the extent of permissible differentials; that is, it establishes the right to unrestricted acquisition of wealth and economic power. Because it is precisely this type of property and mode of distribution that is *absent* from a socialist society, one ponders why Marx, who possessed such a clear understanding of the historically specific features of bourgeois society, described the

proportional distribution characteristic of the first phase of socialism as uniquely *bourgeois*. The idea of distributive justice that gives
unequal rewards to unequal degrees of merit, in exact proportion
to the inequality of the degrees, is at least as old as Aristotle and
also found its way into the moral philosophy of the medieval
canonists (e.g., their commutative theory of the "just price"), few
of whom could be plausibly described as bourgeois thinkers.
Marx is therefore mistaken in his characterization of the norm of
distribution during the period of transition as necessarily or distinctly bourgeois. It can, instead, be suitably *socialist* and constitutes a perfectly reasonable principle of distribution in a circumstance defined by moderate scarcity. It is *not* bourgeois because, at
the same time it issues proportionate rewards, it assumes social
ownership and it strictly circumscribes the range of tolerable inequalities. Thus the principle is rigorously egalitarian.

The market and socialist justice

Is the market compatible with the egalitarian and compensatory
principles of socialist justice? It is if it operates against the background of socialist institutions. As we have seen, the great inequalities of capitalist society stem from its *class structure*. Exploitation is not the consequence of the market *per se,* but of the use of
the market in capitalist society, that is, a society divided into
classes of owners and workers. If the market mechanism were put
to work in a society where the means of production were publicly
owned and where workers controlled the polity and the enterprise, the use of the market need not interfere with the realization
of egalitarian norms of distribution. As already noted, there is no
logical connection between the operation of free markets and the
capitalist ownership of productive facilities. In market socialism,
labor-managed enterprises functioning under market conditions
are neither the property of capitalists nor of the workers who
utilize them. The enterprises belong to society. The right to control the enterprises, vested in their workers, stops short of the
license to hold or sell shares in them; the purchase and sale of
equity shares is nonexistent in market socialism. It is true that the
categories of profit, rent, and interest exist in market socialism,
but these serve solely as accounting prices or efficiency indicators,

providing for a meaningful calculation or rational disposition of resources by indicating their relative scarcity as well as the relative preference of consumers for different products. For example, interest might be charged by banks scheduled for investment by enterprises, but the price assessed on loans would not take the form of an income paid to private owners. The same applies to profit and rent. Profit serves as an evaluator of enterprise efficiency and signals the direction in which future investment will be allocated, but profit is not distributed to shareholders and will affect the distribution of income only if it meets the requirements of egalitarian income policies. The state under socialism, by enacting a variety of redistributive policies stipulated by egalitarian values, prevents a situation from developing in which income differentials exceed an acceptable point. Centrally planned taxation schemes and social welfare provisions operate to institutionalize egalitarian norms of distribution.

This means that the use of market devices does not necessitate material incentives dictated by bourgeois values. Simply, if workers in a socialist society agree to implement egalitarian principles of distributive justice,[7] if politics are in command, then whatever inegalitarian tendencies that are inherent in an unmitigated market distribution will be offset by the redistributional activity of the state. The more efficient workers, including those grouped within the same enterprises, after the redistribution policies have taken their toll, will not be much better off than their less efficient counterparts. Profit making under such an arrangement cannot function as a *motivating* force of production precisely because all workers are in agreement that no individual or group should expect extraordinary benefits as a result of their greater market performance. It is nonetheless true that the idea of profit making looms large in market socialism, but only insofar as it works to let society know where an efficient allocation of resources lies. In market socialism profit does not constitute an incentive to work but serves only as a measure of efficiency. Horvat casts some light on this point in his discussion of the price of labor. He distinguishes between gross and net wages of labor, the gross wage reflecting the marginal productivity of labor and the net wage determined by a political decision consistent with social expectations as to what wage scale constitutes fairness. "The difference between the gross wages and the net wages represents rent which is taxed away by the Planning Authority. One may say that net wage-rates represent the supply price of labor, while the gross wage-rates are its demand price." (1964, p. 130). In the interest of efficiency, it is important that workers seek to maximize the gross wage even though they receive only the politically determined net or fair wage. In this way, justice holds sway in the sphere of distribution while efficiency reigns in the sphere of production. In market socialism the market is used to allocate resources but not to distribute wealth and power.[8] Accordingly, the use of the market is perfectly compatible with the egalitarian and compensatory principles of socialist justice. Of course, material incentives of a bourgeois sort *may* be used in combination with market arrangements, just as they *have* been used in command-type economies, but it should be clear that the decision to rely on such incentives depends on factors other than methods chosen for purposes of allocation.

The market required by socialist justice

It is one thing to argue that the market is compatible with socialism, another that socialist justice *requires* the market. My aim is to defend the stronger claim, and I want to raise some difficult questions about this issue as it relates to the transition to communist society.

Communism defines a society in which the fragmentation of labor has been largely eliminated, individuals are able and willing to realize their unique capacities in the productive process, and the distribution of goods proceeds according to the maxim: To each according to his/her needs, from each according to his/her abilities. Under communism, consumption goods are produced by socially owned enterprises and distributed equally in response to individual need. Equal need satisfaction, of course, entails an unequal distribution of goods because people presumably have different needs and wants of varying intensity. As Mandel states: "It is the full development of the *inequality* among people, of the inequality of their aspirations and potentialities, the inequality of their personalities, that emerges as the aim of communism" (1968, Vol. 2, p. 673). Unequal needs can find equal satisfaction because, under communism, there are more goods available than there are claims for these goods; that is, communism is defined by a circumstance of superabundance. Because there is a complete absence of money, prices, and wages, goods are made available "free for the taking." "Payments" made to individuals bear no connection to what individuals have given in exchange. *All* consumption goods are publicly provided, neither rationed nor purchased by individual wages in a market situation. Mandel tries to clarify what is involved here by distinguishing between individual and social wages, noting that the social wage "foreshadows, at least potentially, the mode of distribution of the future, that is, of an economy directed towards satisfying the needs of all individuals" (1968, Vol. 2, p. 657). Already, in both capitalist and socialist societies, there has appeared the social wage or dividend. Instead of individually purchasing education, medical care, municipal transportation, street lighting, and so on, these goods are provided publicly; that is, individuals pay for these goods collectively through taxes and receive them "gratis" as a social wage or dividend. "The social wage is thus the *socialization of the cost* of satisfying a certain number of needs for all citizens" (Mandel, 1968, Vol. 2, p. 657). Under communism *all* costs would be socialized, or as present-day "welfare economists" would put it, all goods would become "public." This would not square with socialist principles of distributive justice, which call for compensatory payment. This issue becomes inconsequential, because communist society is *beyond* justice.[9]

If socialism is a *transitional* interval, then compensatory principles of justice must gradually give way to communist principles of distribution. Individuals in a socialist society must consent to the substitution of the collective provision of goods for their individual purchase in a market. Sherman points out that this substitution would be piecemeal. Prices of basic necessities would be lowered slowly while noting the reaction of demand to price changes. If demand is fairly inelastic, that is, if demand fails to shoot up as prices are reduced, prices can eventually be lowered to zero. The lowering of prices and their eventual disappearance would be paid for by lowering the money wages paid to individual workers in exchange for their work, by substituting a social wage for an individual wage. For example, instead of a worker receiving twenty dollars daily, he/she might receive eighteen dollars, but his/her bread, salt, and fish would be "free" for the taking at consumer goods outlets. Sherman is aware of the difficulties involved in this substitution: "Obviously, in the continuing expansion of the free public goods sector, each marginal choice is a vital and controversial social decision. It would be imperative to make it as democratically as possible" (1972, p. 342).

Just what is the nature of this difficulty? Simply that the *move* to communism entails not the mere bypassing of socialist distributive principles but their *violation* under circumstances (moderate scarcity) that continue to call for their application. Compensatory principles require rewards proportional to the duration, intensity, difficulty, unenjoyability, risk, etc., involved in different jobs. But the extension of the public goods sector impinges on socialist justice because it upsets this system of proportional rewards designed to govern distribution during the transition period. The increased provision of collective goods in a situation of moderate scarcity compels some individuals to subsidize the unwanted benefits that others desire while necessarily subtracting from the range of want satisfaction available to the former. And to the extent that compensatory principles establish just incentives to work, their attenuation may bring about a slackening in the productive effort to create the material preconditions of communist society. Thus we are faced with a clear-cut opposition between socialist and communist principles, and one that may affect the very likelihood of attaining the goal of communism.

At the minimum, socialist justice prescribes a market in consumption goods. It might be argued as well that socialist justice requires a market in production goods because consumer preferences would of necessity play a large part in determining the direction of production. Furthermore, if individuals are to be compensated for productive contribution as *fully* as possible, and if the market possesses the advantage of efficiency, the case can be made that the market is desirable as an allocative mechanism because it best satisfies the demand that individuals be compensated at a maximum level. But, says Sherman, "a socialist economy, in which payment for consumer necessities is required, reinforces and produces competitiveness in people every day" (1972, p. 343). This is because, according to Mandel, "the continued existence of money and commodity economy in itself *implies* the survival of the phenomenon of *universal 'mercinariness' of life* . . ." (1968, vol. 2, p. 655). Assuming for the moment the truth of these claims, the infraction of socialist justice may be justified by appealing to moral principles of a different order. Justice, after all, is not the sole value and must find accommodation with other, perhaps more important, moral imperatives. Crucial to the moral vision of socialists, built into their picture of the good society, is the elimination of competitiveness, the promotion of social cooperation, and the disappearance of alienation. These aims, ranking first on the scale of socialist values, of necessity override the precedence of justice; only if justice is mitigated can communism be attained, and only under communism can the good life be actualized. Socialist justice may require the market, but more important communist values call for its gradual supercession.

This is fine, as far as it goes, but we should be aware of the profound difficulties, logical and historical, that complicate the move from justice to communism. There is the logical or theoretical problem of reconciling the gradual implementation of communist principles during the transition period with the compensatory type of justice advocated for this period. And there is the historical or motivation problem, for if, as Sherman and Mandel assert, competitiveness and "mercinariness" continue to exist in socialist society, what would prompt its members to execute a program gradually abolishing the commodity production to which both writers attribute these lingering evils? Each decision to substitute public for private goods would test the commitment of socialist citizens to build a communist society and in the course of that construction to surrender the practice of compensating workers in accord with labor performed, and this in a circumstance defined by a moderate scarcity that fosters competitiveness and acquisitiveness! Mandel believes that "it is necessary *first* to see the withering away of money economy through the production of an abundance of goods before the psychological and cultural revolution can fully manifest itself, and a new socialist consciousness bloom in place of the egoist mentality of the 'old Adam' " (1968, vol. 2, p. 655). But surely Mandel has put things in reverse order. The phasing out of commodity producton is not an automatic process, but the result of an undetermined conscious strategy deployed by socialist citizens to overcome the survivals of the capitalist past and to build a new society in conformity with communist ideals. Money and the market are eliminated gradually through a series of "vital and controversial decisions" to extend the public sector, decisions that cannot be the mechanical reflex of a money-market society because, if determinism held, these decisions would be precluded altogether. Without communist ideals occupying a determining place in the transition to the good society, the step-by-step substitution of public for private goods could very well exacerbate the spirit of egoism and envy. We have seen that such substitution effects a redistribution of scarce goods while violating compensatory principles of social justice. Whether there is a market in goods *or* goods are publicly provided, their distribution proceeds under circumstances of scarcity that lay the basis for a competitive scramble. In *this* sense, collective provision holds no advantage over market distribution during the transition period.

Why then the Marxian emphasis on dismantling the market in favor of collective provision and planned allocation? The answer lies in Marx's theory that alienated labor and the market system are inextricably connected. The theme is pervasive in Marx that under communism purposive social control or "conscious regulation in accordance with a settled plan" replaces the autonomy of the market. The market, commodity production, the use of money, and so on, create a "mystical veil" that covers social reality, personifying objects and reifying humans, and transform labor into a *means* for satisfying needs when creative labor itself should be life's prime need. Thus Marx assumed that "the return of man himself as a social, i.e., really human being" can transpire only in a marketless world. Is this assumption warranted?

Alienation and the market

Pursuing a theme introduced in the discussion of justice and the market, this section will suggest that it is the class structure of production, not the market mechanism, that is primarily responsible for alienated labor. This suggestion controverts a contention based on a popular distortion of Marx's theory – the idea that market *efficiency* must necessarily conflict with unalienated labor; it also questions Marx's hypothesis that commodity-producing labor must be alienated labor, that is, the theory of "commodity fetishism."

Market efficiency and alienated labor

Frank Roosevelt (1969) has argued forcefully that market social-ism is a bourgeois idea because it sacrifices work to consumption; that is, it subordinates the satisfaction derivable from work to the efficient production of commodities scheduled for consumption. The market cuts the tie between production and consumption and transforms work into an instrument geared to the maximiza-tion of consumptive utility. The benefits of work are sought outside of work. Labor is "forced," says Marx, and "therefore not the satisfaction of a need; it is merely a *means* to satisfy needs external to it" (1964b, p. 111). Marx understands work or cre-ative activity as "life's principal need," the gratification of which makes it possible for people to express their personalities, objec-tify their inner needs and talents, in short, to realize their human nature. Furthermore, one of Marx's most penetrating criticisms of the capitalist market centers on its possessive individualism and antagonism to community life. Marx uses the concept "capi-talist society" not only to express his condemnation of a social system based on inherent injustice, but also to describe the struc-ture of social order in which some attributes of the communal organization of previous societies no longer exist. In such a soci-ety, at least in its "pure" form, individuals become so isolated and egoistic that they establish contact only when they can use each other as means to particular ends. Communal bonds get supplanted by contractual associations entered into by utility-maximizing individuals. The classical liberals, for instance, made extensive use of a metaphor picturing human society as a vast trading company with each of its members a merchant. More recently, Milton Friedman thought it useful to allude to children as "consumer goods." "The freedom of individuals to use their economic resources as they want includes the freedom to use them to have children – to buy, as it were, the services of children as a particular form of consumption" (1962, p. 33).

Roosevelt's point is that the market mechanism, whether em-ployed in a capitalist or socialist environment, is biased in favor of efficiency to the detriment of humanized work and nonalienated social relations. Not only does efficiency require an enslaving subjection to the division of labor but it lessens the likelihood of community by accentuating the narrowly defined role of *homo economicus* and demanding a high degree of worker mobility organized along vertical lines. The very logic of the market entails the alienation of people from their work and from each other:

> . . . under market conditions a minority of the workers in any industry – perhaps even one enterprise – can impose its preferences on all the rest. All it takes is one firm to choose the more efficient autocratic method of organization, say by signing a Hobbesian type of social contract, and all the other firms must follow suit – or find themselves driven out of business. Thus there seems to be a built-in tendency for a market economy – whether capitalist or socialist – to promote greater efficiency at the expense of humane working conditions whenever the two goals conflict. [Roosevelt, 1969, p. 18]

So goes Roosevelt's critique, which ostensibly takes as its source of inspiration the insight of Marx and the recent prognoses of social philosophers who still think it is important to emphasize the potential benefits of humanizing the work process. Among these prognosticators is Daniel Bell, whom Roosevelt claims has offered an analysis of productivity and work that resembles that of Marx (1969, p. 15). Marx and Bell, however, could not be further apart on the subject of alienation and efficiency, and it is in the radical difference between the two that we can proceed to uncover the essential weakness of Roosevelt's position.

Bell numbers among those bourgeois ideologists who have adopted an attitude of pessimism and highbrow disdain toward certain facts of "advanced industrial society." These facts are expressions of what Bell terms the three "technologics" created by modern industry: the logic of size, the logic of "metric" time, and the logic of hierarchy (1960, p. 225). Each of the three is the product of "engineering rationality" required by "the sociological fact of increased supervision which every complex enterprise demands" (1960, p. 225, 229). Bell explains the huge size of enterprises and the centralization of employment as a consequence of the engineer's belief that large-scale production, conditioned by the development of energy resources, is technologically efficacious. He then attributes to "the inexorable logic of rationalization" the labor regimen so carefully worked out by Frederick Taylor and other theorists of "scientific management." Taylorism, fostering the specialization of labor, the detailed fragmentation of work and the collapsing of skilled labor into simple, repetitive, and easily measurable labor (abstract labor?), is in Bell's view a kind of "social physics" in the service of heightened productivity. The atomization of the work force in turn creates the need for bureaucratic organization staffed by technical coordinators and headed by management; workers whose skills have been downgraded and whose labor has been reduced to the performance of narrow and predetermined tasks *require* hierarchical direction. "Under a complex division of labor these tasks pass out of his control, and he must rely on management to see that they are properly done. This dependence extends along the entire process of production" (Bell, 1960, p. 229).

Bell caps his thesis of the three logics of modern industry by noting their convergence "in that great achievement of industrial technology, the assembly line: the long parallel lines require huge shed space; the detailed breakdown of work imposes a set of mechanically paced and specified motions; the degree of coordination creates new technical, as well as social, hierarchies" (1960, p. 229).

Contrast this to what Braverman says about the assembly line in his Marxist analysis of the labor process under capitalism:

The chief advantage of the industrial assembly line is the control it affords over the pace of labor, and as such it is extremely useful to owners and managers whose interests are at loggerheads with those of their workers. From a technical point of view, it is extraordinarily primitive and has little to do with "modern machine technology." [1974, p. 232]

Braverman arrives at different conclusions about the assembly line because he has not succumbed to any of the prevailing forms of technological determinism. It is not the "logic" of technology, machines, or modernity that is reponsible for alienated labor, but the uses to which technology is put (or *not* put) and the shape it assumes in the *capitalist* mode of production. "Within the historical and analytical limits of capitalism, according to Marx's analysis, technology, instead of simply *producing* social relations, is *produced by* the social relations represented by capital" (Braverman, 1974, p. 20). The notion that machines and "the requirements of efficiency" determine the organization of work under capitalism is

143

actually a reification of the social relations peculiar to capitalism, "nothing but a *fetishism,* in Marx's sense of the term" (Braverman, 1974, p. 229). It is, of course, a convenient fetish for bourgeois thinkers because it lets capitalism off the hook, absolves it of special blame, and shifts castigation in the direction of empty abstraction.

Bell's "logics of modern industry" are in fact the logics of capitalism. The centralization of labor in large-scale production units has its historical genesis not only in the "engineer's concern with efficiency," but principally in the aim of capitalist management to enforce greater discipline over a "free" labor force. Precapitalist productive units, being scattered and allowing producers a considerable degree of autonomy over their work, made it difficult for the capitalist to impose effective supervision over the pace and intensity of work. Bringing workers under a single roof provided capitalists the spatial prerequisite for establishing the tightest possible reins of control over the labor process. "It was not that the new arrangement was 'modern,' or 'large,' or 'urban' which created the new situation, but rather the new social relations which now frame the production process, and the antagonism between those who carry on the process and those for whose benefit it is carried on . . ." (Braverman, 1974, pp. 68–9). Likewise, "scientific management" is not so much a logical outgrowth of industrial technology as it is an attempt to selectively apply the methods of science to the problem of the control of labor in complex capitalist enterprises. Historically, the impulse behind the superfragmentation of work was the capitalists' concern with cheapening the price of labor. The reason for the rapid spread and intensification of the division of labor was that "labor power [could be] purchased more cheaply as dissociated elements than as a capacity integrated into a single worker" (Braverman, 1974, pp. 79–80). The reduction of labor to its simplest form also worked to strip laborers of their power to acquire any modicum of dominion over the entire production process, thus ensuring that management possessed a near monopoly of information and "technique" to execute its plans of production. Taylorism assigns the functions of conception to the brains of management and the task of mindless execution to an increasingly subdivided body of workers. In this way, as Gintis points out, "capitalists can avoid workers gain-

ing enough general expertise and initiative to embark on cooperative production on their own, or to challenge the hegemony of
capitalists in the factory or office" (1974, p. 14; see also Bowles
and Gintis, 1975, and Marglin, 1974).

There is an intimate connection, then, between the atomization
of the work force and the imperative of capitalist domination. The
stratification of roles into managers and managed and the fragmentation of tasks go hand in hand, with the *former* assuming the
determining place. It is the class or power relations of capitalist
society that underpin the technological structure of capitalist production and that come to harness and eventually block the path of
the further development of the forces of production. It is presumably this idea that stands behind Braverman's assertion that the
assembly line is an instance of backward technology and primarily
a method employed by captialists to maintain their dominant social position. It is a form of production compatible with the reproduction of class privilege but hardly likely to unleash the liberating
types of technology that would accompany the all-around development of productive forces. Not efficiency, but control is the
watchword of capitalist production, and the former will usually
lose out to the latter in the event of conflict (see Zimbalist,
1975).[10]

Marx and Engels explicitly view the development of the forces
of production under capitalism as bringing with it the arrival of
the *potential* to revolutionize the nature of work. Marx speaks of
the tendency toward the abolition of the division of labor in modern industry and recognizes that this tendency can be realized only
with the revolutionary transformation of capitalist relations of
production.

By means of machinery, chemical processes and other methods, it
[modern industry] is continually causing changes not only in the technical basis of production, but also in the functions of the laborer, and in the
social combinations of the labor process. At the same time, it thereby
also revolutionizes the division of labor within the society, and incessantly launches masses of capital and of workpeople from one branch to
another. Modern industry, by its very nature, therefore necessitates variation of labor, fluency of function, universal mobility of the laborer . . .
Modern industry . . . through its catastrophes imposes the necessity of
reorganizing, as a fundamental law of production, variation of work,
consequently fitness of the laborer for varied work, consequently the

greatest possible development of his varied aptitudes. It becomes a question of life and death for society to adopt the mode of production to the normal functioning of this law. Modern industry, indeed, compels society, under penalty of death, to replace the detail worker of today, crippled by lifelong repetition of one and the same trivial operation, and thus reduced to the mere fragment of a man, by the fully developed individual, fit for a variety of labors, ready to face any change of production, and to whom the different social functions he performs, are but so many modes of giving free scope to his own natural and acquired powers. [Marx, 1909, vol. 1, pp. 532–4]

Engels comments on these passages in *Anti-Duhring:*

Once more, only the abolition of the capitalist character of modern industry can bring us out of this new vicious circle, can resolve this contradiction in modern industry [between capitalist relations and the requirements of modern industry] which is constantly reproducing itself . . . Certainly, to be able to see that the revolutionary elements which will do away with the old division of labor, along with the separation of town and country, and will revolutionize the whole of production; see that these elements are already contained in embryo in the production conditions of modern large-scale industry and that their development is hindered by the existing capitalist mode of production – to be able to see these things . . . it is necessary to have some knowledge of real large-scale industry in its historical growth and in its present actual form, especially in the one country where it has its home and where alone it has attained its classical development. [Engels, 1947, pp. 441, 443–4]

All of this suggests that there is something seriously defective about the idea that efficiency must necessarily conflict with unalienated labor. The idea turns out to be a corollary of the general theory of technological determinism, a theory that finds little historical support and that rests on the inversion of the relationship between class power and technology. Theoretically, we have little reason to draw the conclusion that technological advance and allocative efficiency rule out the effective democratic organization of work, the breakdown of the fragmentation of labor and the corresponding demystification of technology, and working conditions conducive to the well being and happiness of human beings.[11] There is considerable theoretic appeal in Horvat's contention that workers' control and market efficiency are mutually reinforcing, that administrative planning at the macrolevel and hierarchical relations within the enterprise "exert a depressing effect on individual performers, stifle initiative, undermine the will to work, cause resistance, in short, lower labor efficiency" (1964, pp. 117–18). Empirically, the balance of evidence points to a positive correlation between efficiency and unalienated labor, although in light of the limited number of studies available on the subject and the rather troublesome methodological problems involved, the question is far from being conclusively resolved. Yet Blumberg's extensive survey of the empirical literature on alienation and participation yields this promising conclusion: "there is hardly a study in the entire literature which fails to demonstrate that satisfaction in work is enhanced or that other generally acknowledged beneficial consequences [including increases in productivity] accrue from a genuine increase in workers' decision-making power" (1968, p. 123; see also Jenkins, 1974, and U.S. Dept. of HEW, 1973). Even those organization theorists who display a penchant for Weberian analysis grant that most studies fail to show that cooperative, participatory, and egalitarian organizational experiments negatively affect efficient performance (see Perrow, 1972).[12]

The market and "commodity fetishism"

In market socialism, workers control the workplace, utilize the state to uphold the background institutions that justice requires, and adopt market arrangements to secure the efficient allocation of resources. But, says Marx (1909, vol. 1, p. 84), goods produced for exchange by workers who "do not come into social contact with each other until they exchange their products" are bound to assume a fetishistic quality in the experience of the producers. Commodities take on an independent veneer standing opposed to labor "as an *alien being*, as a *power independent* of the producer" (Marx, 1964b, p. 108).

The product of labor is labor which has been embodied in an object and turned into a physical thing . . . The *alienation* of the worker in his product means not only that his labor becomes an object . . . but that it exists independently . . . and that it stands opposed to him as an autonomous power. [Marx, 1964b, p. 108]

The failure to comprehend the world of commodities as the product of human labor, the inability to pierce the "mystical veil" that shrouds the real social relations underlying the forms of commodity production, has as a consequence the domination of human beings ("living labor") by the products of labor ("dead labor"). Social relations themselves appear as relations among commodities or things, alienating people from each other, transforming specifically human relations into narrowly conceived role relations. Marx is clear that fetishism "attaches itself to the products of labor as soon as they are produced as commodities, and which is therefore inseparable from the production of commodities" (1909, p. 83). Commodity production, simple or capitalist, causes alienation.

Now what of the claim that the *market* is a (although not the singular) cause of much of this? In market socialism, workers participate in decision making on the basis of equality, move to break down the fragmentation of labor, and operate as cooperatives on the enterprise level. The labor of workers is therefore not "forced," and they are able to derive satisfaction both from the work process and from the products produced for the enjoyment of themselves and others in society. The relation of labor to the act of production is not alienated because the productive relations have been stripped of their capitalist integument. The class obstacles to rewarding work having been removed, workers can proceed to develop freely their mental and physical energies, feel at home at work, and carry on a life of "free, conscious activity." If, at any level of the development of technology, there remain tasks that by their very nature cannot offer satisfaction, their performance can be rotated or workers who opt to perform them can be compensated with larger incomes or status. At any rate, it is not the market under socialism, but technological inadequacy, that is responsible for the existence of such tasks, and there is no reason to believe that most work under socialism must fall outside the "realm of freedom." There is much to Marcuse's claim that under socialist productive relations and availed of class-liberated technologies

the realm of necessity will in fact be changed and we will perhaps be able to regard the qualities of free human existence, which Marx and Engels still had to assign to the realm beyond labor, as developing within the realm of labor itself. The rational application of the material and intellec-

148

tual forces of transformation are technically at hand although their rational application is prevented by the existing [capitalist] organization of the forces of production. [Marcuse, 1970, pp. 72, 64]

Not the market, but class structure and class-determined technological misdevelopment, are responsible for alienated labor.

It is true that in market socialism workers produce for exchange and not directly for use, but why *must* production under such an arrangement result in alienated labor, false consciousness, and the estrangement of individuals from one another? Even in a planned economy, regulated by the "whole community," most consumptive goods are exchanged for wages, and wages are exchanged for productive contribution, although because net wages are politically determined (as they are in market socialism), labor itself is not a full-fledged commodity. Perhaps the Marxian argument is that people must be alienated short of fully satisfying their material and psychological needs and that the scarcity of precommunist societies precludes this. But then the problem lies with scarcity, not the market, and it is not at all clear that scarcity implies alienated labor or interpersonal estrangement. If socialist citizens come to some agreement on principles of distributive justice, principles that "provide a way of assigning rights and duties in the basic institutions of society and define the appropriate distribution of the benefits and burdens of social cooperation" (Rawls, 1971, p. 4), the problem of scarcity could be handled fairly and to mutual advantage, delimiting the incidences of competitiveness, envy, and selfishness. Mandel's apparent belief that scarcity is at the basis of egoism implies his acceptance of the view that most people in societies of scarcity (including socialism) are not capable of a sense of justice (1968, vol. 2, p. 668). The plausibility of this view is certainly open to question, suggesting as it does that human nature, previous to communist society, is essentially what Hobbes said it is.

It would seem that if workers succeed in supplanting capitalist control with socialist productive relations they would at the same time abolish the class basis of "commodity fetishism." With the transformation of work and other spheres of social life (e.g., education, community, and political organization), is there any reason to believe that market operation need generate "false consciousness," casting a fog over the social character of production, and subjecting producers to its sway? In market socialism, the working community freely chooses, with a thorough and reasoned comprehension of the automatic workings of market arrangements, to rely on those arrangements for the purpose of allocating economic resources. The idea that production for exchange *must* engender false consciousness is a metaphysical "must," based on a confusion between productive relations and modes of allocation, ruling out *a priori* the distinct analytical fact and historical possibility of diminished alienation in market socialism.

Does workers' democracy require the market?

I began this chapter by focusing on relevant aspects of the recent Cambridge controversies in the theory of capital. This allowed me to show that neither labor nor marginal theories of the market count as theories of exploitation. Following Lange (1968), I derived the Marxian conception of exploitation from an account of the class structure of bourgeois society, a conception that stands independently of the truth or falsity of the labor theory of value. Next, I brought out the ethical assumptions underlying Marx's theory of exploitation and showed them as resting on a sense of justice comprised of compensatory and egalitarian principles. Having demonstrated that the market, as an allocative device, is perfectly compatible with these principles, I then argued that market socialism – the use of market arrangements against the background of socialist productive relations – is required by these principles. This line of argument called into question the consistency of Marx's sense of justice, on the one hand, and his unyielding opposition to the market, on the other, and resolved the inconsistency in favor of the market. Finally, I located the source of Marx's antagonism to the market in his theory of alienation and dealt with the claims that (1) market *efficiency* must necessarily conflict with unalienated labor, and (2) "commodity fetishism" as a form of alienation need be a result of commodity-producing labor. I maintained that the first claim is false and, incidentally, non-Marxist, and that insofar as Marx attributes alienation to the market, he fails to make good on his theory of "commodity fetishism." My argument has thus emerged as both an account of Marx's sense of justice and a defense of market socialism.

The tension between Marx's antagonism to market arrangements and other important aspects of his theory appears also in a consideration of Marx's concept of revolution and the place he assigns to the proletariat as the ruling class under socialism. Selucky (1975) has argued that the rejection of the market is incompatible with the concept of self-managing economic systems. "Any consistently nonmarket economy must be by definition: centralized; run by command plan; controlled by a handful of planners rather than by workers themselves; based on manipulation of producers by the planning board" (1975, p. 58). The idea that the market is *necessary* to sustain workers' democracy under socialism goes beyond the scope of my argument, and it would be inappropriate to introduce an additional and controversial thesis. However, Selucky's treatment of the relation of Marxist theory to the idea of the market is of considerable relevance to a defense of market socialism. He notes that if Marx's account of the market "had been meant seriously, it by no means favors any self-managing economic socialist system," and that "the concept of self-management could not be either accepted or rejected without a substantial revision of the original Marxist theory" (1975, pp. 58, 60). Selucky sees a contradiction in Marx's theory: Marx calls for workers' democracy, control of the political economy by the "direct producers," but Marx iterates the need for central planning, which (to Selucky) entails bureaucratic domination. Selucky concludes that "the Marxist concept of the market is far less important for the whole doctrine than is the Marxist concept of revolution" (1975, p. 61). Workers' ownership and control, socialist justice, the historical role of the proletariat are of greater significance in Marx's scheme of things than his critique of the market, and if the former cannot be reconciled with the latter, then the latter must go. Selucky states the point forcefully:

In order to overcome the key contradiction within the Marxist theory, a revision of original Marxist doctrine is unavoidable. Admitting this we suggest that the revision of the Marxist concept of the market is less harmful to the whole doctrine than the revision of the rest." [1975, p. 61]

Notes

1 Paul Samuelson, for example, wishes to leave it to "the citizenry to ultimately decide moral issues" and, presumably, he hopes the "citizenry" defaults to the "expert" in the matter of "pointing out the feasible alternatives and the true costs that may be involved in different decisions" (1964, p. 8).

2 In contrast to precapitalist societies, this payment proceeds automatically, "invisibly," and without deliberation, because the nature of capitalist production tends to obscure the division of the working day into necessary and surplus labor time.

3 According to James Weinstein (1968, p. 40), from 1880 to 1900 an estimated 700,000 workers were killed and 10,720,000 injured in U.S. industry. According to HEW (1973), some 14,000 workers died in industrial accidents in 1968, 90,000 suffered permanent impairment, 2,100,000 suffered total but temporary disability, and an untold number contracted an assortment of occupational diseases ranging from heart and lung disorders to deafness and hypertension.

4 These passages assist in clarifying Marx's treatment of "fair distribution" in *Critique of the Gotha Programme*. Marx rejects the "fair distribution" (the social fairness of capitalist political economy) of bourgeois apologists as so much "verbal rubbish," and although he is understandably impatient with utopians who propose principles that have no chance of implementation at given stages of economic and cultural development, he does not reject the idea of justice or its compensatory component (for support of this interpretation, see Van De Veer, 1973). The claim is mistaken that Marx provides a purely descriptive or sociological treatment of justice, that he limits himself to explicating the content of the norms of distribution mirrored by different modes of production. On this account, "the Marxian critique of justice may be viewed as an attempt to clarify the role of the concept of justice in social life and to prevent its ideological abuse" (Wood, 1972, p. 245), but Marx is not understood as issuing any first-order moral judgment of capitalism as unjust. This relativistic reading of Marx has it that capitalism *is* just because "it accords with the juridical or moral rules and practices which govern distribution" in that particular mode of production (Wood, 1972, p. 268). Against this interpretation, I maintain that Marx's characterization of capitalism as exploitative implies a theory of justice; it is a clear case of taking issue with the distributive norms of bourgeois political economy and rendering a negative assessment of them. Marx is saying that bourgeois "fairness" is not fair. Hanna Pitkin refers to such terms as "fairness," "legitimacy," "obligation," "authority," etc., as performing performative functions. To say that something is fair is to adopt a position toward it, not to say merely that something is commonly considered fair by other individuals employing the term. See Pitkin's critique of Weber's use of the term "legitimacy" (Pitkin, 1972, pp. 280–6).

5 When Tawney said (1953, p. 39) that "the last of the Schoolmen was Karl Marx" he had in mind the medieval concern that tied social reward to the performance of social function.

6 Of course, nothing prevents workers who undergo greater disutility from voluntarily contributing their surplus labor. Altruism is a noble practice and is encouraged under socialism, but it is not enforced. On the distinction between justice and altruism, see J. O. Urmson (1958).

7 In the *model* of market socialism, workers *would* agree. I am not concerned here with the *historical* problem of getting workers to substitute egalitarian for bourgeois ideas of justice.

8 The idea that the market be employed to efficiently allocate resources while at the same time utilizing a socialist norm of distribution is in no way at odds with Marx's insistence that production and distribution are two sides of a single economic process in which production assumes the dominant and determining place. Marx argues that "to treat production apart from the distribution which is comprised in it, is plainly an idle abstraction," and he derides the "insipidity of the economists who treat production as an eternal truth and banish history to the domain of distribution" (1904, p. 286). For Marx, "distribution is itself a product of production . . . since the definite manner of participation in production determines the form under which participation in distribution takes place" (1904, p. 284). Marx's criticism was prompted by J. S. Mill's abstraction of the laws of distribution from the relations of production. Mill expresses the idea that "the laws and conditions of the production of wealth partake of the character of physical truths," whereas the distribution of wealth is "a matter of human institution only" (1864, pp. 257–8).

9 As the ingenious Rawls writes: A society of superabundance "in which all can achieve their complete good, or in which there are no conflicting demands and the wants of all fit together without coercion into a harmonious plan of activity, is a society in a certain sense beyond justice. It has eliminated the occasions when the appeal to the principles of right and justice is necessary" (1971, p. 281). Nicholas Rescher writes: ". . . the workings of the concept of distributive justice are a function of scarcity . . . In an economy of superabundance where everyone has all that he needs and wants, the question of distributive justice no longer arises" (1966, p. 107).

10 The same can probably be said about the Soviet system. Of course, to the extent that it *can* be truthfully said, the USSR is distinctly not socialist. I am struck by the applicability of the argument of the theorists of "totalitarianism" – that "totalitarian" control goes hand in hand with the fragmentation of the labor force – to the economic dimension of capitalist society.

11 Similarly, little theoretical support can be accorded to another platitude in the stock of conservative metaphysics – the idea that there "must" exist a conflict between efficiency and an egalitarian distribution of income. For one of the most recent expositions of this view by an economist and Wall Street consultant, see Arthur Okun's *Equality and Efficiency: The Big Tradeoff.* The title tells it all.

12 For a good survey of the literature on worker participation, see Greenberg (1975), and Tautsky (1970).

References

Bell, Daniel (1960). "Work and Its Discontents: The Cult of Efficiency in America." In Daniel Bell, *The End of Ideology*. Glencoe, Ill.: Free Press.

Blumberg, Paul (1968). *Industrial Democracy: The Sociology of Participation*. London: Constable.

Bowles, Samuel and Gintis, Herbert (1975). "Class Power and Alienated Labor." *Monthly Review* 26.

Braverman, Harry (1974). *Labor and Monopoly Capital*. New York: Monthly Review.

Dobb, Maurice (1960). *Political Economy and Capitalism*, 2d, rev. ed. London: Routledge and Kegan Paul.

　(1947). *Studies in the Development of Capitalism*. New York: International Publishers.

Engels, Friedrich (1967). "Articles from *The Labour Standard*." In W. O. Henderson, ed., *Engels: Selected Writings*. New York: Penguin.

　(1947). *Herr Eugen Duhring's Revolution in Science*. Moscow: Foreign Languages Publishing House.

Friedman, Milton (1962). *Capitalism and Freedom*. Chicago: University of Chicago Press.

Gintis, Herbert (1972). "Alienation and Power." *Review of Radical Political Economics* 4.

Gordon, Scott (1968). "Why Does Marxian Exploitation Theory Require a Labor Theory of Value?" *Journal of Political Economy* 76.

Greenberg, Edward (1975). "The Consequences of Worker Participation: A Clarification of the Theoretical Literature." *Social Science Quarterly* 56.

Hollis, Martin and Nell, Edward (1975). *Rational Economic Man: A Philosophical Critique of Neo-Classical Economics*. Cambridge: Cambridge University Press.

Horvat, Branko (1964). *Towards A Theory of Planned Economy*. Belgrade: Yugoslav Institute of Economic Research.

Hunt, E. K., and Schwartz, Jesse, eds. (1972). *A Critique of Economic Theory*. New York: Penguin.

　and Sherman, Howard (1972). "Value, Alienation, and Distribution." *Science and Society* 36.

Jenkins, David (1974). *Job Power: Blue and White Collar Democracy*. Baltimore: Heinemann.

Lange, Oskar and Taylor, Fred M. *On the Economic Theory of Socialism*. Minneapolis: University of Minnesota Press.

Lange, Oskar (1968). "Marxian Economics and Modern Economic Theory." In David Horowitz, ed., *Marx and Modern Economics*. New York: Modern Reader Paperbacks.

Lebowitz, Michael A. (1974). "The Current Crisis of Economic Theory." *Science and Society* 37.

154

Leontiev, A. (n.d.). *Political Economy*. New York: International Publishers.

Macpherson, Crawford Brough (1962). *The Political Theory of Possessive Individualism*. London: Oxford University Press.

Mandel, Ernest (1968). *Marxist Economic Theory*, 2 vols. New York: Monthly Review.

Marcuse, Herbert (1970). *Five Lectures*. Boston: Beacon Press.

Marglin, Stephen (1974). "What Do Bosses Do?" *Review of Radical Political Economics* 6.

Marx, Karl (1906). *Capital*, 3 vols. Chicago: Kerr.

(1904). *A Contribution to the Critique of Political Economy*. Chicago: Kerr.

(1955). *Critique of the Gotha Programme*. In Marx and Engels, *Selected Works*, 2 vols. Moscow: Foreign Languages Publishing House.

(1971). *Theories of Surplus Value*, 3 vols. Moscow: Progress Publishers.

and Engels, Friedrich (1964a). *The German Ideology*. Moscow: Progress Publishers.

(1964b). *Economic and Philosophical Manuscripts of 1844*. New York: International Publishers.

Mayer, Kurt and Buckley, Walter (1970). *Class and Society*, 3d ed. New York: Random House.

Meade, James E. (1965). *Efficiency, Equality and the Ownership of Property*. Cambridge, Mass.: Harvard University Press.

Mill, John Stuart (1864). *Principles of Political Economy*, vol. 1, 5th ed. New York: Appleton.

Nell, Edward (1972a). "Property and the Means of Production: A Primer on the Cambridge Controversy." *Review of Radical Political Economics* 4. Reprinted in Warner Modular Publication, No. 511, 1973.

(1972b). "The Revival of Political Economy." *Social Research* 39.

O'Connor, James (1976). "A Note on Independent Commodity Production." *Monthly Review* 28.

Okun, Arthur (1975). *Equality and Efficiency: The Big Tradeoff*. Washington, D.C.: Brookings.

Ollman, Bertell (1971). *Alienation: Marx's Conception of Man in Capitalist Society*. Cambridge: Cambridge University Press.

Perrow, Charles (1972). *Complex Organizations: A Critical Essay*. Glenview, Ill.: Scott, Foresman.

Pitkin, Hannah (1972). *Wittgenstein and Justice*. Berkeley: University of California Press.

Rawls, John (1971). *A Theory of Justice*. Cambridge, Mass.: Harvard University Press.

Rescher, Nicholas (1966). *Distributive Justice: A Constructive Critique of the Utilitarian Theory of Distribution*. New York: Bobbs-Merrill.

Robinson, J. (1966). *An Essay on Marxian Economics*. 2d ed. London: Macmillan.

(1962). *Economic Philosophy*. Chicago: Aldine.

and Eatwell, J. (1973). *An Introduction to Modern Economics*. New York: McGraw-Hill.

Roosevelt, Frank (1969). "Market Socialism: A Humane Economy?" *Journal of Economic Issues* 3.

Samuelson, Paul (1964). *Economics: An Introductory Analysis*. 6th ed. New York: McGraw-Hill.

Selucky, R. (1975). "Marxism and Self-Management." In Jaroslav Vanek, ed., *Self-Management: Economic Liberation of Man*. New York: Penguin.

Sherman, Howard (1972). *Radical Political Economy*. New York: Basic Books.

Smith, Adam. (1910). *The Wealth of Nations*. vol. 1. London: J. M. Dent.

Sweezy, Paul (1942). *The Theory of Capitalist Development*. New York: Oxford University Press.

Tautsky, Curt (1970). *Work Organizations: Major Theoretical Perspectives*. Itasca, Ill.: Peacock.

Tawney, R. H. (1920). *The Acquisitive Society*. New York: Harcourt, Brace and World.

   (1950). *Religion and the Rise of Capitalism*. New York: Mentor.

U.S. Department of Health, Education, and Welfare. (1973). *Work in America*. Cambridge, Mass.: MIT Press.

Urmson, J. O. (1958). "Saints and Heroes." In A. I. Melden, ed., *Essays in Moral Philosophy*. Seattle: University of Washington Press.

Van De Veer, Donald. (1973). "Marx's View of Justice." *Philosophy and Phenomenological Research* 33.

Vanek, Jaroslav (1975). *Self-Management: Economic Liberation of Man*. New York: Penguin.

Vickrey, W. S. (1964). *Microstatistics*. New York: Harcourt, Brace and World.
   (1973). "An Exchange of Questions between Economics and Philosophy." In Edmund S. Phelps, ed., *Economic Justice*. New York: Penguin.

Weinstein, James (1968). *The Corporate Ideal in the Liberal State*. Boston: Beacon Press.

Wood, Allan W. (1972). "The Marxian Critique of Justice." *Philosophy and Public Affairs* 1.

Zimbalist, Andrew (1975). "The Limits of Work Humanization." *Review of Radical Political Economics* 7.

7

Marković on critical social theory and human nature

DAVID A. CROCKER

Introduction

For almost twenty years a group of Yugoslav philosophers and sociologists has been developing an independent, critical, and humanistic version of Marxism.[1] Commonly called "the Praxis Group" or Praxis Marxists because of the centrality in their thinking of the concept of praxis, these theorists have sought to understand and evaluate conditions in postwar Yugoslavia in the light of a humanistic interpretation of Marx and an original theory of democratic socialism. The result has been a critical social theory whose significance extends far beyond Yugoslavia. For, as a young student of the Praxis Group has recently stated:

If there is one central tenet of Praxis Marxism it is this: Marxism is pre-eminently a body of thought which is uncompromising in its rejection of all forms of human alienation, exploitation, oppression and injustice, regardless of the type of society – bourgeois or socialist – in which these phenomena occur.[2]

In the early sixties the Praxis Marxists initiated their approach by rejecting orthodox dialectical materialism in favor of an outlook and reading of Marx informed by Heidegger's existential ontology. Especially important in this initial phase was Gajo Petrović, Professor of Philosophy at the University of Zagreb and editor-in-chief of *Praxis*.[3] Petrović's book, *Marx in the Mid-Twentieth Century: A Yugoslav Philosopher Reconsiders Karl Marx's Writings,* was originally published in Yugoslavia in 1965 and appeared in English translation in 1967.[4] This volume introduced many Anglo-Americans to the new currents in Yugoslav thought.

In recent years the Praxis Group has become less interested in the exegesis of Marx's writing and less committed to an ahistorical, existential philosophical anthropology. Instead its members have sought to develop a critical social theory by which they could understand contemporary societies and confront social dilemmas. This development has increasingly involved the critique of sensitive aspects of Yugoslav society, such as "market socialism" and the bureaucratic and technocratic features of Yugoslav political institutions. Such social criticism has also been extended to include the nondemocratic aspects of both advanced capitalist and bureaucratic socialist societies. Finally, the Praxis Group has progressively elaborated an original normative model for a democratic socialism: "integral self-managing and self-governing socialism."

Particularly prominent in this latest phase of the Praxis Group has been Mihailo Marković, until recently Professor of Philosophy at the University of Belgrade. Marković has given the social criticism of the Praxis Group sophisticated philosophical articulation and defense. This chapter will explicate and show the relation between two themes in Marković's writings: (1) the aim, nature, and methods of critical social theory, and (2) his descriptive or nonnormative conception of human nature.

Apart from the importance of Marković in the recent phase of the Praxis Group, three considerations justify singling him out for attention. First, because he studied in England and has taught at American universities, he provides Anglo-American thinkers, especially those trained in analytic philosophy, with a good point of contact with Praxis Marxism. Marković, born in 1923, was a partisan during World War II in the Yugoslav struggle for national and social liberation. Following the Yugoslav break with Stalin in 1948, Marković spent five years trying to root out Stalinist dogmatism. His academic study of philosophy culminated in Ph.D. degrees at both the University of Belgrade and University College in London. At the latter he spent two years studying under A. J. Ayer and wrote a doctoral thesis entitled "The Concept of Logic." The young Marković found Ayer's stress on scientific and logical objectivity a valuable weapon against Stalinist mystifications. Although he came to recognize the inadequacy of analytic philosophy (and especially logical positivism) in diagnosing and solving contemporary social problems, Marković's writing continues to reflect the analytic tradition's commitment to clarity and its concern for foundational issues in logic and philosophy of science.[5] But Marković is also influenced by the existentialist tradition and is deeply rooted in the neo-Marxist tradition of Lukács, Bloch, Korsch, Gramsci, and the Frankfurt School of Critical Social Theory. His debt to (and critique of) existentialism is most visible in his philosophical anthropology and especially his concept of freedom, whereas his neo-Marxism is apparent in his critical social theory and model of democratic socialism.

The recent appearance in English of some of Marković's major writings is a second reason for attention to his work.[6] In 1974 two collections of Marković's more important essays were published in English: *From Affluence to Praxis: Philosophy and Social Criticism*[7] and *The Contemporary Marx: Essays on Humanist Communism.*[8]

Third, Marković, together with seven of his Belgrade colleagues,[9] has been at the center of recent political turmoil in Yugoslavia. On January 28, 1975, the "Belgrade Eight," as they have come to be called, were fired from their posts at the University of Belgrade on charges of political deviance and "corrupting the youth." This ouster culminated a seven-year campaign against the Praxis Group by the Party, government officials, and the state-controlled mass media.[10] Since the fall of 1972, the focus of the often vicious campaign has been to remove the "Eight" from their positions of academic influence and to "muzzle" if not silence them. Where (unconstitutional) changes in university law, the "packing" of university councils with nonuniversity Party members, and various forms of political pressure failed in getting the "Eight" "legally" fired,[11] the implementation of a new law passed in November 1974 by the Republic of Serbia was finally successful. This law, which the Praxis Marxists argue is in clear violation of constitutional guarantees for self-managing autonomy in educational and cultural institutions, authorized the Serbian Parliament to dismiss university teachers on grounds of (lack of) moral and political fitness. A few weeks following the ousters the journal *Praxis* suspended publication when state subsidies were cut off and printers, under political pressure, refused to print the journal. In the summer of 1975, for the first time since its inception in 1963, the Praxis Group's internationally famous summer school on the Adriatic island of Korčula was not held.

In 1976 the "Eight" unsuccessfully challenged, in the Yugoslav Constitutional Court, the law under which they were fired. Prospects for reinstatement appear bleak. In the meantime the "Eight" are either in Yugoslavia, receiving their salaries – at the 1975 level – but unable to teach or publish, or are serving as visiting professors abroad. Their fate, as well as that of Yugoslavia itself, may well hinge on what happens in the post-Tito period.

The causes of the firings and prolonged governmental hostility to the Praxis Group are complex and can only be suggested here. We have seen that the social criticism of the Praxis Marxists became increasingly concrete and challenged problematic features of Yugoslav society. At the same time Yugoslav society had become more laissez faire in economics – with such attendant problems as unemployment, foreign debts, increasing social differences, and divisive regionalism – and more authoritarian in politics, partially as a response to resuscitated regionalism. Moreover, student demonstrations in Belgrade in June 1968 protested these conditions. While Tito initially gave a public show of support for the student demands and even promised to resign if they were not met, with the passing of the crisis the students' Belgrade professors were blamed for leading them into political opposition. In fact the Praxis Marxists, unlike Milovan Djilas, have never constituted a disloyal opposition. Rather, in their "critique of all existing conditions" they have argued that the Yugoslav ideals of self-managing socialism should be made a reality instead of being used as ideological justification for autocratic government and laissez faire economics.

What is tragically ironic about events in Yugoslavia is that the very country that broke with Stalin and initiated important steps toward an independent and democratic socialism is now using Stalinist methods to repress the critical views and open dialogue it once honored in practice as well as principle.[12] The current struggle underscores the truth of Stojanović's judgement of 1971:

The Yugoslav revolution is far from resolving the agonizing question that has confronted every socialist revolution until now: how to undertake the necessary modernization without allowing it to kill the prospects for achieving social equality, justice, and democratic participation at all levels of society.[13]

The nature of critical social theory

According to Marković the aim of critical social theory or critical social philosophy is both to understand a social formation and to contribute to its humanization. Moreover, the two tasks are related: An understanding of what-is is relevant to both the projection and realization of what ought-to-be. Given this view of the purpose of social inquiry, Marković seeks to distinguish his approach from both positivistic social science and antiscientific utopianism.

Both Marxist and non-Marxist social scientists, influenced by philosophical positivism, conceive social inquiry as a science that provides value-free descriptions, explanations, predictions, and control of social phenomena. Normative questions concerning a good or more humane society are ignored or viewed as extratheoretical issues to be settled by arbitrary decision or preference. Given social ends, the social scientists can employ social laws to identify effective means. What one cannot do as social inquirer is to criticize or revise social goals: "science loses power to supersede existing forms of social reality and to project new, essentially different humane historical possibilities" (CM 3). The result is that social inquiry contributes to (1) the loss of society's critical self-consciousness, and, thereby, (2) the maintenance of the status quo (whether in capitalist or in socialist societies) (CM 94–5).

In contrast to positivistic social science, some utopian social theorists embrace an ideal future and condemn both present social reality and its scientifically explicated regularities. Among this group Marković includes some humanist Marxists, such as Max Horkheimer of the Frankfurt School, antiestablishment social theory informed by existentialism, and Theodore Roszak's utopian mysticism (CM 3, 104, 188). In this approach social laws are perceived and rejected as apologies for a dehumanized status quo. Instead of accepting the present social framework or forecasting a single, inevitable future, these theorists imaginatively project an ideal future radically discontinuous with present trends and behavior. For it is assumed that all possibilities are open to human beings who have no definite structure and who exist in a historical process with no causal linkages (CM 4; AP 211–12). The defect in this sort of "absolute utopianism," aside from positing a naïve picture of a future in which all human problems are resolved, is that "scientific theory building need not play an apologetic role" (CM 104) and that ideal futures may be excluded by present realities.

Critical social theory, as explicated and practiced by Marković, is designed to mediate between these one-sided approaches by dialectically relating science and philosophy, the real and the ideal, nomological explanation and critique, theory and practice. Such a social theory has five interrelated aspects.

1. A critical social theorist seeks to understand and explain a particular social configuration.[14] The theorist assumes that the social formation is a totality or "meaningful whole" (AP 33) that cannot be adequately studied in either piecemeal or static fashion. The theorist seeks causal links among the social system's present structure of elements[15] (treated separately and hence incompletely by economists, sociologists, political scientists, etc.). A social law, here, is conceived as a generalization that "establishes constant relations among certain variables under given conditions, and implies an extrapolation for an unspecifiable future (or past) interval of time."[16] To be causally explained is how the system maintains its identity in relation to changes in its external environment and conflicting tendencies among its own components.[17] Not only is the present structured functioning of the system to be explained but so are (1) its historical origins in earlier social formations and (2) limitations on its future development.[18] These limitations are of two sorts: limitations beyond which the system cannot change without becoming a different sort of system, and limitations on the system's capacity to fulfill genuine human goals and needs (AP 24). Axiological assumptions are involved in this scientific aspect of social theory not only because, as in natural science, public truth, clarity, and so forth, are assumed to be good (CM 95) but also because the identification of at least the second sort of limit is dependent on valuation as to genuine human needs and appropriate goals.[19]

This first descriptive and explanatory aspect of social theory may be executed on various levels. For example, the United States can be "totalized" as a social system of technocratic welfare capitalism, of welfare capitalism, or of capitalism. Each layer of analysis and synthesis identifies the formation's origin, dynamics, and limits. The most basic levels would involve social laws for social systems of an entire epoch (such as capitalism) or several epochs of social evolution. In any case social laws are not universal in scope but deal with an historical context of lesser or greater spread.[20]

For Marković, social laws are not completely without exception even when their scope is limited to a particular social formation (at a particular time). There are two reasons why exceptions occur and why social laws "should be conceived as tendencies and not inevitabilities" (CM 119). First, social laws often fail to treat a social or behavioral system's many variables and those that are included as boundary conditions are seldom quantifiable. As a result the degree of experimental confirmation "is usually not very high" (CM 119). Second, social laws often formulate only probabilistic tendencies because some human beings act in ways that creatively transcend the dominant causal patterns: "social laws are flexible and open because man is able to learn, to introduce novelty into his behavior, and change the very conditions under which certain laws hold" (AP 11–12). Often this novel action occurs precisely because the agent understands and rejects the causal law. The less human beings use their capacity for law-transcending action, the more thinglike (reified) they and their social system become and, consequently, the more closely social laws approach "inevitabilities." But the greater the number of agents who are not reified, the more would social laws formulate tendencies and the less probable would be the predicted behavior patterns.

2. That present social agents and systems have more than one path to the future brings us to the second aspect of a critical social theory. The critical theorist goes beyond description and explanation of a given social formation to an "extensive exploration of real possibilities" (AP 3). Some futures are logically or factually impossible, for "the past lives in the present and sets limits for the future" (AP 35). But within these limits, several futures are possible. Moreover, these possible futures may include the radical change or surpassing of the entire social formation. For a social formation's tendencies may be disintegrating or destructive as well as integrative or system maintaining. Whether and under what conditions crisis tendencies emerge and can be avoided, displaced, or promoted by collective action are matters of empirical knowledge (AP 214).[21] It follows that rather than necessarily playing a conservative, system-supporting role, social knowledge can contribute to system transformation (CM 104, 96).

A social system's possible futures may be roughly ranked with respect to likelihood. However, the most probable will not occur if and when human agents understand the probabilities and act to bring about an option that they view as less likely but still – perhaps barely – possible (AP 210–211). Moreover, because of contribution of these unexpected human intentions and efforts, it follows that "we cannot draw a sharp boundary line between historical possibility and impossibility"; for it sometimes happens that "we cannot know if a project is possible until we try to achieve it" (AP 84).

Although Marković does not consider the point, it would also seem to follow that the social theorist could (roughly) forecast how people would act in response to earlier social forecasts. A "higher-order" forecast might predict with more or less probability how people will respond to a "lower-level" forecast, and this probability factor could enter into the consideration of the likelihoods of the various possible futures. The point to be stressed is that tendential social laws and "the exploration of future possibilities" can take human intentions and actions into account.[22]

In this second aspect of inquiry, then, the critical social theorist, on the basis of knowledge of social tendencies, identifies alternative social futures of varying likelihood.

3. Possible social futures differ with respect to good and evil as well as with respect to likelihood. Accordingly, the social theorist adds critical evaluation to forecast and identifies that future that is ideal in the sense of "the optimal real possibility of an essentially open historical process" (AP 245, n. 2). This normative aspect of social theory is executed on different levels; for just as an understanding and explanation of present social formations involves a multilayered analysis, so projection of the best future will have a shorter and longer time dimension:

A series of successive steps, projected . . . by critical theory, mediates between the actual situation at present, and the vision of an optimal historical opportunity over the whole given epoch. Without this mediation, a humanist vision of an optimal future remains only a matter of faith or hope. Humanism needs science in order to transcend its utopian and arbitrary character, i.e., to translate its theoretical aspirations into a practice. [CM 104]

For example, Marković argues that the best short-run future for Yugoslav socialism is a more rationalized and democratically controlled commodity production with distribution, to some extent, according to work. In the more distant future, however, it is possible and desirable for production to be for the filling of needs, rather than for profit, and for distribution to be solely according to need.

This "vision of an optimal future" (CM 35) is meant to avoid utopian fantasizing not only because the optimal future is historically achievable in a sequence of steps, but also because these future possibilities help illuminate (1) past and present social formations, and (2) the course of historical development.

Concerning (1), in light of an optimal future, the social theorist can understand both a present social formation's essential limitations on authentic human life and those beneficial but embryonic achievements that could more fully develop in a better society (CM 35–36). Dialectical critique of the present is not total rejection, for the surpassing of a present formation toward a better future is a negation of the present's limitations ("negation of the negation") without destroying its humane accomplishments. For Marković, as for Hegel and Marx, dialectical surpassing [*Aufhebung*] involves a preserving on a higher level as well as a negating and a going beyond (AP 35–36). Absolute utopianism errs not only in positing an impossibly perfect future but in finding nothing of value in the present.

In the case of (2), the overall course of history or social evolution can be illuminated in terms of an optimal but not inevitable future. For Marković, this involves a view that history should be (and sometimes is) a development "from the reified to the increasingly free society."[23]

4. What is the basis for judging one possible future as optimal? The criterion for such a judgment can be derived neither from descriptions and explanations of particular (sorts of) societies nor from forecasts of possible futures. For Marković accepts that we cannot deduce an ought from what was, is, or might be. Marković concedes that the distinction between factual and value statements is not always sharp and that some statements are either ambiguous with respect to the speaker's intention or simultaneously inform and evaluate. Yet he maintains that factual and value statements (or informative and evaluative dimensions of statements) should not be confused and that objectivity is a regulative ideal (AP 36–

43). Although the "totalization" of a social formation and the identification of its essential limitations on human development presuppose a conception of the good life, that conception can always be challenged or viewed as hypothetical. For example, someone might agree to identify society X as a system of alienation and *then* ask if alienation is bad.

Nor can the critical social theorist derive an ultimate social norm from what *has* to be, for Marković conceives historical process as neither inevitable nor necessarily progressive. Many positivistic Marxists claim to avoid but actually presuppose (unargued) normative commitments by assuming both inexorable historical laws and that they (the Marxists) are "on the side of history."

For Marković the critique of a present social formation and the projection of an optimal future are both grounded in an explicitly articulated and *defended* conception of the good life: Human beings can and should be beings of praxis.

By praxis Marković means neither nontheoretical doing nor, more specifically, productive labor. Rather, praxis is an explicitly normative concept for activity that realizes one's best potentialities. These optimal potentialities include (1) the humanly generic dispositions of intentionality, self-determination, creativity, sociality, and rationality, and (2) one's relatively distinctive abilities and bents compatible with (1). One acts intentionally when he or she acts on purpose and for a purpose. One's action is self-determined when, subject to neither external nor internal compulsions or constraints, one unpredictably and autonomously chooses from among a range of alternatives. An action is creative when it is both novel and beautiful. An action is social when it realizes one's disposition for a coordinated effort, open communication, and reciprocal nurturing of individual self-realization. Finally, an act of praxis is also rational in the three-fold sense involving knowledge of what is, of the best means to obtain a given end, and of the best end, that is, praxis.[24]

This norm of praxis provides Marković with more than a standard for individual excellence; it also functions in critical social theory as an axiological principle for social critique of present societies and projection of optimal futures. Those futures are constructed in the light of the standard of a praxis society. A praxis society is a society whose basic structure and institutions would

(1) maximally exemplify social principles (such as freedom, equality, justice, and community) derived from and rendered in terms of the norm of praxis,[25] and (2) maximally promote lived praxis in contrast to its opposite, alienating activity.

5. The final aspect of critical social theory points beyond scientific and normative theory to social action that transforms society. The typically Marxist doctrine of "the unity of theory and practice" is understood by Marković in three related ways, each of which involves the rejection of the notion that theory is merely the passive reflection of economic practice. First, as we have already seen, theory and practice are linked on the level of theory because scientific explanations and forecasts of likely futures take into account and may influence human action (positively or negatively).

Second, one reason for doing social theory is to promote social action that attempts to actualize optimal future possibilities. The critical theorist constructs his theory in order that members of a society can both understand their society's merits and limitations and be normatively guided in their efforts to bring about a better future society. While the theorist strives for theoretical truth and normative correctness he or she has, as Habermas would put it, the "practical intention" that the theory play an "emancipatory role" in the actual surpassing of the investigated social formation.[26] For Hegel, the point of theory was to show that the world was (necessarily) rational. For Marković, following Marx, the point of theory is to make an irrational social world more rational (CM 5, 23, 28). This theoretical guide to social practice is offered not as a directive from above but as a proposal for discussion and possible consensus. For, of course, a crucial dimension of the normative component of the theory is that societal members should finally determine, through public discussion and democratic decision making, the ends and means of their life together.[27]

A third connection between theory and practice concerns critical social theory's norm of individual excellence in relation to the theorist's own life: "[the philosopher's] task is not only to derive philosophical principles from human life, but also to try to raise human life to the level of philosophical principles" (AP 6). On the one hand, a philosopher's normative principles are the theoretical expression of "the general practical orientation of the author (in the sense of Fichte's *dictum* that the character of a philosophy depends on what kind of man the philosopher is)" (CM 162). This claim would have to be examined in more detail in considering how Marković seeks to justify the norm of praxis.[28] On the other hand, a philosopher "should live *his* philosophy" (AP 6). Not only does the effort to change the world help the philosopher understand it, but to be a "theoretico-practical being" is part of the meaning of praxis (AP 6, CM 71).

The descriptive conception of human nature

We have seen that Marković conceives critical social theory as having scientific, normative, and practical dimensions. As a part of this social theory, Marković has developed in some detail a theory of human nature or a philosophical anthropology that also has both scientific or "descriptive" and normative components. To understand what a social formation is and should be we must understand what human beings are and should be. And in both cases the "is" and the "ought" are mediated by the concept of potentiality. In a fuller treatment, the following discussion of Marković's descriptive concept of being human would be followed by a detailed consideration of his normative conception, whose central feature is the concept of praxis.[29]

Marković succinctly summarizes his view of the nonnormative component of human nature in the following way: ". . . human nature is a structure of conflicting latent dispositions that evolve in time and may be manifested, suppressed, or modified in ways appropriate to historical conditions" (CM 158–59). This suggests that Marković conceives human nature as (1) more than actual behavior, (2) involving opposing potentialities, and (3) historically variable.

Dispositions and behavior

A crucial distinction in Marković's social philosophy is that between actuality and potentiality. Just as the social theorist must discover what a society *can* be, so he or she must not reduce human beings to their actual existence or behavior. Although present behavior provides important evidence about human beings and although one's actions may sometimes belie what one says, human beings have a subjective "inside" as well as a behavioral "outside." This subjectivity involves not only beliefs, desires, and wishes but also various potentialities or dispositions both for these episodes and for overt behavior (including purposive behavior). To seek to explain human behavior solely in terms of environmental conditions and stimuli is to neglect the agent's contribution to a particular action and his or her capacities to act or act differently in the same or other circumstances. Natural science also deals with more than present properties and environmental causes. To ascribe "solubility in water" is to ascribe *possible* behavior under present conditions (such as, holding the sugar in a spoon) and (very) *likely* behavior under certain specifiable (future) conditions (such as placing the sugar in water).

Marković distinguishes three types of human dispositional properties: (1) *universal* or generic latent dispositions, (2) *particular* dispositions: actual tendencies and abilities by and large common to members of a social group, and (3) *individual* dispositions: actual tendencies and abilities (relatively) distinctive of an individual.

Universal dispositions. Anthropological evidence, contends Marković, indicates that, in addition to certain generic biological, social, and psychological needs, human beings have certain "universally latent dispositions" (CM 98), "latent predispositions" (AP 12), or "potential human capacities" (CM 85). Examples are dispositions to communicate, reason, be creative, and be self-determining as well as dispositions to be irrational, destructive, and submit to authority.

These dispositions are genetic and latent. They are genetic, for they are grounded in, if not identified with, biological gene patterns. Like Aristotle, Marković in effect is holding that actuality is ontologically prior to potentiality in that dispositions are manifestations or results of an actual state of affairs even though we may not yet understand that state of affairs. The brittleness of the glass may be the manifestation or effect produced by a certain molecular structure of the glass in conjunction with a certain kind of impact. Unlike D. M. Armstrong, however, Marković holds that in human beings the genetic basis only sets *general* limits and is not rigidly determining (CM 152).[30] These dispositions are also *universal* or *generic* in the sense that they are part of the native endowment or

169

"equipment" of every human being.[31] Finally, these genetic and generic dispositions are also *latent* in the sense that they are not (yet) manifest as actual behavioral abilities or tendencies but will likely become so at a certain stage of growth and/or under certain conducive conditions (CM 98). But actualization is not a necessity. Given unfavorable social conditions or brain damage a child may never actualize (and may lose altogether) his natural disposition to master symbols or communicate. Learning a particular language can be said to realize one's latent linguistic competence. Marković characterizes this realization or actualization as a *specification* of the generic disposition. I learned English as a child, but the *more general* generic competence could have been specified in other ways. Generic competencies do not rigidly determine but rather make possible options within limits. These generic competencies could also be said to be (higher-order) dispositions for (lower-order, behavioral) dispositions. Like any disposition they designate possible behavior under present circumstances and likely behavior under specific circumstances – circumstances that include the acquisition of some actual ability or tendency. Unlike a dog or a plant, a human infant has the possibility of speaking and will most likely realize that latent disposition (by learning a specific language) under the circumstances of normal growth and socialization.

Particular dispositions. Particular dispositions are, for Marković, those actual behavioral capacities and tendencies that an individual shares with other members of the same social group, such as family, region, class, nation. Particular dispositions are made possible by and specify latent generic (or nongeneric) dispositions. That I grew up speaking English was made possible by my genetic and humanly generic linguistic competence but was concretely caused by particular socialization patterns in an English-speaking language community. Once acquired, actual dispositions need not be actualized in behavior (because of unfavorable circumstances) and may be extinguished. But that members of the same social group can and under specifiable circumstances do exhibit the same sort of behavior is explicable by the acquisition of the same actual dispositions. One task of a critical social theory is to explain causally the acquisition and manifestation in behavior of such particular dispositions.

Individual dispositions. Finally each individual has actual dispositions that are individual as well as those that are particular. Like particular dispositions, these individual abilities or tendencies specify latent or genetic (usually nongeneric) potentialities. But unlike particular dispositions, these individual ones are (relatively) distinctive talents and bents that more or less distinguish the individual from other members of his or her groups. For example, Ms. Jones stands out from other members of her various groups by virtue of her natural ability for quickly learning a foreign language or her acquired ability to construct a "private language." Of course, Jones may also differ from Smith when both are members of group *A*, because Jones (but not Smith) is a member of group *B* and has some particular dispositions that she shares with other members of *B* but that Smith does not have. Moreover, a dispositional property that begins as individual would seem to be capable of becoming particular in so far as an idiosyncratic person established a new group whose members possessed and promoted the idiosyncrasy (see AP 222).

Like particular dispositions, individual dispositions need not be actualized or realized in behavior because of unfavorable social circumstances, one's free choice, or both. Moreover, although socialization patterns may nurture, block, or even extinguish these idiosyncratic natural or acquired abilities, such abilities are (relatively) peculiar to the individual.

We can summarize Marković's three kinds of dispositions and our addition of latent nongeneric dispositions with the following schema:

Latent or genetic dispositions	I. Generic or universal dispositions		II. Nongeneric dispositions	
	A_1 Particular dispositions	B_1 Individual dispositions	A_2 Particular dispositions	B_2 Individual dispositions
Actual dispositions				
Behavior				

In this schema Marković's universal latent dispositions are I, his particular dispositions are A_1 and A_2, and his individual dispositions are B_1 and B_2. For the sake of completeness I have added II: nongeneric but latent and genetic dispositions (see note 31).

Marković needs to differentiate those actual dispositions (whether particular or individual) that are abilities or capacities from those that are propensities or tendencies. Although both sorts of dispositions refer to likely behavior under certain circumstances, propensities seems to add a motivational factor (desire, want) not present in abilities. Johnny can both do math and play football; but he hates the former and loves the latter. Do propensities differ from abilities in that they are behaviorally realized in a greater range and number of circumstances (*ceteris paribus*)? Johnny is likely to do math only in math class and while figuring the pass completion record of his favorite quarterback, but is likely to play football every chance he gets. But what if he does not get much of a chance?

A related problem in Marković's anthropology is the relation between the concept of disposition and the concept of need (see CM 98, 125, 137, 150–51, 164). Actual tendencies seem to presuppose needs, because one wants what one (thinks one) needs or lacks. But the relation between needs, on the one hand, and either latent dispositions or actual abilities, on the other, is not so clear. Does one have a (true) need to realize one's (optimal) latent dispositions and (optimal) actual abilities as well as one's (optimal) tendencies? Marković seems to suggest so (CM 151, 164), but the topic needs more attention.

Opposing dispositions

For Marković dispositions often come in conflicting or opposing pairs. Human beings are generically capable of both creativity and destructiveness, altruism and selfishness, rationality and irrationality, self-determination and flight to authority.[32] And in the course of history these opposing latent capabilities have often become specified as conflicting actual behavioral tendencies (AP 73–5). It follows that human beings should be viewed neither as essentially good nor as essentially evil. Marx, Rousseau, and Marcuse err in construing human beings as essentially good but prone to evil because of contingent and alterable social structures.[33] In contrast, Hobbes thought that greed and destructiveness were essential human traits that could be mitigated only by an "artificial" but absolute sovereign.

For Marković human nature is a mixture of good and evil generic dispositions – the specification, realization, nurturing, and inhibition of which depend on contingent social institutions (CM 143). Accordingly, social theory must reject both an unqualified optimism and unqualified pessimism concerning the human prospect: Human beings are capable of both good and evil and which becomes dominant depends to some extent on contingent and (in principle) changeable social structures. Moreover, it follows from this "mixed" picture of human nature that self-realization *sans phrase* is too general as an individual or social ideal; for, realization can be of the self's bad as well as good dispositions (CM 125). What is needed is a normative theory that recognizes the complexity of human nature, identifies (and proposes ways to actualize) the good (latent and actual) human propensities, and identifies (and seeks to inhibit or modify) their bad counterparts. For Marković the concept of praxis plays the central role in such a normative theory.

Historical variability

Marković's philosophical anthropology can also be characterized, with certain qualifications, as historicist and antiessentialist. Human nature, in his view, is an historical and not a transcendental category designating an eternal (platonic) essence that exists independently of human beings and that they instantiate or approximate (CM 152). Yet what it means to be (generically) human, the *defining* characteristics of human beings, has *not* changed in the course of *human* history.

Generically human dispositions, whether good or bad, have not always existed. They are the (contingent) result of biological evolution. Presumably an historical anthropology would seek to explain why these generic (and nongeneric) dispositions emerged and why they (usually) come in opposing pairs. We must be careful here, for Marković does not seem to be saying that what it means to be generically human has changed over the course of successive historical epochs (see CM 35; AP 35).[34] Rather, although he could be clearer here, Marković's claim is that generi-

cally human dispositions and needs are biologically evolved properties that were once possessed by no beings and that could in the
future disappear. Just as *human* history began as *homo sapiens*
emerged in the evolutionary process, so could human history end
with the disappearance of beings with humanly generic properties.
"In between" the (proposed) concept of human nature has concrete exemplification.

Although latent generically human dispositions remain constant
throughout *human* history, actual tendencies and abilities, whether
particular or singular, exhibit greater or lesser variability in the
course of a person's life or between successive generations of persons. What accounts for these alterations? What explains changes
in actual dispositions in contrast to generic human nature? We can
distinguish two sorts of "formal" conditions for and two sorts of
"efficient" causes of such change.

One formal condition for the alteration of a person's actual
disposition is the polarization of latent dispositions: "Change is
possible because human nature is nothing but a very complex and
dynamic whole, full of tension and conflict between opposite features and interests" (AP 222). A merely latent disposition may
become manifest and specified as an actual disposition. And, con-
versely, the actual specification of the opposing universal disposition may altogether cease. A second formal condition for change
in concrete human nature is that latent dispositions, as we have
seen, can be specified in a variety of ways with a variety of intensi-
ties. It is formally possible that a person's actual disposition (1) be
eliminated and succeeded by an alternative specification or (2) be
strengthened or weakened in itself or in relation to other actual
dispositions in a person's dispositional repertoire.

In addition to these two formal conditions for changes in concrete human nature are two sorts of efficient causes: socialization
and self-determination. I acquire many of my actual dispositions
by virtue of being socialized into various groups (narrower in
scope than mankind). This set of socialized dispositions includes
all of my particular dispositions and some of my individual dispositions. If these groups change or disappear, either through
natural or social forces or through collective or individual action,
then sometimes my actual dispositions (or those of my descen-
dants) change as well. Moreover, actual dispositions – acquired in

groups that have passed from the scene or of which I am no longer a member – may have no opportunity to issue in behavior in the new social setting. Continual blockage may result in a gradual weakening and even extinction of the actual disposition in question.

Let us briefly look at some of Marković's examples of changes in actual human dispositions and values brought about by changes in social structures and socialization patterns (see AP 223–26). First, the biologically basic need for and disposition to acquire adequate food, clothing, and shelter has been specified in our epoch as a greedy drive for material possessions. This acquisitiveness is not essential to human nature but is a compensatory mechanism due to such historical factors as economic scarcity, physical deprivation, and the free market. In a changed society with a socially controlled economy of abundance and an adequate level of material well being, this "goods hunger" would gradually phase out and, perhaps, altogether cease.

In our epoch lust for political power over others has also been a dominant motive. Although Marković is not clear on this point, I think he would say that this will-to-power is a specification of one's universal dispositions for egoism and for self-determination. But an actual will-to-power is not essential to human nature; it is a mechanism of defense and compensation in a hierarchical society in which insecurity for all and powerlessness for most is endemic. In a society characterized by the deprofessionalization, decentralization, and equalization of political power, the universal disposition for egoistic self-assertion would remain latent and the universal disposition for self-determination would be specified in, *inter alia,* capacities for democratic decision making.

Finally, the love of social approval or personal glory becomes a dominant motive (realizing one's universal disposition for egoism) in a society marked by work in which technical activity is routine and controlled by others. The love of social success becomes a compensatory motive in a society that affords little hope to realize one's universal dispositions for creativity and self-determination. In a social system that provided an abundance of creative professional and leisure-time opportunities, personality structures are apt to be quite different. Approval for achievements in "science, art, politics, or personal relations" would not be "regarded as supreme and worthy of any sacrifice" (AP 225). Such praise would be a "natural consequence" of those abilities and performances that realized one's universal capacities for self-determination, creativity, and sociality.

So far, Marković has not provided much empirical evidence to back up these particular claims of the effects, on actual dispositions, of such changes in social structure. (He also needs to consider whether there are situations in which thwarted actual dispositions would *increase* in strength and/or find other forms of expression rather than gradually phase out.) If Marković's general point about the conditioning role of social structures on actual disposition is correct, however, the implications for critical social theory are clear. Among the social laws sought by critical social theorists would be (tendency) laws explaining the acquisition, realization in behavior, inhibition, and extinction of actual dispositions in particular social settings.

A person's self-determination is a second source of change in his or her actual dispositions. When I become aware, perhaps on the basis of nomological social knowledge, of my actual abilities and tendencies, I may decide to supplement them or to alter or eliminate one or more of them. Put another way, I may decide to actualize, block, or specify in new ways one or more of my latent dispositions. For given the openness of latent dispositions to alternative specification, a human being, like a social system, faces alternative futures:

We have a chance to choose, within certain limits, what kind of man we are going to be. While practically bringing to life one of several possible futures we, at the same time, consciously or involuntarily mold our own future by fixing some of our traits, by modifying others, by creating some entirely new attitudes, needs, drives, aspirations, and values. [AP 223; cf. CM 121]

We can both further our grasp of Marković's notion of self-determination and summarize our discussion in this chapter by indicating that self-determination, as a latent generic disposition, nicely illustrates each feature of Marković's descriptive concept of human nature.

First, like any disposition for behavior, the power of self-determination can exist without being manifested in behavior (see CM 120). (The sense in which this would be true would be different for an infant and for a reified person.) Second, the generic disposition for freedom is opposed by the generic capacity for escape from freedom and responsibility. This means that humans are susceptible to being controlled by others and to accepting the status quo. But it also means that a reified person can exercise his or her latent capacity for self-determination. Third, while the latent power of self-determination emerged in biological evolution, some societies are better than others in nurturing it as an actual ability and in providing opportunities for its manifestation in behavior. Moreover, one's actual power of self-determination might be exercised to change one's concrete self, including the relative importance of self-determination in one's character and action. Finally, it is possible that an individual could altogether lose the latent capacity for self-determination; but that would be tantamount to no longer being human.[35]

In this chapter we have discussed Marković's descriptive concept of being human. In addition we have deepened our understanding of critical social theory. In its empirical aspect such a theory seeks to explain the origin, actual specification, and behavioral manifestation (or inhibition) of human beings' latent dispositions. This includes explaining and predicting (or understanding) changes in actual dispositions and behavior. In its normative aspect, critical social theory (1) distinguishes good from bad latent dispositions and (2) identifies social structures that inhibit or mitigate the latter while promoting the best possible specification and realization of the former.

Notes

1 I wish to thank Mihailo Marković, Svetozar Stojanović, and Zagorka Golubović for helpful criticisms of preliminary drafts of this paper, access to unpublished materials, and continual encouragement. I am also indebted to my colleagues Richard Kitchener, Daniel Lyons, and Bernard Rollin for extensive comments. Any remaining inaccuracies in interpretation or wrongheadedness in appraisal are my own responsibility. In the spring of 1975 an earlier version of the present essay was read at the Departmental Colloquium of the Department of Philosophy, Colorado State University; and a more general study, "*Praxis* and Democratic Socialism: The Critical Social Theory of Marković and Stojanović," was presented at the University of Washington Colloquium in Social Theory. The paper in its present form was also read in

November 1976 at the Conference on the Current State of Marxism, University of Nebraska at Omáha, and at a meeting of the Rocky Mountain Chapter of the Conference of Political Thought, the University of Denver.

2 Gerson Sher, "Tito Muzzles the Loyal Opposition," *Nation* 220 (March 15, 1975): 294. For interpretations of the history of the Praxis Group see Mihailo Marković, "Marxist Philosophy in Yugoslavia. The *Praxis* Group" in *Marxism and Religion in Eastern Europe,* ed. Richard T. De George and Thomas Scanlan (Dordrecht and Boston: D. Reidel, 1976), pp. 63–89; and Gerson Sher, *The Dialectic of Dissent: Praxis and Marxist Critique in Socialist Yugoslavia* (Bloomington: Indiana University Press, 1977).

3 The journal *Praxis,* the theoretical organ of the Praxis Group, was founded in 1964 and, until 1975, regularly appeared in both Serbo-Croatian and international editions, the latter in English, French, and German translation.

4 Gajo Petrović, *Marx in the Mid-Twentieth Century: A Yugoslav Philosopher Reconsiders Karl Marx's Writings* (Garden City, N.Y.: Doubleday & Company, Inc., 1967).

5 Marković's main publications in Serbo-Croatian reflect these interests: *Logic* (1954), presently banned in Yugoslavia, and *Dijalektiška teorija Značenja* [Dialectical Theory of Meaning], (Belgrade: "Nolit," 1961).

6 Major writings by many other Praxis Marxists remain in Serbo-Croatian or German. Svetozar Stojanović's *Between Ideals and Reality: A Critique of Socialism and Its Future* (New York: Oxford University Press) appeared in English translation in 1973. Stojanović's *Geschichte und Parteibewusstsein: Auf der Suche nach Democratie in Sozialismus* (München und Wien: Carl Hanser Verlag, 1978) will be published in English in 1980 by Oxford University Press. Two recent English-language anthologies consist of essays by various members of the Praxis Group: Gerson S. Sher, ed., *Marxist Humanism and Praxis* (Buffalo, N.Y.: Prometheus Books, 1978); and Mihailo Marković and Gajo Petrović, eds. *Praxis: Yugoslav Essays in the Philosophy and Methodology of the Social Sciences* (Dordrecht: D. Reidel, 1979). See also the Praxis Marxists' contributions to the following volumes: Branko Horvat, Mihailo Marković, and Rudi Supek, eds., *Self-governing Socialism: A Reader,* vol. 1 and 2 (White Plains, N.Y.: M. E. Sharpe, Inc., 1975).

7 Mihailo Marković, *From Affluence to Praxis: Philosophy and Social Criticism* (Ann Arbor: The University of Michigan Press, 1974); hereafter cited in the text as AP. This volume, which includes some papers written in 1968 and 1969, is largely based on Marković's lectures in 1969–70 at the University of Michigan.

8 Mihailo Marković, *The Contemporary Marx: Essays on Humanist Communism* (Nottingham: Spokesman Books, 1974); hereafter cited in the text as CM. The bulk of the essays in this collection are papers presented and/or published in 1970–3. A German translation of some of Marković's essays written in Serbo-Croatian between 1960 and 1967 has been published as *Dialektik der Praxis* (Frankfurt: Suhrkamp Verlag, 1968).

9 Svetozar Stojanović, Ljubomir Tadić, Zagorka Golubović, Dragoljub Micunović, Miladin Zivotić, Nebojša Popov, and Trivo Indjić.

10 For a more detailed recounting of the chain of events leading to the ousters and for a more comprehensive account of their causes and wider significance, see Sher's writings cited in Note 2. Also indispensable are "Repression at Belgrade University," *New York Review of Books* 19 (February 7, 1974): 32–3; "Yugoslav Notes" privately circulated by Robert S. Cohen of Boston University; Oskar Gruenwald, "The Silencing of the Marxist Avant-garde in Yugoslavia," *Humanist* (May–June 1975): 32–6. For the official Party line on the "Eight" see "The Extreme Left – Actually the Right," *Socialist Thought and Practice* 14 (March 1974): 83–108.

11 The "Eight" have been continually supported by faculty and students within the Faculty of Philosophy and Sociology, the University of Belgrade, and other Yugoslav universities. For example, faculty committees, who investigated the "Eight" in the spring of 1974, commended their academic qualifications and dismissed all charges against them. In July 1974 these judgments were approved by the University of Belgrade's Faculty of Philosophy and Sociology by a vote of 150 for, none against, and one abstention.

12 As members of the Praxis Group wrote in February 1974: "[The events in Belgrade are] one of the last battles for survival of free, critical, progressive thought in the present-day socialist world, in a country which is still open to democratic development and where until recently it seemed to have every chance to flourish" ("Repression at Belgrade University," *New York Review of Books* 19 [February 7, 1974]: 33; CM xviii).

13 "Marxism and Socialism Now," *New York Review of Books* 16 (July 1, 1971): 21.

14 For Marković, explanation [*Erklärung*] can and should be synthesized with understanding [*Verstehen*] based on "direct, personal, intimate contacts with many individuals who live in that community" if the "full meaning of what is going on" (AP 20) is to be grasped. While explanation "provides abstract analytical information about the facts and external, objective, structural characteristics of certain isolated social phenomena" *Verstehen* "supplements these informations by a concrete, qualitative, historical understanding of the subjective dimensions of a social whole" (AP 20–21); see also Marković's, "The Problem of Reification and the *Verstehen-Erklären* Controversy," *Acta Sociologica* 15, 1 (1972): 27–38.

15 Unlike many Marxists, Marković and other Praxis Marxists do not give any a priori causal priority to economic factors.

16 Marković, "The Problem of Reification," p. 30.

17 Cf. Habermas's notion of the organizational principle of a social formation [*Gesellschaftsformation*]: "The formation of a society is, at any given time, determined by a fundamental principle of organization [*Organizationsprinzip*], which delimits in the abstract the possibilities for alterations of social states. By 'principles of organization' I understand highly abstract regulations arising as emergent properties in improbable evolutionary steps and characterizing, at each stage, a new level of development. Organizational principles limit the capacity of a society to learn without losing its identity" (*Legitimation Crisis* [Boston: Beacon Press, 1975], p. 7).

18 "After centuries of static structuralism (since Plato) and descriptive historicism (since Thucydides) Hegel achieved the great intellectual breakthrough by showing how all structural features are changeable and all historical processes structured" (CM 22).

19 An inquirer could, it seems, stay neutral with respect to a *particular* valuation of human needs and goals – viewing them only as *hypothetical goods*. However, for Marković, "universal human values which express the interests and needs of mankind as a whole are by no means incompatible with truth and scientific method. Without them science would be reduced to mere positive knowledge and devoid of true critical spirit" (CM 119; see also CM 95–100).

20 For Jürgen Habermas, it is legitimate for a critical social science to seek *universal* social laws, but it also must identify those patterns of social action that *seem* universal but are actually capable of alteration: "The systematic *sciences of social action,* that is economics, sociology, and political science, have the goal, as do the empirical-analytic sciences, of producing nomological knowledge. A critical social science, however, will not remain satisfied with this. It is concerned with going beyond this goal to determine when theoretical statements grasp invariant regularities of social action as such and when they express ideologically frozen relations of dependence that can in principle be transformed." (*Knowledge and Human Interests* [Boston: Beacon Press, 1971], p. 310; footnote in text omitted).

21 Habermas's book, *Legitimation Crisis,* is an attempt to clarify and appraise various empirical hypotheses about possible crisis tendencies in advanced capitalist societies. See also Thomas McCarthy, *The Critical Theory of Jürgen Habermas* (Cambridge, Mass., and London, England: MIT Press, 1978), Ch. 5.

22 See David A. Crocker, "The Humanistic Value of a Science of Human Action," *Proceedings of the XVth World Congress of Philosophy 17–22 September 1973 Varna (Bulgaria),* vol. 2 (Sofia, Bulgaria, 1973), pp. 273–9. Cf. AP 37, CM 122, "The Problem of Reification," p. 34.

23 Mihailo Marković, "Self-determination in Theory and Practice" in *For Dirk Struik,* ed. Robert S. Cohen, J. J. Stachel, and Marx W. Wartofsky, vol. 15 of *Boston Studies in Philosophy of Science,* ed. Robert S. Cohen and Marx Wartofsky (Dordrecht: D. Reidel, 1974), p. 547; hereafter cited in the text as SD.

24 For a detailed analysis and evaluation, see David A. Crocker, "Marković's Concept of *Praxis* as Norm," *Inquiry* 20 (1976): 1–43.

25 In the manuscript mentioned in acknowledgments, I treat Marković's and Stojanović's renderings of these social ideals, show how they are informed and constrained by the norm of praxis, and argue that they would be realized in institutions of self-managing socialism.

26 Jürgen Habermas, *Theory and Practice* (Boston: Beacon Press, 1973), pp. 1–3. Habermas conceives critical social theory as accounting for its own origins as well as for its emancipatory applications.

27 Although Marković does not deal with the question directly, it would seem that this nonelitist conception of social theory would itself be subject to rational discussion.

28 Crocker, "Marković's Concept of *Praxis* as Norm," pp. 24–30.

29 Ibid., pp. 1–43.

30 See *Metaphysics* 1049 b5–1050 b5 and D. M. Armstrong, *A Materialist Theory of Mind* (London: Routledge & Kegan Paul, 1968), pp. 57–9.

31 Although Marković does not do so, he could distinguish genetic generic dispositions, like the capacity to communicate, from genetic but nongeneric dispositions, like the capacity to wiggle one's ears or have perfect musical pitch. In contrast to the universality of generic dispositions these nongeneric dispositions would be possessed by only some human beings.

32 In a personal communication Marković has indicated that some dispositions are not polarized, e.g., the generic disposition to communicate. Why should only some dispositions – either latent or actual ones – have opposites? Is this just a contingent fact of biological and social evolution? Don't some people have the actual tendency to withdraw from communication, perhaps to protect their privacy? Wouldn't this actual tendency not to communicate be made possible by and specify a genetic and generic potentiality?

33 Instead of Marx's and Marcuse's use of "human essence" as a term indicating "true potentiality" (AP 248, n. 9) or what human beings ought to be, Marković construes human essence as a descriptive concept designating opposing potentialities. For, as Marković argues, a *normative* concept of essence "slides over" the real problem for critical theory, viz., "which among many potential human faculties may be considered true" (AP 248, n. 9).

34 Presumably all (and only) human beings would be sorts of beings who not only had the generically human dispositions but also were such that the generic dispositions could (often) come in pairs and could either remain latent or be specified by actual abilities and tendencies.

35 Cf. Frederick Ferré's illuminating comparison of human powers of self-determination and speech:

(a) This power, of creative self-determination within various contexts of multiple real possibilities for future courses of action, is (like the power of speech) neither racial nor cultural but intrinsic to our species. (b) It (like speech) is not apparent at birth, but if all necessary conditions are met it will develop within the normal child. (c) In some it develops (like verbal aptitude) to a higher level than with others, for reasons not all of which are clearly understood. (d) It (like the power of speech) is a natural and organically related power which is subject to inhibition or even destruction under unfavorable circumstances. (e) It (like speech) is by no means constant throughout life and may gradually fail in old age. (f) And while it (like speech) may not be without rudimentary analogues in other animal species, it is so vastly different in scale as to be qualitatively unique to man as (like speech) a prime mark of his humanity and a prime source of his distinctive dignity ("Self-Determinism," *American Philosophical Quarterly* 10 [July 1973]: 172).

8

Marxism and dissent in the Soviet Union

LYMAN H. LEGTERS

One of the irritating byproducts of Stalinism, merely a nuisance as distinct from the horrors associated with the dictatorship, is the conceptual confusion that pervades discussion of protest and dissent in the Soviet Union. At the center of the difficulty is the widespread outside acceptance of Stalin's own claim, backed domestically by an apparatus of enforcement and terror, to the authority to define Marxism for the twentieth century. Where the claim could be enforced – generally in the Soviet Union, for certain periods of time in other countries, and at least intermittently in fraternal parties abroad – it is not surprising that the claim was honored, in public discourse at any rate. It is not so obvious why enemies and critics of Stalinism elsewhere should be so prone to treat Stalin as the authoritative spokesman for Marxism.

To take a single glaring example from the post-Stalin era, it was not uncommon among outside observers to see in the Soviet invasion of Czechoslovakia in 1968 a clash between Western democratic values and Marxism – as if the public statements of the Czechoslovak leaders were hollow and the professions of Marxist orthodoxy in Moscow should be taken at full value.[1] Aside from the patent absurdity of analysis couched in such terms, commentaries of that sort left in mystery the eloquent protests of some of the world's leading Marxist thinkers. The widespread acceptance of such a view would nevertheless suggest that one of Stalin's greatest successes lay in the realm of persuasion and beyond the reach of his enforcement system.

Among serious Marxists and students of Marxism this kind of confusion has of course long since become tedious and unworthy of additional consideration. But as long as public discussion and much academic discourse is disfigured by these distorted perceptions, the effort must continue to clarify matters, and especially –

in light of contemporary developments in Eastern Europe – to clarify the relationship between Marxism and dissent.

The first step may be to recall certain well-known facts. One of these, of which we are reminded not least by the current revival of interest in Bukharin,[2] is that serious theoretical discussion did not die in the Soviet Union with Lenin. The theoretical sterility of Marxist discourse in the era of Stalin's dictatorship was of such duration that we need to be reminded of the vigorous theoretical discussion surrounding Soviet policymaking in the 1920s. Whatever one may think of the quality of Bolshevik understanding of Marxism in Lenin's time, the seriousness of the intellectual commitment to genuine Marxism is undeniable. And then it took a while for Stalinist sloganeering to empty Marxist discourse of its critical content. Indeed that process was probably more prolonged, more difficult to accomplish, than Stalin's consolidation of power itself. The question that remained, once Stalinist orthodoxy had established its monopoly of public discourse, and its authority to define a particular version of Marxist theory as orthodox, was whether the old intellectual habits had been extinguished or merely driven underground.

For the decade or so following the revolution, a period that retains such appeal for many of the current Soviet dissenters, it is proper to speak of dissent only in connection with those elements of the population that had not accepted a revolutionary transformation of Russian society, the class enemy in revolutionary rhetoric. Within the party, and indeed throughout the left side of the political spectrum, there was abundant disagreement and even organized opposition (such as the Left Opposition to Brest-Litovsk, the Workers' Opposition, etc.[3]), but there was not dissent in the sense of fundamental objection to the revolutionary project.[4] Although it is important not to give an idealized appearance either to Lenin's or to Trotsky's tolerance of disagreement, it is vital to recognize the contrast between the first period and the Stalinist era that ensued. Dissent was anathema at all times on grounds of being counterrevolutionary; opposition on the other hand was at first only an extreme form of intraparty disagreement until Stalin obliterated the distinction.

Another well-known but crucial fact in this connection is that, within the growing range of Stalinist repression – which had the

effect of merging class enemy and intraparty opposition by treating them alike – dissent of all the kinds now discernible in the
Soviet Union were constant accompaniments of the increasingly
maniacal dictatorship.[5] Intraparty disagreement thus became an
aspect of dissent by reason of its exclusion from what was left of
public discourse. When there was no longer room for even the
debate that Leninism allowed prior to a final party decision, disagreement became subversive and thus fundamentally at odds
with the character of the regime as Stalin defined it – in effect a
reversion to tsarist attitudes toward public discourse. By the dictator's fiat, then, it ceased to be important whether a deviation in
opinion was modest or militant, radical or reformist, Marxist or
anti-Marxist.

In this connection the postwar discussion of totalitarianism has
been less than helpful. Arising out of pertinent perceptions that
Hitlerism and Stalinism had common features, that discussion im-
planted in our vocabulary a term defined essentially by degree of
revulsion. Despite the enumeration of the characteristics shared by
both dictatorships,[6] none of these was a defining characteristic in
the sense of firmly distinguishing those two systems from other,
perhaps slightly less repugnant, political orders known to modern
history. On the other hand, the new category obscured not only
differences between the two dictatorships but also, at least in the
usage that soon emerged, much that was imperfect (hence normal)
in the operation of both systems. The term "totalitarianism" came
to imply not only that systems so designated differed absolutely
from all others but also that their workings approximated perfect
efficiency. Such an image was poor preparation for the recognition that central control over the content of human minds is never
complete, at least not on the scale of an entire society. Because
thought control is a (perhaps *the*) salient characteristic of what we
have come to mean by totalitarianism, the most that can be said of
a regime or movement is that it embodies a totalitarian tendency.
Control over the means of access to public discourse and expression thus becomes a second-best kind of achievement for such a
regime, adequate to the normal requirements of autocratic governance but never fully satisfying – as Hitler's or Stalin's megaloma-
nia amply testify – the demand for willing obedience. In any case,
mere control over public discussion fails to qualify as a distin-

guishing feature of modern totalitarianism, for it is found with varying degrees of effectiveness in autocratic regimes of all ages.

The point of these distinctions in the present context is to be able to speak with some precision about Stalinist repression and the panorama of dissent that it evoked, both in the realm of public discourse and within party councils. As an autocratic system, improved over time by the "refinements" of terrorism, Stalinist repression was certainly one of the most efficacious that history had known, although the documented existence of multiform dissenting and protesting movements signify how imperfect the system was. If it is useful to apply the term "totalitarian" here at all, then it is to be found as a tendency in Stalin's dissatisfaction, not just with the marginal inefficacy of repression but also with the very need for repression, with the system's inability to graduate to the enforcement of willing obedience. This was nowhere clearer than in Stalin's relationship to the party, for if a dictator of totalitarian tendency may provisionally blink at public dissatisfaction so long as it remains quiescent he cannot tolerate even the suspicion of deviant persuasion within his own party. It follows, less paradoxically than might at first appear, that unfettered intraparty discourse among serious Marxists would have first priority among the targets of a Soviet autocrat's program of repression. In this perspective, the survival of nationalistic longings within a multinational state or the persistence of religous belief amongst a predominantly peasant population is less threatening than even the suspicion that the dictator's own party harbors alternate or deviant conceptions of the reigning ideology. In other words, repression begins with the inner circle and proceeds, if at all, through concentric circles of the most advanced and privileged sectors of the population. When the two processes are telescoped together – as in Stalinism – then dissent becomes the correct term for all deviation from official policy. If this is a correct understanding of Stalinism, then it makes it somewhat less surprising that, in a state claiming a privileged Marxist status, many other forms of dissent should appear in advance of any revival of authentic Marxist debate.

But the question of "appearing" is of course not a simple one, especially in an analysis that stresses the distinction between subterranean dissent and open or public opposition. Intraparty debates and even opposition were an element of public discourse for purposes of policymaking in party circles; but they never "appeared" in the sense of a democratic public discussion featuring freedom of utterance. Dissent in the sense of basic hostility to the prevailing order or to the direction of development never "appeared" at all, neither under Lenin nor during the interregnum nor in the period of Stalin's ascendance, for it was regarded in all three stages as counterrevolutionary. What changed was not the treatment of dissent but rather the determination of what was to count as dissent.

Yet it can be argued that in the post-Stalin era of *Samizdat* and the *Chronicle of Current Events* the phenomenon of dissent entered the arena of public discourse, irrespective of thaws and counter-thaws, in as decisive a way as intraparty discussion had in Lenin's era. If sufficient allowance be made for Stalin's dual accomplishment – eliminating the possibility of opposition and widening the inclusiveness of dissent – this is not as paradoxical as it may seem. Functionally speaking, what was initially tolerated as opposition and "appeared" as such in the circumscribed arena of public policy debate had either to die or reappear as dissent. And when it did not die, its reappearance, albeit as a formally disallowed expression, during what someone has called the "post-totalitarian" phase of Soviet development reinstated the function of offering policy options. And these, because they were noticed by the authorities and by sympathetic fraternal parties and by less sympathetic foreign observers, became at least as public, for purposes of articulating interests and criticizing prevailing policy, as the earlier forms of intraparty opposition had been.

The case may be made somewhat clearer by reference to the partially contrasting experience of other countries of Eastern Europe. As serious theoretical discussions surfaced in these lands, employing a recognizable vocabulary and displaying a recognizable intellectual filiation with the unbroken Western tradition of Marxist thought, students of Eastern Europe have been forced to wonder what became of authentic Marxist discourse in the homeland of the revolution. All of these other countries had experienced the impress of Soviet versions of Marxist orthodoxy in the interwar period; and all, except for Yugoslavia, had undergone a surrogate form of revolution under the tutelage of the Soviet army. Yet they were the arenas of genuine Marxist debate within a few years, whereas the frozen Marxism-Leninism of the Soviet mentors exhibited almost none of the openness, the flexibility, the critical cutting edge that has properly been attributed to the Marxist intellectual tradition.

It was of course true that first-rank Marxist thinkers of these Eastern European countries suffered exile – enforced or self-imposed – as a result. Bloch and Kołakowski spring to mind. Others – the Praxis philosophers, for example – were silenced or deprived at times. Lukács underwent the well-known oscillations between acclaim and opprobrium. And Karel Kosík was reduced to a shadow existence. Lesser figures too, more noteworthy for their protests than for lasting theoretical contributions, suffered in varying degree: Djilas, Schaff, Svitak, Hegedus, and others.[7] Finally, silence was imposed on the single most impressive outlet for serious Marxian theorizing, the journal *Praxis*. Virtually all were stigmatized at one time or another as revisionist, signifying at bottom nothing more than a discomfiting degree of deviation from official party lines.

Yet from the time when Djilas broke ranks, and in spite of resulting hardships and penalties, the lands of Eastern Europe have not been without serious Marxian discourse. If one state silenced or exiled its public spokesmen for authentic Marxism, similar voices would arise in another country to take their place. And now, one suspects, it would take something on the order of a regionwide renewal of Stalinism at its worst to terminate a discussion that has grown habitual.

Only very recently has something similar begun to appear in the Soviet Union. From the time when intraparty discussion was effectively stilled, from the time when old Bolsheviks such as Bukharin were finally straitjacketed, the Soviet Union has offered nothing comparable in the way of Marxian dissent. The major exception, discernible only to close observers of particular branches of scholarship, has been a quiet, at times indeed surreptitious, pursuit of genuine Marxian inquiry. This form of surviving Marxism, to be found in the other Eastern European countries since World War II as well, succeeded in much the same way as *Capital* passed the Russian censorship. Only *in potentia* does such Marxist scholarship pose a challenge to the official orthodoxy and it has rarely entered into public discourse, even to the extent that the underground press has in recent years. The public challenge that did emerge finally, when Trotskyism had become a faint memory and Bolshevik intraparty debates were found only in hidden memoirs, was not in any immediate sense an alternative to the Marxist orthodoxy found in *Pravda* or *Izvestia* but was rather an alternative to Soviet political practice, a rebuke to repression and the denial of civil and human rights.[8]

This was the initially undifferentiated form in which Soviet dissent was perceived in the West. It would surely not be wrong to surmise that the initial failure to differentiate among forms of dissent was conditioned by wishful thinking surviving from the Cold War era – to the effect that dissent was uniformly anti-Soviet and that, as the tip of a presumed iceberg, it foreshadowed serious crises for the Soviet regime. Nor would it be implausible to suggest that Western observers often preferred to view the Soviet internal order as the inevitable outcome of Marxism and all protest against it as being, therefore, anti-Marxist. The faulty totalitarian image also undoubtedly came into play: If such a regime cannot contain and silence protest, it must be a sign of impending disaster. Here again we witness the curious alliance between Stalinists on the one hand and the most vigorous spokesmen for anticommunism on the other. The very identification of serious Marxism with official party lines that Kołakowski, the Praxis philosophers, and Kosík had made all but impossible in their countries, the neo-Stalinists and Western anticommunists preserved for the Soviet Union by equating protest with anti-Marxism.

Gradually, however, and not least because of the precedents recorded in neighboring countries, commentators on Soviet dissent developed a more sophisticated taxonomy, one that could distinguish between dissenters who wished to dismantle the Soviet system and revert to prerevolutionary models and those who sought to discern where the revolutionary project had gone wrong. There are of course those who would limit the application of the term "dissent" to the former, to the critics who reject every aspect of the revolution and long for some manner of restoration. In a curious parallel to the condemnation heaped upon reform socialists by their revolutionary brethren, this viewpoint attempts to portray those who would refurbish and reinstate the values of the revolutionary movement as reformers of a scheme that was wrongheaded from the start. The Solzhenitsyn of more recent political observations is, from this perspective, the epitome of dissent and his militancy gets highest marks.[9] One would like, in reply, to invoke the Marx of the post-1848 period, for he too seemed less militant than his romantic associates in the Communist League. The seeming militancy of a romantic reliance on sheer will, whether in a revolutionary or a counterrevolutionary cause, makes hardheaded realism look bland. Yet it would be difficult to argue that any sort of *Schwärmerei* is more basic, and hence more radical, than a clearsighted appraisal of possibilities. Romantic militancy is, then, chimerical, and true radicalism consists in perceiving what kinds of change are actually possible. This does not restrict realistic dissent to Marxists by any means, but it does tend to exclude those who cling to romantic notions of turning the clock back. And it serves to remind us that, by his adoption of a system that enforced a frozen orthodoxy by chilling ordinary disagreement, Stalin made it possible as the Tsars had earlier for moderate reformers, civil libertarians and Leninists alike, to count as fundamental critics and proponents of radical change.

But Western social scientists have not commonly made this kind of distinction. Among the schemes, diagrams, and classifications that have been proposed to account for Soviet dissent,[10] few have given any special recognition to the impact of Marxist criticism on a self-proclaimed Marxist system. Instead of attending mainly to the intellectual or political positions from which the dissent emerges, Western observers have usually placed their emphasis on the aims, purposes, and directions of change advocated. Such analysis is necessary and has the particular merit of revealing the manner in which variant persuasions can and do unite or coalesce around particular objectives. Thus, liberals and Marxists join in advocating democratization; nationalists and Marxist critics of nationality policy may coalesce in behalf of minority rights; civil libertarians and religious believers unite against discriminatory treatment of religious institutions. In the most general cases of all, dissenters of all persuasions are at one in favoring freedom of expression and deploring illegal deprivation of civil and human rights. (It does not follow of course that their argument would survive if basic change really did take place.)

But there are also reasons for insisting on the sources of dissenting sentiment, especially when they are Marxist, not least because this focus helps to elucidate the knotty (and partly artificial) issue of system rejection versus system modification. The most conspicuous reason, more perceptible in the neighboring socialist states than in the Soviet Union, is that Marxists supply the most trenchant criticism of the prevailing order. This is because Marxists are *prima facie* members of the family and hence harder to dismiss as hostile critics (true as well of foreign communists and intellectuals, such as Berlinguer, Fischer, or Garaudy, but felt most acutely when the critic is homegrown). Moreover, because of shared vocabulary and critical method, Marxists are usually more penetrating in their diagnoses of the prevailing system (which is also why they sometimes seem less militant than do those who reject the revolutionary project altogether).

Most crucial of all the reasons, however, is the insistence by authentic Marxists throughout Eastern Europe and in some fraternal parties elsewhere that democracy is a defining characteristic of the socialist "good society," and that autocracy is its obverse.[11] From the standpoint of bourgeois capitalism this observation may seem a less fundamental attack on the system than a thoroughgoing rejection of socialism would be. Solzhenitsyn then sounds more radical than Roy Medvedev. But here the issue of system rejection reveals its artificiality, for the only way to maintain that the elimination of socialism is more basic than the elimination of autocracy is to hold that autocracy inevitably results from socialism. If instead one holds that autocracy and genuine socialism are incompatible, then the insistence by native Marxists on fulfillment of the socialist promise is a more radical and fundamental atack on the existing order than any yearning for the *status quo ante*.

The evidence we have from Eastern Europe, scanty as it is, does suggest both that democratization is a live option – even though it has occurred only fitfully – and that creative Marxist thinkers can, as in the Prague Spring or in relation to Yugoslavia's system of workers' self-management, contribute actively and importantly to movement toward democratic socialism. Kosík and Svitak, the Praxis philosophers, and the students of Lukács also suggest, moreover, that Marxists can, given even moderately favorable circumstances, make the crucial move from criticism of existing conditions to creation of new perspectives that arise from their intellectual tradition but that are fitted to contemporary situations, for the improvement of the social order.

In the Soviet Union it is harder to discern corresponding developments. The most suggestive case so far seems to be Roy Medvedev, whose move from criticism of Stalinism to a plea for socialist democracy begins to parallel the efforts of Marxists in neighboring countries.[12] Furthermore, his work has opened up a dialogue with Western Marxists, a form of reinforcement that has been important to the vitality of theoretical work elsewhere in the region.[13]

Medvedev is of course not the only Marxist among the prominent Soviet dissenters, but there are certain features of his recent history that make him distinctive – and distinctive in ways that fit particularly well with some of what has been argued in this chapter. Although he was identified as a Marxist in his first major publication in the West, the historical exposé of Stalinism called *Let History Judge,* his work was perceived in the West primarily as an element of a still undifferentiated body of dissent. One aspect of the case was the continuing effort to unmask the horrors of Stalin's dictatorship; the other, revealed in the author's inability to get the work published in the Soviet Union, was the resurgence of Stalinism.

Three years later, with the publication of *On Socialist Democracy,* the contours of the situation became clearer. The unwillingness of Soviet authorities to publish was hardly surprising, but it was no longer possible to regard Medvedev simply as another dissenter gradually moving toward the prominence already enjoyed by Solzhenitsyn and Sakharov. Here plainly was a Marxist perspective being applied critically to the Soviet social order, the equivalent functionally perhaps of Djilas's *The New Class* of an earlier period but at the same time a more ambitious theoretical statement. For the first time, a Russian theorist of Marxist persuasion was counterposing to the vapid orthodoxy of official Soviet Marxism a widely noticed alternative. Although the work could circulate in the Soviet Union only in subterranean fashion, it precipitated the aforementioned theoretical discussion, *Detente and Socialist Democracy,* with Western Marxists and established that an authentic Marxism had survived – and not just in the obscure corners of arcane scholarship – in the Soviet Union.

It was then no longer possible to regard Soviet dissent as a homogeneous plea for civil liberties and due process of law. It became much clearer than it had been before that the prominent intellectuals among the dissidents, not to mention the movements for religious freedom and national-cultural autonomy, started from widely disparate political premises and aimed at sharply differing outcomes. The disparities did not demolish the coalition in behalf of civil liberty, as is eloquently witnessed by Zhores Medvedev's *Ten Years after Ivan Denisovich*[14] (which appeared just as Solzhenitsyn's political position was becoming quite explicit). But they did demolish the lingering notion that Soviet dissent signified agreement about the dismantling of the revolution. For Medvedev's entire project, evidently shared by numbers of other dissenters, was to discover where the revolution had gone wrong and what it would require to redirect it in democratic fashion. If he seemed to yearn for the early years of the revolution, it was quite a different species of yearning than that which sought to refurbish and restore the prerevolutionary order.[15]

Interestingly enough, as a veritable stream of subsequent publications has disclosed, Roy Medvedev and his brother Zhores Medvedev have chosen a procedure that seems, at first glance, the very obverse of militancy. Without abandoning the enunciation of theoretical alternatives to the prevailing order, they have invested their greatest energies in the task of correcting the history of the revolution. To some of Medvedev's early readers, his historical work seemed, paradoxically, more radical than his theoretical statements. The reason for this, possibly, is that an authentic account of a systematically distorted revolutionary history may be the most radical move that can be taken against a still lively autocracy. And in concentrating on political history (Roy Medvedev) and science (Zhores Medvedev), with incidental glances by both at literature, the brothers have singled out the subjects on which the Soviet regime is most sensitive and ambitious in its claims.

If this work appears less sophisticated than the Marxist philosophy predominant among the dissenters in other countries of Eastern Europe, the difference is explained by the still significant differences in political climate between the Soviet Union and its neighbors. The brothers Medvedev have, I want to argue, chosen appropriately, and the Marxism that Roy in particular represents is well served in the prodigious task that he has undertaken. All of the Eastern European Marxists are often lonely and beset, sometimes actively persecuted, never free to work and publish as they would wish. But the dismantling of autocracy is, as Lenin knew, a slow and arduous process.

Notes

1 Henryk Skolimowski, for instance seems to operate on such an assumption when he speaks of Marxism suppressing the reform program in Czechoslovakia. "Are There No Consequences of Open Marxism?" *Studies in Comparative Communism* 4, no. 1 (1971): 51.

2 As evidenced by the reissuance of his theoretical works in translation, by reported renewal of discussion of the still unrehabilitated theoretician in the Soviet Union, and by the excellent biographical study, *Bukharin,* by Stephen Cohen (New York: Random House, 1973). Especially significant here is Roy Medvedev's essay, "Bukharin's Last Years," *New Left Review* 109 (May–June 1978): 49–73.

3 See especially Robert V. Daniels, *The Conscience of the Revolution* (Cambridge, Mass.: Harvard University Press, 1960).

4 This distinction between opposition and dissent is obviously not a semantic or etymological one. I am simply underscoring a usage that terms intraparty factions "oppositions" and the wide array of critical opinion expressed currently without official sanction "dissent." For references to other reflections on the terminological questions see Rudolf L. Tökes, ed., *Dissent in the USSR* (Baltimore: Johns Hopkins University Press, 1975), pp. 16–19.

5 The Tökes volume treats dissent mainly as a phenomenon of the postwar period. But a documentary collection, *Samizdat* (New York: Monad Press, 1974) edited by George Saunders, quite plausibly extends the notion backward in time to include fascinating materials from the whole of the Stalin era illustrating my point that dissent did not suddenly appear at or near the end of Stalin's rule.

6 Carl J. Friedrich and Zbigniew K. Brzezinski, *Totalitarian Dictatorship and Autocracy* (Cambridge, Mass.: Harvard University Press, 1956), pp. 9–10. Whether or not one accepts their conceptualization (and I do not), the authors should not be held responsible for careless usage that ensued, and especially not for the now common habit of applying the term promiscuously to any regime one does not like.

7 I want here to express my indebtedness to several students whose graduate research has instructed me on some of these figures and on much that is otherwise unfamiliar to me about scholarly discussion in the Soviet Union.

8 In addition to sources already cited, see Abraham Brumberg, ed., *In Quest of Justice* (New York: Praeger, 1970) and Cornelia Gerstenmaier, *The Voices of the Silent* (New York: Hart, 1972), as well as the rich material of the *Arkhiv*

Samizdata described by Tökes (pp. xiii–xiv), and available in several European and U.S. repositories.

9 See for example, his *Letter to the Soviet Leaders* (New York: Harper & Row, 1974) and *A Lenten Letter to Pimen Patriarch of All Russia* (Minneapolis: Burgess, 1972).

10 Daniels, *The Conscience of the Revolution*, pp. 434–8; Tökes, *Dissent in the USSR*, p. 15, and the extensive secondary literature cited in his Introduction, pp. 1–31.

11 This is not to suggest that the Marxists monopolize the antiautocratic front; to the contrary, this is one of the items of broadest agreement among dissenting elements. The Marxists are emphasized here because they are arguing the point about socialism and with a socialist regime.

12 Roy Medvedev, *Let History Judge* (New York: Knopf, 1972) and *On Socialist Democracy* (New York: Knopf, 1975).

13 Ken Coates, *Detente and Socialist Democracy* (New York: Monad Press, 1976) in which Marxists from several countries comment on Roy Medvedev's essay, "Problems of Democratization and Detente," and he then responds to the comments.

14 Zhores Medvedev, *Ten Years after Ivan Denisovich* (New York: Vintage Books, 1973).

15 See Medvedev's own characterization of the dissident movement, "The Soviet Dissident," *Marxist Perspectives* 2, no. 1 (Spring, 1979): 92–103.

9

Science, Soviet socialism, and the good society

LOREN R. GRAHAM

In 1960 Alexandr Solzhenitsyn, Russia's most noted writer of this generation, wrote a play entitled *The Candle in the Wind* in which he expressed certain attitudes toward science and technology that I would like to describe as an introduction to a more general consideration of opinions about science in the Soviet Union and the West.[1] The issue Solzhenitsyn raised is no less than the question of the role that science should play in any future "good" society. It is a question that has, in recent years, been asked in many places.[2] To what degree should scientific inquiry and technological application be limited in order to protect certain human values?

The play is one of the few works of Solzhenitsyn that do not take place in Russia; its setting is a contemporary or slightly futuristic society that is not named. In 1967 Solzhenitsyn told a journalist, "The action takes place in an unknown country at an unspecified period, and the heroes have international names. I did not do this in order to conceal my thought. I wanted to treat the moral problems of society in developed countries, independently of whether they are capitalist or socialist."[3] What is clear is that the society is a technological one, with the familiar establishments of all powerful modern societies: industry, the military, higher educational institutions, intelligence organizations, and finally – and most importantly – a well-developed scientific research establishment.

One of the main characters of the play is a young girl, Alda, who suffers from a strange mental disorder. A kind and sensitive person who takes delight in nature and music, Alda is subject to debilitating seizures of fear and despondency. She frequently loses the train of her thoughts in the middle of a sentence. The worse attacks are provoked by violent sights or sounds, especially those common to industrial civilization. While walking in the woods with the other protagonist of the play, Alex, Alda breaks into uncontrollable sobbing when upset by sonic booms overhead or by the whistle of commuter trains.

Alex proposes that Alda submit to treatment in the neurocybernetics laboratory where he works. There scientists have worked out a way of altering the patterns of synaptic transmissions in the brain so that the behavior of persons suffering from mental disorders is "stabilized." Alda is at first reluctant, but Alex and his friends persuade her to be treated, although Alex himself has previously revealed his own reservations about cybernetics research. There is, for example, a mercenary competition going on in the laboratory between two groups of cyberneticists for a government subsidy. The first group wants to produce programmed individuals who would be useful for certain societal roles, and this group's interests are being promoted by the army, which seeks a secure supply of fearless individuals. The second group, which eventually loses out in its efforts to secure a grant, is seeking to establish the laws of an ideal human society.

Both Alda and Alex become convinced that treatment of Alda's case is justified, whatever their reservation about some of the institute's other endeavors. Alex is obviously very fond of Alda, and Alda herself wants to believe that the treatment will free her from the crippling malady.

The treatment is administered and it is successful. Alda experiences no more seizures and begins to live a happy and untroubled life. But although she is evidently pleased with her new disposition, Alex finds that she has lost her most human qualities. She now converses wittily and plays the piano brilliantly, but she seems somewhat mechanical and uninteresting. The sight of a dog being run over by a bus would previously have destroyed her equanimity for days; now it hardly fazes her. Alex is deeply disturbed. The "candle in the wind" has been snuffed out. However, an exceedingly traumatic experience – the witnessing of her father's death – interrupts the still incomplete stabilization process and returns Alda to her previous unstable, vulnerable, and human state.

In the course of the play, Alex expresses on several occasions a sharp moral critique of scientific research. In a conversation with his old friend and convinced cyberneticist, Philip, the following dialogue takes place (which I have slightly condensed). Philip has urged Alex to commit himself to science.

Alex: But if you could answer just one question for me . . . one question . . . *What for?*[4]

Philip: How do you mean – what for? What is science for in general?

Alex: Yes. *What* is science *for?*

Philip: You must be pulling my leg? Where is the problem? It's all so elementary! Well, first of all, it's devilishly interesting! It's so supremely enjoyable, surely you . . .

Alex: Well, then? Is it just for yourself? Out of egotism?

Philip: But wasn't all the material wealth created by humanity created through science?

Alex: But that's not an answer either. What do we want wealth for? Does wealth better a man? I haven't noticed it.

Philip: You've really seized on a word I used! Well, not wealth, but all the material goods we possess on our planet, our entire civilization, our entire culture – everything was created by science, everything!! What is there to argue about?

Alex: We can argue about the fact that when we boast about the quantity of material goods we collectively produce, no one mentions what their production costs us . . .

Philip: You've clamped onto me like a tick. After all, the twentieth century without science wouldn't be the twentieth century any more. Science is its soul!

Alex: Or do you mean its soullessness?

Philip: You shouldn't have doubts about it, but instead go down on your knees before it! You should worship science!

Alex: "Oh, great science!" That's the same as saying, "Oh, we great minds!" Or even more precisely, "Oh, great me!" People have worshipped fire, the moon, and wooden idols – but I'm afraid that worshipping an idol is not so pitiful as worshipping oneself.

The views expressed in this play are not at all new to non-Soviet readers, who find frequent expressions of Faustian and Promethean themes in modern literature. But in 1960, when this play was written with hopes that it would be staged (it was first accepted for production at a leading Moscow theater, then cancelled), such a deep questioning of science was nearly unheard of in the Soviet Union; indeed, even in the United States – then experiencing the post-Sputnik exuberance for the expansion of science and technology – such views were much rarer than they are today.

The more typical Soviet attitude toward science is that given by the historian of science S. R. Mikulinsky at the International History of Science Congress in Moscow in 1971, when he said: "In our country there is no ground for political and intellectual reaction directed against science and technology. Our activities are based on the thesis that communism is inseparable from science and that an all-sided development of science and technology is a prerequisite for building a communistic society."[5] Yet we will see that in the years since Mikulinsky spoke, other Soviet authors have begun to raise questions about science and technology, including the issues of recombinant DNA research and nuclear power, so much debated in the West.

The citation from Solzhenitsyn's play (and similar citations could be given from his other words, such as *Cancer Ward*), provides us with an opportunity to compare attitudes toward science in the United States and the Soviet Union. It is well known now that in the United States science and technology are believed by many of their practitioners to be in a state of depression. Enrollments in science courses and majors dropped in the early seventies at many universities, including the best ones. The average age of university scientists is increasing as fewer younger scholars are hired. Throughout the seventies funds for research were no longer available on the scale of previous years, and laboratory equipment was not replaced at an appropriate rate. By 1980 it appeared that the downward trend of federal support for research had been halted, but many American scientists and engineers feared that long-term indicators of decline, such as a diminishing share of American patents on the international market, still were cause for pessimism.

In the early seventies the most alarming threat perceived by many American scientists was the turn of the young toward alchemy, astrology, Eastern religions, the occult systems, and to the more fundamentalist streams of their religious traditions. The magic phrase among many groups in those years was "other ways of knowing," a reference to the claim that there are avenues to reality that are forever closed to scientific inquiry and are, in fact, in fundamental contradiction to the methodology of science. The popular authors Theodore Roszak and Carlos Castaneda pointed, each in his own fashion, toward the limitations of science, and presented separate romantic or mystical visions of a world inadequately described by objective methods.[6]

By the late seventies and the beginning of the eighties these alternatives to science seemed to be declining in strength in America, but other issues, such as genetic engineering and nuclear power, continued to motivate critics of science and engineering. The newer issues were obviously serious ones on which many scientists and engineers themselves differed. Nonetheless, many members of the scientific community expressed the fear that the general public would become so suspicious of science and technology that government support of research and development would falter.[7] The National Science Foundation reacted by expanding the activities of its Office of the Public Understanding of Science, making grants aimed at buttressing the case of science before the American public.

Is the USSR undergoing a questioning of science and technology similar to that in the United States?

Many Americans take an almost perverse satisfaction from the fact that whenever a certain ailment appears in American society it is likely to be developing in the Soviet Union as well. For some American observers it is almost a balm to their spirits to learn, for example, that however badly the air and rivers in the United States are polluted, the Soviet Union seems headed down the same path. In their moments of trouble, Americans are attracted to a theory of economic determinism nearly as rigid as that of a scholastic Marxist: The Soviet Union and all other societies *must* encounter the same problems as the United States because the United States is leading the way down the unavoidable path for all modern states. If an attack on science has not yet developed in the Soviet Union, it soon will. Derek Price, historian of science at Yale, turned to Mikulinsky and other Soviet colleagues at the 1971 history of science congress in Moscow and told them: "I must suppose that increasingly during the next several years the Soviet Union must experience a political and intellectual reaction against science and technology in some form or other . . ."[8]

I, like Price, have followed the upward growth curves of budgets for science and technology in the Soviet Union long enough to believe, as he does, that the discrepancy between the annual growth rates for research and that of the economy as a whole cannot be continued indefinitely. Already a flattening of the curve has begun, comfortably before every member of the Soviet population is a scientist and all the budget goes to research.[9] But this flattening of the growth curves is not in itself an intellectual reaction against science and technology of the order that we have witnessed in the United States. The thesis that the impulse toward an intellectual and emotional turn against science and technology is equally strong in the USSR and the United States is questionable. As a result of their very different histories and intellectual traditions, attitudes toward science and technology are rather different in the two countries (indeed, it would be quite remarkable if they were identical). The commitment to science still has deep reserves in the Soviet Union, probably deeper than in the United States.

One of the first things a Westerner who studies the Soviet Union notices is the degree of commitment to scientific rationality that exists among many Soviet dissidents. This commitment is often disconcerting to the Westerner, and seen by him as simplistic, especially at a time when science is being questioned so deeply in the West. A physicist told me a story that in a small way may illustrate my point. While in Moscow he visited a group of intellectuals who considered themselves radical social reformers, people who had little sympathy with the political authorities in the Soviet Union. These Russians hoped to create a new and just society that would sharply contrast to the one in which they currently lived. Among their projects was a "city of the future," an ideally designed metropolis. The model city that they presented was drawn up on strictly scientific and rational lines. Throughways encircled and penetrated the heart of the city, the citizens' places of work were integrated with their places of residence. The entire environment was synthetic, manmade, plastic, and concrete, the type of city that Roszak would call "the air-conditioned nightmare," a technocratic "world's fair." But to these young Soviet dissidents this model represented the goal of all their efforts, something that might be possible if only they could free themselves from the orthodox and bureaucratic restraints of the Soviet political system. If this story reveals accurately a characteristic of a significant portion of the antiestablishment Soviet reformers, then we would be tempted to conclude that *both* the Soviet bureaucracy *and* their opponents share a continuing commitment to science and social planning. These dissidents rejected not the goal of a scientific society, but the possibility of achieving it under the present regime.

The memorandum "Progress, Coexistence and Intellectual Freedom" issued by Andrei Sakharov, the Soviet physicist who helped to organize the Committee for the Defense of Human Rights, is one of the most programmatic statements of a future society to come from Soviet critics. It is not surprising, perhaps, that a distinguished Soviet scientist would produce an architecture for the future of the world that is based explicitly upon scientific analysis. It may be surprising, however, to realize how deeply committed this critic of the Kremlin is to the very principle of the application of science to *all* of life that the Kremlin itself has officially supported throughout the years of its rule. Sakharov called for the application of the scientific method not only to the economy, but even to international affairs, education, and the arts. Although he recognized the danger inherent in the great power that science gives to man, he saw science as the *only* solution to the problems that man faces. This memorandum was based on the scientific methodology and the universal commitment to science that are now so deeply questioned by critics in the West.

Summing up his prediction of a convergence of the socialist and capitalistic systems at the end of this century, Sakharov wrote:[10]

In the fourth stage, the socialist convergence will reduce differences in social structure, promote intellectual freedom, science, and economic progress and lead to creation of a world government and the smoothing of national contradictions (1980–2000). During this period decisive progress can be expected in the field of nuclear power, both on the basis of uranium and thorium, and, probably, deuterium and lithium.

During this period the expansion of space exploration will require thousands of people to work and live continuously on other planets and on the moon, on artifical satellites and on asteroids whose orbits will have been changed by nuclear explosions.

The synthesis of materials that are superconductors at room temperature may completely revolutionize electrical technology, cybernetics, transportation, and communications. Progress in biology (in this and subsequent periods) will make possible effective control and direction of all life processes at the levels of the cell, organism, ecology, and society, from fertility and aging to psychic processes and heredity.

Many people would account for Sakharov's enthusiasm for science entirely on the basis that he is himself a scientist. A physicist in the United States might very well write a similar document. One could maintain that Sakharov's views will not support the case that there is a deeper commitment to science among the Soviet intelligentsia than their Western counterparts. What about the views toward scientific rationality of humanists, writers, poets, and philosophers in the Soviet Union? What prescription for the future of Soviet society would the intelligentsia give if they could express themselves freely?

Certainly some members of the Soviet intelligentsia were offended by the technocratic flavor of Sakharov's memorandum. Solzhenitsyn responded to it directly. Although these two most famous of the Soviet Union's dissidents share an antipathy to the Soviet regime, they differ radically in their visions of the world and in particular, in their opinions about scientific progressivism. After quoting Sakharov's hopes that progress in biology would lead to control of "psychic processes and heredity," Solzhenitsyn remonstrated, "Such prospects come close to our idea of hell on earth."[11] And in his Nobel Lecture, Solzhenitsyn accused scientists of backing "away from the sufferings of others; it is more comfortable [for them] to stay within the bounds of science."[12]

But Solzhenitsyn's fears of science do not seem widespread in the Soviet Union, even among those of his fellow dissidents who criticize socialism. Consider, for example, Igor Shafarevich, co-editor with Solzhenitsyn of one of the most influential collection of essays by dissidents yet to be published.[13] Whereas Solzhenitsyn sees the commitment to science (to the detriment of religion) as one of the primary flaws of socialism, his colleague Shafarevich, a distinguished mathematician, criticizes socialism for "casting off" its links to science and acting instead on "irrational instinct."[14] To Shafarevich, socialism is not scientific enough, while to Solzhenitsyn it is too scientific. Both Shafarevich and Solzhenitsyn believe Soviet socialism is leading Russia to disaster. To Shafarevich the danger of Soviet socialism lies in an instinctual irrationality spurning science; to Solzhenitsyn Soviet socialism is the apotheosis of the materialist worldview born with the scientific revolution.

Among other Soviet dissidents the ideal of a rational and scientific socialism, genuinely democratic in its nature, still has strong appeal. The reform movement in Czechoslovakia in 1968 has often served as their model. This movement was one in which writers, philosophers, and poets played important roles. Their goal was to give socialism "a human face," to eliminate Stalinism in their society, and to replace it with a just and free socialist system. Their efforts immediately caught the attention of the Soviet dissidents. Certainly one of the reasons the Soviet government felt compelled to suppress the Czechoslovak experiment was its fear that the principles of this socialism with a human face would spread to the Soviet Union itself, where intellectuals were chafing under the same sort of controls that the Czech intellectuals had revolted against. The speech that Alexander Dubček gave on April 1, 1968, has often been called Czechoslovakia's "Blueprint for Freedom," and was published in the West as a volume with that title. The speech contained frequent references to science, including the following statement:

The importance of science in our society is growing. Socialism originates, lasts and wins by the connection of the working movement with science. There is no relationship of subordination and compromise between these forces. The more resolute and impartial is the advancement of science, the more is it in harmony with the interests of socialism; the greater are the achievements of the working people, the bigger is the scope opened up to science. In the relationship to the development and application of science in the life of socialist society is reflected how much the working people are aware of their historical tasks, to what extent they really enforce them. Socialism stands and falls with science, just as it stands and falls with the power of the working people.[15]

We in the West are now so suspicious of scientistic ways of thinking and so accustomed to reading Communist and socialist documents of this type that we have great difficulty taking such statements seriously, even if they are issued by an obviously authentic group such as the socialist reform movement in Czechoslovakia, a movement later repressed by the Soviet Army.

It is my opinion, however, that this commitment to science on the part of dissident socialists is at least as serious a continuing force in the world as is the disaffection from science of the new critics in the West. However simplistic this socialist commitment to science may seem, it probably rests on firmer intellectual grounds than the flight from science among the seekers of "other ways of knowing" in the United States.

In order for one to become disenchanted with rationality, one needs to believe that one has tried rationality and it has failed. It is probably easier to believe this in the United States today than in the Soviet Union. During the past twenty-five years the United States government has applied the talents of America's best specialists in every field to domestic and international problems. The administration of John F. Kennedy, with its heavy reliance on professors from the best universities in the country, was probably the most striking illustration of this effort to apply the finest intellects and the latest technical and scientific expertise to national problems, whether they be the problems of urban education, rural poverty, race relations, or guerrilla warfare. Any assessment of the results of these efforts would have to be pessimistic. On a whole series of problems – improving children's reading skills, diminishing the gap in living standard between the wealthy and the poor, asserting the national will overseas – we were told that the "best and the brightest" were not enough. Few people believe that more of the same will change the situation. The present administration's disinclination to engage in progressive social planning evidently accords with a widespread disillusionment among the American populace about the effectiveness of such planning.

One would assume that the vestiges of decades of imposed five-year plans in the Soviet Union would cause a similar disillusionment with the social engineers. Undoubtedly, a great deal of disenchantment does exist in the Soviet Union; writers like Solzhenitsyn have spoken powerfully of the revulsion of Soviet citizens against years of being treated as building materials in the hands of the social architects. But there are other powerful countercurrents in the Soviet Union as well, issuing from the general knowledge that socialism was never given a truly fair trial in the Soviet Union, that the best intellects and latest scientific knowledge have never actually been enrolled in the service of the Soviet government. There has never been anything remotely resembling a Kennedy administration in the Soviet Union, although someone like Sakharov would very much like to see one. The rulers of the Soviet Union have never given scientists, engineers, economists, and social scientists weighty and genuine influence in policymaking. Instead, they place them under heavy political and ideological controls. No one, for example, has been permitted to question the rationality of the collective farm system, or the basic principles of the Soviet economy. Relatively tame suggestions, such as the de-centralization of control over industrial enterprises, were treated with the utmost caution by the political authorities and eventually emasculated.

Alexander Gerschenkron once spoke of the "advantages of backwardness" when referring to Russia's underdeveloped econ-omy of decades ago, an economy that permitted the skipping of intermediate stages of technology during the modernization ef-fort. In a similar paradoxical way, the patent irrationalities and political authoritarianism of the present Soviet state may have the advantage of preserving the belief of numerous Soviet intellectu-als – even many dissidents who are in deep disagreement with the Soviet establishment – that if rationality and science were ever given a real chance in influencing the Soviet state, great progress might be expected. In such an event, many of them seem to have a reservoir of faith in the potential of a socialist society for solving its major problems.

As individuals, these dissidents are often very pessimistic, but their pessimism seems to center on the political possibility of ra-tionality ever gaining a voice in the Soviet Union, not the efficacy of rationality itself. Among established scientists the appeal of an unfettered rationalism is thus greater than among their Western colleagues: As Ravetz commented, "In the Soviet Union the po-litical pressures on intellectuals are so crude, that the leaders of science have a natural social and political role as spokesmen for an Enlightenment in classic eighteenth-century terms."[16]

An interesting reason that science has so far not been attacked as strongly in the Soviet Union as it has in the United States may be that "reductionism" – the belief that all phenomena, including hu-man emotions, can be explained in physicochemical terms – has not gone as far there as it has in the United States and conse-quently has not generated the impassioned counterattack we are witnessing in this country. Reductionism is highly criticized by the majority of Soviet scientists and philosophers of science, who carefully distinguish themselves from what they call the "vulgar materialists" in the West. In the biological sciences, in particular, Soviet scientists have been quite skeptical of the possibility of explaining thought in elementary physicochemical or cybernetic terms. The development of matter during the history of the earth from the simplest nonliving forms up through life and eventually to man and his social organizations is regarded as an evolutionary series of quantitative transitions involving correlative qualitative changes. Thus, there are "dialectical levels" of natural laws, or what J. D. Bernal once called "the truth of different laws for different levels, an essentially Marxist idea."[17]

According to this view, social laws cannot be reduced to biological laws, and biological laws cannot be reduced to physico-chemical laws. The scientist, such as the ardent cyberneticists in Solzhenitsyn's play, who draws too close a parallel between the behavior of computers and the human mind is ignoring these very significant differences, however valuable the comparison may be in certain limited ways. Even to draw too close an analogy between humans and animals, as the popular Western ethologists today often do, is to commit the same error. As the American Marxist and Nobel Prize laureate H. J. Muller once observed, such scientists are "forgetting the special laws which apply to social processes and structures, that put the latter on a different level, as it were, from the simple biological relationships of non-social, non-intelligent organisms."[18]

If one examines the writings of the Soviet Union's most prominent authors on the nature of human consciousness and the place of reductionism in scientific explanation, it soon becomes clear that the target of Solzhenitsyn's criticism in *The Candle in the Wind* is more properly the mechanistic materialists of the West than the dialectical materialists of his own country. I. T. Frolov, a recent editor of *Problems of Philosophy,* the leading Soviet philosophy journal, wrote that dialectical materialism "defines a dual responsibility: on the one hand, it opens the way for complete freedom for the intensive use of the methods of physics and chemistry in studying living systems: on the other hand, it recognizes that biological phenomena will never at any point in time, be fully explained in physico-chemical terms."[19] The influential Soviet Marxist psychologist S. L. Rubinshtein maintained that within the framework of Soviet psychological theory "the psyche retains its qualitative specificity: it is not reduced to the physical properties of matter and is not converted into an ineffective epiphenomenon."[20] The Soviet psychologist L. S. Vygotsky, whose work is recognized widely in the West, relied heavily on the "dialectical levels of laws" model in explaining the nature of human thought and he carefully distinguished the physical, biological, and social realms. Speaking of Piaget's views on child psychology and the moment when a child discovers that every object has a name, he wrote, "*The nature of development itself changes,* from biological to socio-historical. Verbal thought is not an innate natural form of behavior but is determined by a historical-cultural process and has specific properties and laws . . ."[21] The Soviet biochemist A. I. Oparin, one of the initiators of theories on the origin of life in this century, wrote, "Regarding life as a qualitatively special form of the motion of matter, dialectical materialism formulates the very problem of understanding life in a different way than does mechanism."[22] Indeed, the most appropriate criticism of Oparin's philosophy of nature is not his "scientism" or "reductionism," but his occasionally unbridled antireductionism, which has led him rather close to romantic organicism. Established philosophers of science in the Soviet Union often frown upon these exaggerations in Oparin's views, but they agree with him that life and thought can not be understood entirely from physical or biological viewpoints.

Compare these prevailing opinions in the Soviet Union on the nature of life and thought with the opinions of two of the most prominent Western commentators on the same topics in recent years: Jacques Monod and B. F. Skinner. The Nobel laureate Monod, in his best-selling book *Chance and Necessity,* stated outright, "Living beings are chemical machines."[23] Monod's opinions on the debate between "holism" and "reductionism" were equally straightforward: "A most foolish and wrong-headed quarrel it is, merely testifying to the 'holists' profound misappreciation of scientific method and of the crucial role analysis plays in it." The question of whether thought processes differ qualitatively from physical processes Monod considered "not a meaningful question." Only at one point did Monod reveal his doubts about the case of reductionism against Marxism; speaking of the nature of human thought he observed that "Nothing warrants the supposition that the basic interactions are different in nature at different levels of interaction. But if a case exists where the first law of the dialectic is applicable, this indeed is it."[24] Monod's case, however, was clearly based on reductionist assumptions.

Skinner is another prominent and successful exponent of the potency of reductionist analysis for explaining human consciousness; the "science of behavior" that he calls for is a much more serious threat to people of Solzhenitsyn's convictions than the views of any prominent Soviet psychologist. Whereas Solzhenitsyn spoke of "the light which is in thee" (Luke 11:35),[25] the autonomous human soul, Skinner maintained that "as a science of behavior adopts the strategy of physics and biology, the autonomous agent to which behavior has traditionally been attributed is replaced by the environment – the environment in which the species evolved and in which the behavior of the individual is shaped and maintained." To Skinner, "The intentional design of a culture and the control of human behavior it implies are essential if the human species is to continue to develop." And further, "What is needed is more control, not less, and this is itself an engineering problem of the first importance."[26]

As one would expect on the basis of their views on reductionism, many Soviet scholars have been critical of Monod and Skinner. Frolov, the philosopher already mentioned, has called Monod's book "an absolutization of scientific knowledge and its ethic," an ignoring of humanism.[27] A Soviet reviewer of Skinner reproached him for "lumping together the social milieu with the milieu of nature, believing that in both cases the technology of control is the same."[28]

Whereas scholars in the Soviet Union have been trying to maintain a sophisticated middle position between the views, on the one hand, that mental functions can be described in terms of physical science and on the other hand, that they are in some way uniquely and inexplicably human, Western thought has broken down even more dramatically than before into the camps of the mechanists and the romantic mystics. The mechanists have gained new strength through the writings of such talented exponents as Skinner and Monod, while Western youth flee from such views to anything that will give them a sense of the uniqueness and mystery of life, whether it be Eastern religions, fundamental Christianity, magic and the occult arts, or romanticized science fiction.

Seen from this perspective, the Soviet Marxist view of nature is not nearly as guilty of "scientism" as is often thought. Through its nonreductionism it offers a way of remaining stoutly loyal to science without responding to enthusiastic calls by Skinner for a "technology of human behavior" or subscribing to Monod's view that "living beings are chemical machines."

The most serious fault in the Soviet attitude toward human nature seems to be not the theoretical conceptions contained in the Marxist philosophy of science, but the use that the party leaders have made of these conceptions. These leaders and their official ideologists have appropriated for themselves the right to define the "laws on the social level" and to enforce acquiescence to these laws. It is important to note that because science is based on the assumption of free debate and communication, this control over the discussion of societal norms that the party has asserted is not an excess of "scientism," but a denial of the scientific ethos. Unorthodox Soviet scientists know this very well and hence, do not believe that the prestige of science is damaged by "scientific" assertions of the leaders.

Of course, it is possible that we are discussing not one but two faults in Soviet attitudes. That is, not only is the Soviet political system an incorrect one for the most effective promotion of knowledge, but also the very philosophy of nature that Soviet scholars have developed may also be incorrect in its assertion of nonreductionism. Perhaps all aspects of nature, including human thoughts and emotions, *are* explicable in terms of physics and chemistry. Maybe the cyberneticists in Solzhenitsyn's play are correct and the Soviet Marxist scholars are wrong. We have an interest in hoping, however, that the Soviet Marxist intellectuals are the ones who are correct on this issue. For if they are wrong, we are left with the rather grim conclusion that there is little available to us as explanations of ourselves and nature other than mechanism and mysticism. Solzhenitsyn not only wishes us to recognize the inevitability of that choice, but invites us to turn to mystic Christianity for our explanation and sustenance, an invitation to which, it is to be hoped, many Westerners, sufficiently graduated from their own rich heritage, will reply, "Thanks, but no thanks."

I would not wish to exaggerate the strength of scientific rationality as a philosophic commitment in the Soviet Union. Many of the same signs of frustration with millenarian visions of the future scientific society are visible there as in Western countries. Streams of mysticism deep in the Russian religious tradition are recurring more strongly, sometimes uniting with right-wing nationalist movements. Solzhenitsyn has moved strongly into the traditional Orthodox Christian stream as both his personal beliefs and his letter to the Moscow patriarch so clearly indicate.[29] Interest is also growing among Soviet students and intellectuals in Eastern religions, Taoist philosophy, and Yoga.

Among Soviet artists and writers alarm is growing about the progressive destruction of traditional Russian villages and rural customs by encroaching suburbs and modern technology. Both novelists and short story writers nostalgically compare the old "unspoiled" countryside to "corrupt and busy" Moscow. The movement toward preservation of churches and national monuments frequently displays antiurban and antitechnology themes. Indeed, an American specialist on Soviet literature recently maintained that "Soviet literature today can be understood best through an awareness of the dialectical relationship between rural and urban thematics."[30]

Quite belatedly, compared to the United States, writers in the Soviet Union are now beginning to ask critical questions about the future development of such technologies as genetic engineering and nuclear power. On genetic engineering some of the most pointed criticisms have been advanced by orthodox Marxist philosophers, people who are normally thoroughly acquiescent to the government's scientistic programs and visions.[31] On nuclear power, the few criticisms yet to appear in print have come from physicists and economists.

In a 1978 article entitled "The Ideological Significance of Modern Biology," the Soviet philosopher of science R. S. Karpinskaia observed:[32]

The sense of social responsibility of scientists already cannot be intuitive, it must have a scientific ideological base. The philosophical interpretation of the perspectives of biology is becoming an integral part of scientific research, and the more deeply the creators of the brilliant experiments in genetic engineering realize this fact, the more hopeful is the possibility of turning the invincible development of genetic engineering to the benefit of mankind.

Philosophers like Karpinskaia are calling for the moral examination of genetic engineering within a Marxist framework. Still smarting from the loss of reputation that Soviet philosophers of biology suffered during the Lysenko affair, they are now trying to move the discussions onto a higher moral plane where Marxist philosophers and literary humanists can find common cause in their anxieties about such prospects as genetic engineering, cloning, and "surrogate motherhood" by *in vitro* fertilization. Academician N. P. Dubinin, an establishment Marxist who is also a leading geneticist in the Soviet Union, criticized genetic engineers for trying "to convert humans into an experimental herd."[33]

Another somewhat similar debate is beginning to emerge over nuclear power. For years Soviet authorities have maintained that their nuclear power plants were absolutely safe; they placed responsibility for the Three Mile Island incident in the United States on the selfish interests of the private power company, and contrasted that system of control with their own state ownership of all utilities. But in late 1979 two Soviet scholars published an article in one of the main Communist Party journals pointing to the ecological dangers of nuclear power plants and calling for their construction in the future in remote underpopulated areas where the dangers would be less.[34]

The Soviet Union, then, is beginning to witness the questioning of science and technology that is already so prevalent in the West. It is becoming increasingly clear in all countries that any person who is interested in the issue of what a future "good society" would look like must ask about the proper roles of science and technology. It is no longer adequate merely to say that "science and technology must serve human beings." Almost every thoughtful person would agree with that statement, but it does not solve the questions we face as we move into an ever more technological civilization. Nor does the observation that "socialism inherently leads to a more humane science and technology than capitalism" seem nearly as persuasive as it did to many intellectuals of a generation ago. If we could be certain that science and technology were merely tools to be used according to unchanging societal values, we might be able to accept the earlier simple formulas. We know now that our social values change, that science and technology are among the forces that change those values, and that we have no secure means of predicting which of those changes will later be considered beneficial and which will be considered harmful.

The current discussion in all scientifically advanced societies – whatever their political and economic systems – about the importance that should be assigned to science and the implications of science for human values are much more complex than commonly thought. The common view is that the Soviet Union has pushed the idolatry of science to extremes unknown in other parts of the world, whereas the West has recognized the limitations of a scientific worldview. On the superficial level of analysis that a Westerner gains from Soviet newspapers that opinion is not only understandable but probably justified.

A negligible portion of Soviet intellectuals, however, turns to such pronouncements when they are attempting to resolve for themselves the old and pressing questions about the legitimacy of science for an explanation of nature, man, and society. When they do turn to the writings of serious Soviet scholars about the nature of human consciousness and the legitimacy of scientific methods for explaining it they find a Soviet literature that is much less simplistic than is usually thought in the West and that actually allows more room for human autonomy than many recent writings in the West by reputable psychologists, physiologists, and biologists. In my opinion, there are no Soviet equivalents to Western scientists like Monod and Skinner in terms of devotion to reductionist methods for explaining the human personality on the basis of physics and chemistry. In the writings on the nature of man by authentic scholars (who, after all, should attract our attention at least as much as *Pravda*) the apogee of scientism in recent years has not occurred in the Soviet Union, but in the West. Against this background, the greater interest in the West than in the Soviet Union in mystical and romantic escapes from science is not surprising.

Notes

1 "Svecha na vetru," *Student* (No. 11/12, 1968), London, pp. 22–3. Also available in English: Aleksandr Solzhenitsyn, *Candle in the Wind,* trans. Keith Armes (Minneapolis: University of Minnesota Press, 1973).

2 See for example Loren R. Graham, "Concerns about Science and Attempts to Regulate Inquiry," *Daedalus* (Spring 1978): 1–22, and the other articles in this issue.

3 Quoted in Keith Armes, "Introduction," in Solzhenitsyn, *Candle in the Wind*, p. 9.

4 Solzhenitsyn, *Candle in the Wind*, pp. 48–9.

5 S. R. Mikulinsky, "Is a Decline in Science an Inherent Law of its Development: *à-propos* the paper of Prof. Derek Price," paper read at XIII International Congress for the History of Science, Moscow, 1971.

6 See Theodore Roszak, *Where the Wasteland Ends: Politics and Transcendence in Postindustrial Society* (Garden City, N.Y.: Doubleday Anchor, 1972), especially pages xxiv and 168; and Carlos Castaneda, *The Teachings of Don Juan: A Yaqui Way of Knowledge* (New York: Pocketbooks, 1968), especially p. 183.

7 See especially the "Newsletter of the Program on Public Conceptions of Science," nos. 1–6, William A. Blanpied, ed., Jefferson Physical Laboratory, Harvard University.

8 Derek J. de Solla Price, "Is There a Decline In Big Science Countries and in Big Science Subjects?" paper read at the XIII International Congress for the History of Science, Moscow, 1971.

9 See the decline in graduate study growth cited in Loren R. Graham, "The Place of the Soviet Academy of Sciences in the Overall Organization of Soviet Science," in *Soviet Science and Technology,* John Thomas and Ursula Kruse-Vaucienne eds., (Washington, D.C.: National Science Foundation, 1977), pp. 44–62, esp. p. 50. See also Louvan E. Nolting and Murray Feshbach, "R & D Employment in the U.S.S.R.," *Science* (February 1, 1980): 493–503.

10 Andrei D. Sakharov, *Progress, Coexistence, and Intellectual Freedom* (New York: Norton, 1970), pp. 82–3.

11 Alexandr Solzhenitsyn, "As Breathing and Consciousness Return," in A. Solzhenitsyn et al., *From Under the Rubble* (Boston: Little, Brown and Co., 1975), p. 16.

12 Alexandr Solzhenitsyn, *Nobel Lecture* (New York: Farrar, Straus and Giroux, 1972), p. 27.

13 Solzhenitsyn et al., *From Under the Rubble.*

14 Igor Shafarevich, "Socialism in Our Past and Future," Solzhenitsyn et al., *From Under the Rubble,* pp. 65–6.

15 Paul Ello comp., *Czechoslovakia's Blueprint for Freedom* (Washington: Acropolis Books, 1968). For citation given here, Michael Csizmas, *Prag 1968: Dokumente* (Bern: Verlag Schweizerischer Ost-Institut, 1968), p. 104.

16 Jerome R. Ravetz, *Scientific Knowledge and its Social Problems* (Oxford: Oxford University Press, 1971), p. 410.

17 Cited from transcript of discussions in Sidney W. Fox, ed., *The Origins of Prebiological Systems and of Their Molecular Matrices* (New York and London: Academic Press, 1965), pp. 53–5.

18 H. J. Muller, "Lenin's Doctrines in Relation to Genetics," published in En-

glish and Russian in *Pamiati V. I. Lenina: sbornik statei k desiatiletiiu so dnia smerti, 1924–1934* (Moscow and Leningrad: 1934), pp. 565–79; reprinted in Loren R. Graham, *Science and Philosophy in the Soviet Union* (New York: Knopf, 1972); this citation from Graham, p. 464.

19 I. T. Frolov, *Genetika i dialektika* (Moscow: "Nauka," 1968), p. 253.

20 S. L. Rubinshtein, *Osnovy obshchei psikhologii* (Moscow: State Educational Publishing House, 1946), p. 19.

21 L. S. Vygotsky, *Thought and Language* (Cambridge, Mass.: MIT Press, 1962), p. 51.

22 A. I. Oparin, *The Origin and Initial Development of Life* (NASA TTF-488), (Washington, D.C.: 1968), p. 4.

23 Jacques Monod, *Le hasard et la necessité* (Paris: Éditions du Seuil, 1970), p. 59.

24 Ibid., pp. 93, 164.

25 Solzhenitsyn, "Svecha na vetru," p. 71.

26 B. F. Skinner, *Beyond Freedom and Dignity* (New York: Knopf, 1971), pp. 158, 185, 175, 177.

27 I. T. Frolov, "Sovremennaia nauka i gumanizm," *Voprosy filosofii* 3 (1973): 13.

28 I. I. Antonovich, "Antopologicheskoe izmerenie sotsial'nogo progressa i burzhuaznyi gumanizm," *Voprosy filosofii* 10 (1973): 165.

29 *A Lenten Letter to Pimen Patriarch of all Russia* (Minneapolis: Burgess Publishing Co., 1972).

30 George Gibian, "The Urban Theme in Recent Soviet Russian Prose: Notes Toward a Typology," *Slavic Review* (March 1978): 41.

31 Loren R. Graham, "Reasons for Studying Soviet Science: The Example of Genetic Engineering," in *The Social Context of Soviet Science,* Linda L. Lubrano and Susan Gross Solomon, eds., (Boulder: Westview Press, 1980), pp. 205–40.

32 R. S. Karpinskaia, "Mirovozzrencheskoe znachenie sovremennoi biologii," *Voprosy filosofii* 4 (1978): 95–106.

33 Quoted in Graham, "Reasons for Studying Soviet Science," p. 217; see also references to Dubinin's articles on genetic engineering given on p. 237, note 16.

34 N. Dollezhal' and Iu. Koriakin, "Iadernaia elektroenergetika: dostizheniia i problemy," *Kommunist* 14 (1979): 19–28.

10

Theory and practice in the Mao period

PAUL M. SWEEZY

Marxism grows and develops through the historical experience of class struggles and their reflection in the thoughts of leaders and participants. The two greatest periods and sources of such advance have been the Russian and Chinese Revolutions. Although it is, of course, much too soon to come to any final conclusions, the death of a great leader like Mao Tse-tung inevitably marks a turning point and invites consideration of what has been accomplished during his lifetime.

When the time comes to attempt an overall evaluation of the Maoist period, it may well be concluded that its most important contribution to the advance of Marxism was to break what may be called the tyranny of the Soviet model. The very foundation of this model was "primitive socialist accumulation" at the expense of the peasantry, and its emphasis was the building up of heavy industry while concomitantly downgrading the development of light industry and the production of consumer goods.[1] The application of this model had (and has) many implications: the ending of all hope of an effective worker-peasant alliance and hence (in countries with peasant majorities) the necessity of a severely repressive state. And this in turn meant the renunciation of any possibility of transforming social relations in the direction of communism. In the Marxist orthodoxy of the Stalinist period – from the 1920s to the 1950s – this problem, to the extent that it was not dealt with in a purely propagandistic way, was put off until some future time when the forces of production would presumably have developed to the point of making general abundance a reality. In this way, development of the forces of production was turned into a sort of universal panacea for all the ills and contradictions of society, and from this it followed that for a socialist society the highest and overriding objective for the foreseeable future must be the most rapid attainable development of the forces of production.[2]

In the first years after they came to power the Chinese Communists set out to follow the Soviet model, but soon discovered that it put demands on the agricultural sector that could not be met. In a similar situation in the 1920s the Russians decided to squeeze the needed surplus out of the peasants, with the fateful consequences already noted. Quite apart from any reluctance on the part of the Chinese leadership to follow this course, the option did not exist as a realistic possibility. Unlike the Russian case, the surplus to be squeezed out of the peasantry was simply not there.[3] A different course had to be adopted. And it was here that Maoist ideas, based on long years in governing the border regions and conducting the wars against the Kuomintang and the Japanese, came into their own as policy guides for the whole country. Priorities were reordered: Industry was to be geared to the needs of agriculture and developed not only in the cities but also and especially in the countryside, employing surplus rural labor and beginning the process of introducing the peasantry to modern technology. The absolute priority accorded to heavy industry in the Soviet model was abandoned, with the development of heavy industry also being integrated into a strategy that placed agriculture (and the 80 percent of the people dependent upon it) at the top of the nation's concerns. This meant that the "capital" needed to develop the Chinese economy was to come not from any preexisting source of surplus – as both bourgeois economic theory and the Soviet orthodoxy of the period believed essential – but from a general increase in the productivity (agricultural and industrial alike) of the Chinese labor force. In this way the imposition of a special burden on any particular section of the population could be avoided and the whole issue of primitive socialist accumulation rendered irrelevant and meaningless. And politically this would permit the maintenance and even strengthening of the worker-peasant alliance, which in turn would make the build-up of a specially repressive state apparatus as unnecessary as it would be irrational.

Carrying through this new strategy of development was by no means easy. It required a vast and historically unprecedented institutional innovation in the form of the agricultural communes; it suffered severe setbacks in the hard years of 1959–62; and it finally got on track only with the introduction in 1962 and after of a

Chinese version of the Green Revolution.[4] After that, however, it worked remarkably well: China became essentially self-sufficient in agricultural production, and industry developed, in terms of both rapidity and geographical distribution, in quite satisfactory fashion. It was thereby shown once and for all that the Soviet model, far from being an embodiment of the "laws" of socialism, was merely one possible path to economic development and in all probability one that was in irreconcilable contradiction with the requirements of a socialist transition toward communism. Never again, after the Chinese experience in the period 1955–65, will a newly liberated country feel compelled to choose between the classical capitalist and Soviet roads to economic development.

This was the first momentous achievement of the Maoist period. But it was not the only one. The Cultural Revolution was yet to come, and the issues involved, although closely related to the strategy of economic development, were of a different order.

The basic problem can perhaps best be understood if set in the perspective of orthodox Soviet political theory of the 1930s. According to this theory, the proletarian revolution overthrows capitalism and/or other forms of class society by abolishing private ownership of the means of production. The government that presides over this process and at the same time takes in hand the task of developing the forces of production is a dictatorship of the proletariat, in the specific sense that it represses the old possessing classes and thwarts their inevitable counterrevolutionary efforts. Vis-à-vis the working class and its peasant allies, however, the revolutionary government is a democracy much more genuine than even the freest of bourgeois democracies. From these premises it follows that with the dying out of the old bourgeois and feudal ruling classes, the development of the forces of production, and the continuous elevation of the standard of living of the mass of the people, the class struggle will diminish in intensity and gradually disappear, and the state as a special apparatus of repression will, in the classical Marxian phrase, "wither away." To be sure, these processes will not be able to work their way through to completion as long as capitalism exists on an international scale and the world bourgeoisie continues to support the counterrevolutionary ambitions of the overthrown classes: During this period the state will continue to exist as a repressive apparatus against outside intervention. But this will not affect the basic tendencies at work as far as the internal structure and dynamics of the postrevolutionary society are concerned. Here democracy will flourish, and the path to a future transition to communism will be mapped out, subject only to the requirement of an adequate development of the forces of production.

The trouble with this theory, of course, was that it was in no way borne out by the experience of the Soviet Union. From the earliest days of the revolutionary government, repression was directed at large sections of the population, not only the deposed exploiting classes, and this repression became an increasing, not a decreasing, characteristic of Soviet society with the passage of time. There were several kinds of responses to this situation. Orthodox Stalinists simply denied that there was any massive internal repression, their propaganda becoming more and more strident in proportion to its obvious belying of the facts. The other main responses were those of the various brands of Trotskyists, all of whom were agreed that what was happening in the USSR was an aberration from rather than a refutation of the basic theory, and all of whom stressed the backwardness of traditional Russian society as the underlying cause. According to this view, a backward society inevitably inherits and/or breeds a large bureaucracy to perform economic and political managerial functions. Either this bureaucracy will be kept under the democratic control of the workers and their allies until, with the development of the productive forces, it is no longer necessary and can be dispensed with. Or it will grab the levers of power and repress the masses, which is what happened in the Soviet Union under Stalin. At this point there was a division between those who, following Trotsky himself, believed that sooner or later a second, this time purely political revolution would be necessary to restore power to the masses. Others, of whom Isaac Deutscher was perhaps the leading representative, took the position that after the death of Stalin, as the educational and cultural level of the Soviet peoples rose under the impact of the developing forces of production, a gradual process of democratization would set in that would eventually bring the Soviet Union into line with orthodox Soviet political theory.

It is important to recognize that none of what may be called these "aberration theories," no matter how scathingly critical of developments in the Soviet Union, had any place for the idea that the results of the October Revolution had been or were in the process of being negated. The bureaucracy was seen as an unavoidable excrescence on an otherwise healthy body politic, one that could and would be removed, either violently or peacefully, when the consequences of backwardness had been sufficiently overcome.[5]

However plausible this view may have seemed in the 1930s, or even two decades later, it certainly appears in a very different light today, seventy years after the October Revolution and more than a quarter of a century after the Second World War. The extreme methods of repression in use under Stalin were abandoned after his death, but Deutscher's optimistic expectation that a gradual process of democratization had been initiated proved to be without foundation. And above all, the notion that the combination of state ownership of the means of production plus rapid development of the forces of production would somehow open the socialist road to communism has turned out to be the grand illusion of the Marxism of the period of the Third International. The Soviet Union is now the world's second industrial power with a high level of popular education and a vast trained intelligentsia, and yet its working class has no access to political power, is barred from any form of self-organization, and probably has less influence on its conditions and methods of work than the working classes of the advanced European capitalist countries.

Evidently there was something radically wrong with the political theories of the Stalin period, including both those of the official Stalinists and those of their main opponents. The Soviet Union was neither a developing socialist democracy, modified only to the extent necessary to defend itself against external counterrevolutionary intervention, nor was it basically a healthy workers' state temporarily deflected from its natural course of development by the rule of an overweening bureaucracy. In reality it had become a social formation that was neither foreseen nor easily accounted for by any of the existing versions of Marxian theory. To illuminate this situation and lay at least the foundations for a more adequate Marxian theory of postrevolutionary society was the second great accomplishment of China under Mao's leadership.

Here, as in the case of the rejection of the Soviet model of economic development, it was practice that led the way and theory that lagged behind. "Learning from the Soviet Union," which was a cardinal principle in China in the first years after the takeover of power in 1949, naturally meant copying much in addition to the central strategy of economic development. Bureaucratic and elitist practices permeated all sectors of Chinese society, including the economy, government, and education. These practices were very much in the tradition of age-old Confucian habits of thought and action and hence were easily assimilated by those newly in authority. On the other hand, they were in sharp contrast to many of the ways of doing things that had evolved in the years of civil strife, resistance to Japanese invaders, and governance of large border regions in the 1930s and 1940s. Chinese Communism thus developed a kind of split personality, deeply rooted in the history of China as well as in its own history as a revolutionary movement. Both tendencies were, of course, represented in the ruling Communist Party, with Liu Shao-ch'i as the most prominent figure in the conservative or right-wing camp and Mao Tse-tung holding the same position in the radical or left-wing camp. Not that this division was altogether new – in one form or another, indeed, it went back to the very beginnings of the party – but its full and fateful significance could only come to the fore after the seizure of power and the assumption of responsibility for the future course of the country as a whole.

This is not the place for a review of the history of what later came to be known as the "two-line struggle" in the period between 1949 and the Cultural Revolution. Suffice it to say that as long as the problem was one of overthrowing the old order and securely establishing the new, the differences remained in the background. But the more attention had to be focused on what the shape of the new order was to be, the more the differences came to the fore, with the Liuist tendency embracing the Soviet model and all that went with it, and the Maoists struggling to deepen the revolution and carry it forward from one stage to the next, always in the direction of greater equality and fuller participation by the masses in controlling and managing their own lives. The Maoists scored an important victory with the Great Leap Forward and the immediately following fall of P'eng Teh-huai, but the opposition made a strong comeback in the "hard years," and the early 1960s witnessed the proliferation of elitist tendencies in both economics and politics.

This was the setting for the Cultural Revolution. It originated in a revolt of university students – comparable to similar movements in the West – against exaggerated forms of elitism deeply rooted in Chinese tradition, and from there it spread to the schools and other sectors of the younger generation. Mao, whose dominance in the country's leadership had suffered a partial eclipse in the rightward movement of the early 60s, saw in this uprising of the youth his opportunity to regain the initiative for the left. Using such slogans as "It is Justified to Rebel" and "Bombard the Head-quarters," he embarked the country on a three-year voyage through stormy seas and rocky shoals that came perilously close to shipwreck on more than one occasion. The schools and universities were closed while students roamed the country with the revolutionary message; many leaders were dismissed and disgraced; party committees were disbanded and replaced by new "Revolutionary Committees"; the People's Liberation Army had to be called upon in numerous situations to prevent factional struggles from degenerating into civil war. And all the while the post-Great Leap move to the right was being reversed, and the initiative in matters of economic and social policy was passing into the hands of those who stood for propelling the revolution forward in the direction of greater equality and greater mass participation.

It would take someone far more knowledgeable than the present writer to trace the impact of these tremendous social upheavals in the realm of theory. I shall therefore focus entirely on one aspect and one outcome that seem to me to have fundamentally and definitively transformed Marxian political theory as it had taken shape in the period of the Third International.

Among the Chinese themselves there has never been any doubt that all the struggles that have taken place since 1949 have been in one way or another manifestations of class struggle that, since the appearance of the *Communist Manifesto,* has been seen by Marxists as the motor force of historical change since the period of primitive communism. But precisely what is meant by class struggle in a modern postrevolutionary society has never to this day been satisfactorily analyzed or explained. There are three strands of thought concerning class struggle that need to be clearly distinguished.

(1) The overthrow of a bourgeois and/or feudal regime does not do away with the old exploiting classes. These will, of course, strive by every available means to defeat their conquerors and to return to power. In the course of doing so they will wage fierce class struggles that can be expected to continue until the old exploiting classes have died out. All Marxists, whatever their differences, agree that in this sense class struggle is an inevitable feature of postrevolutionary society.

(2) The ideas, values, and habits of thought and behavior of the old ruling classes – which, Marx insisted, have always been the ruling ideas of a society – do not die out with their progenitors. They are deeply imbedded in all strata of society, especially the educated elements, which naturally play a prominent role in revolutionary leaderships. The struggle to get rid of this inherited and necessarily counterrevolutionary mental baggage is also in a very real sense a class struggle, although Marxists have not always identified it as such.

(3) The third strand is the most complicated and the least understood. Running a postrevolutionary society requires administrators, managers, technicians, experts of various kinds; compared to ordinary workers and peasants, the people occupying these positions have higher incomes and dispose over substantial perquisites and power. And regardless of class origin or degree of subjection to the dominance of old ideas, those who enjoy such privileged positions soon develop a vested interest in maintaining them and seek, consciously or unconsciously, to pass them along to their children. (To a considerable extent this intergenerational transmittal of privileged position happens anyway because children of favored households have an important headstart in school. This, on the average, means that the chances of following in the parents' footsteps are better than those of their less favored classmates.) All of this, of course, has long been known to sociologists, and (so far as I know) has never been denied by Marxists. But given the premises of the orthodox political theory of the Stalin period, these questions of relative power and privilege were treated as part of the problematic of bureaucracy rather than class,

classes being entirely defined and circumscribed by the property system. According to this theory, in a socialist setting the very existence of a bureaucracy, whatever its undesirable qualities and tendencies, was a temporary and transitional phenomenon. With the inevitable development of the productive forces (unleashed by the abolition of private property in the means of production) the conditions necessitating a bureaucracy would gradually disappear and the stratum itself would follow in due course. In the meantime – and this is a crucially important point – the struggle against bureaucracy would take the form of measures to control excesses and inculcate in bureaucrats a greater sense of social responsibility. The argument in a nutshell is that elites are inevitable for a long time to come (until they more or less automatically disappear), but they ought to be well-behaved elites. On the other hand, if one takes the position that the managerial stratum is not a bureaucracy in this sense, but rather an incipient ruling (and exploiting) class, then the struggle against it must be a class struggle in the full sense of the term with the ultimate objective not of controlling it and making it more socially responsible, but of eliminating it altogether and achieving a genuinely classless society. This in turn implies the belief that workers and peasants, through prolonged struggle lasting a whole historical epoch but beginning immediately, can themselves master and assume responsibility for functions that are carried out by the privileged managers and bureaucrats in the first postrevolutionary phase.

Against this background, the thesis that I am concerned to uphold can be briefly stated. In the Chinese political discussions, debates, and polemics of the 1950s and 1960s, the meaning of the term class struggle gradually shifted from almost exclusive emphasis on the first sense to a combination of the second and third senses, with the third having acquired clear predominance by the end of the Cultural Revolution. In other words, the class enemy that the workers and their allies were being exhorted to struggle against started out being the old ruling classes, increasingly became elites (and others as well) still dominated by the ideas and values of the old ruling classes, and ended up by being a "new bourgeoisie" produced (and incessantly reproduced) by the social formation that had emerged from the revolution itself.

That this last conception of classes and class struggle in postrevolutionary society is as applicable to the Soviet Union as to China is obvious: Indeed the evidence and reasoning to support it came at least as much from Soviet as from Chinese experience. It is also obvious that its implications for the political theory inherited by China from the Soviet Union are devastating. The notion that abolition of private property of the means of production ushers in an essentially classless society that, given a sufficient development of the forces of production, will evolve in a harmonious way toward communism is exploded once and for all. In its place we have a conception of socialism as a class-divided society like all that have preceded it, and one that has the potential to move forward or backward depending on the fortunes of a class struggle through which alone the human race can aspire to leave behind the horrors and miseries of the past and lay the foundations for a future worthy of its capabilities.

Many will find this a discouraging conclusion. Revolution, they firmly believe, would mark a decisive turning point, after which progress, however slow and painful, could only be in the direction of the higher stage of communism that Marx described in *The Critique of the Gotha Program*. What had to be overcome was the terrible heritage of the past, not the inherent contradictions of the new society. The experience of the Mao period shattered this optimistic illusion. Postrevolutionary society contains not only contradictions inherited from millennia of class-riven society, it produces and reproduces its own contradictions. The revolution provides no final solutions. It only opens the possibility of moving forward *in the direction* of eliminating classes. But the existence of this as a possibility implies its opposite, the possibility of moving backward toward the reentrenchment of an exploiting class based not on private property of the means of production, but on control of an all-encompassing repressive state apparatus.

According to the theory developed in the Mao period this is precisely what actually happened in the Soviet Union. Would it also happen in China after Mao was gone? That it might was inherent in the theory itself. Whether it would could only depend on the still unknown future course of a class struggle the meaning and importance of which must now be recognized and pondered by all who seek to understand the historical period in which we live.

Notes

1 The term "primitive socialist accumulation" was Preobrazhensky's, but it was far more appropriate to the Stalinist practice than to the relatively mild program advocated by Preobrazhensky himself.

2 The counterpart to this theory of the productive forces – as the Chinese have called it – is that the fatal flaw of capitalism was that it had finally become, in Marx's phrase, a fetter on the development of the forces of production, a proposition that seemed self-evident in the 1930s. Note that this theory had the effect of making analysis of other contradictions of capitalism unimportant or unnecessary. (One example that readily comes to mind in the nuclear age is that capitalism might *overdevelop* the forces of production in self-destructive ways without being able to provide any effective controls. Another is that in its unlimited urge to expand it might in effect destroy its own natural base and environment.)

3 This problem and its implications are analyzed by Harry Magdoff in an important article, "China: Contrasts with the USSR," *Monthly Review* (July–August 1975): 12–57, especially pp. 29–32.

4 See the article by Harry Magdoff cited in note 3, and Ben Stavis, "China's Green Revolution," *Monthly Review* (October 1974): 18–29.

5 A logical corollary, which however need not concern us in the present context, is that a postrevolutionary society in an already developed country would not be subject to the evils that had befallen the Soviet Union.